NSW Targeting Maths

Year 3

Garda Turner

PASCAL
PRESS

Contents

New Edition

Targeting Maths Australia's Favourite Maths Program

Australian Curriculum/ NSW Alignment

This NEW Edition fully aligns each student page with both the new NSW Syllabus (2024) and the new Australian Curriculum: Mathematics F-10 version 9.0. The NSW Syllabus outcome codes and content groups appear with the Australian Curriculum strand and code on each student page.

iPad Apps

With an app for each year, from Foundation/Kindergarten to Year 6, the Targeting Maths Apps include all the essential maths content that children need to know in an amazing app that makes learning maths fun, motivating and full of rewards. Look for it in Apple's App Store today! Made especially for the iPad and aligned to each student page in this book.

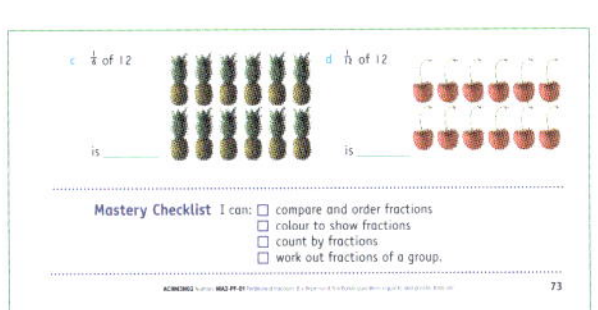

Mastery Checklists

Each unit has a Mastery Checklist. These checklists engage students in visible learning as they recognise and reflect on the specific maths skills learnt in each unit.

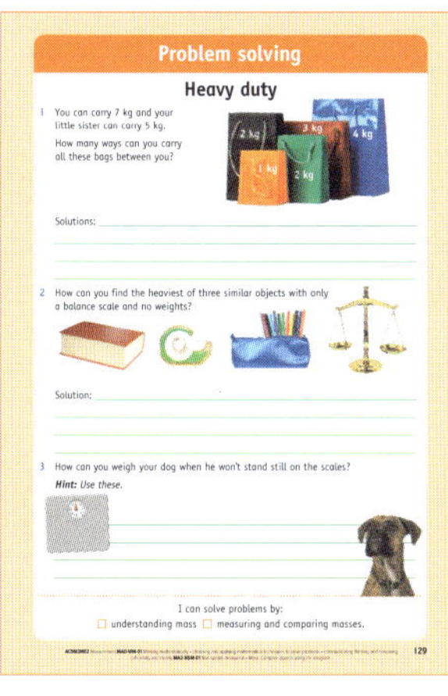

Integrated Problem-solving Program

Includes an integrated problem-solving program that actively builds students' problem-solving capabilities.

In-stage Topic Alignment for Composite Classes

Great for composite classes too, the contents of each book in one stage, eg Year 3 and Year 4, match topic by topic.

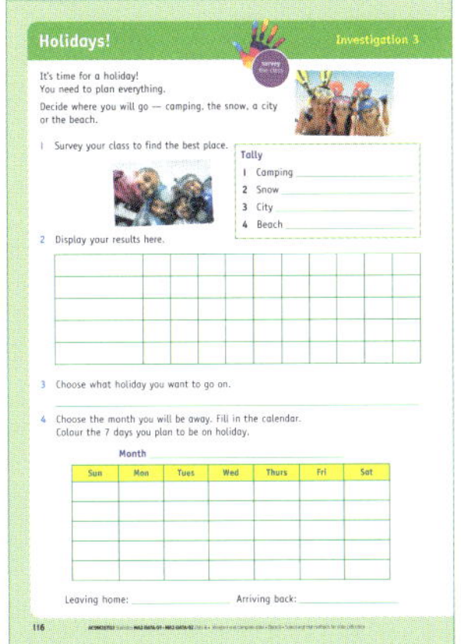

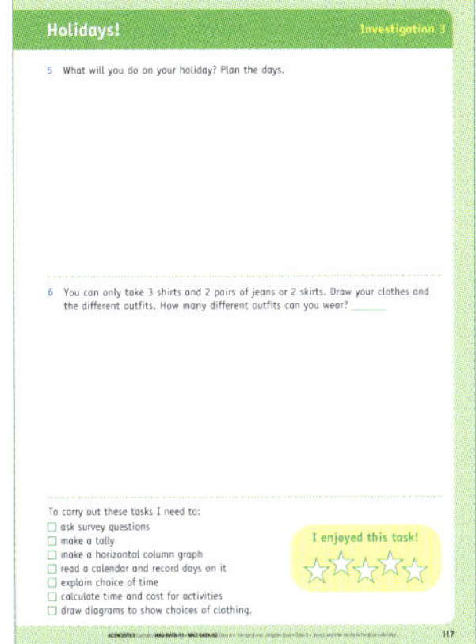

Term Investigations

Each term includes an investigation that will get students planning and working through an extended problem.

Regular Revision

Revision pages appear both at mid term and at the end of each term to revise key concepts.

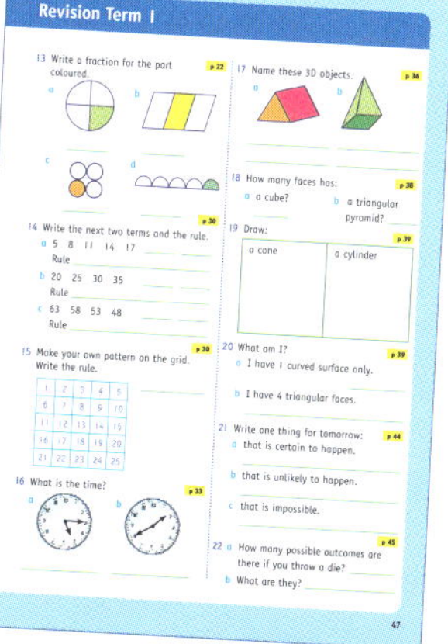

Hands-on Activities

Various hands-on activities are included in each term, asking students to measure and make, count and compare, using objects from around the classroom or home.

Year 3 Outcomes

	NSW Syllabus Outcomes	Student pages
Working Mathematically	**MA1-WM-01** develops understanding and fluency in mathematics through exploring and connecting mathematical concepts	2–184
	MA1-WM-01 develops understanding and fluency in mathematics through choosing and applying mathematical techniques to solve problems	23, 24, 25, 31, 40, 43, 70, 74, 75, 107, 111, 115, 116, 117, 129, 147, 151, 161, 164, 165
	MA1-WM-01 develops understanding and fluency in mathematics through communicating their thinking and reasoning coherently and clearly	16, 23, 24, 25, 40, 70, 74, 75, 84, 107, 111, 115, 116, 117, 126, 129, 151, 161, 164, 165, 178
Number and Algebra	**Representing numbers**	
	MA2-RN-01 applies an understanding of place value and the role of zero to represent numbers to at least tens of thousands	2, 3, 4, 5, 6, 8, 56, 57, 58, 152, 153, 154
	MA2-RN-02 represents and compares decimals up to 2 decimal places using place value	156
	Additive relations	
	MA2-AR-01 selects and uses mental and written strategies for addition and subtraction involving 2- and 3-digit numbers	7, 9, 10, 11, 12, 13, 14, 15, 16, 63, 64, 65, 66, 67, 69, 70, 78, 79, 80, 83, 96, 97, 98, 99, 100, 148, 151
	MA2-AR-02 completes number sentences involving addition and subtraction by finding missing values	12, 13, 14, 28, 29, 30, 31, 68, 97, 99, 168, 169
	Multiplicative relations	
	MA2-MR-01 represents and uses the structure of multiplicative relations to 10 × 10 to solve problems	28, 30, 59, 61, 84, 101, 102, 103, 104, 105, 106, 107, 108, 109, 110, 111, 121, 142, 143, 144, 145, 146, 147, 148, 150, 169
	MA2-MR-02 completes number sentences involving multiplication and division by finding missing values	60, 81, 82, 83, 105, 106, 111, 142, 143, 144, 145, 146, 147, 149, 150, 151, 168, 170
	Fractions	
	MA2-PF-01 represents and compares halves, quarters, thirds and fifths as lengths on a number line and their related fractions formed by halving (eighths, sixths and tenths)	20, 21, 22, 23, 71, 72, 73, 74, 75, 112, 113, 114, 115, 155, 157
Measurement and Space	**Geometric measure**	
	MA2-GM-01 uses grid maps and directional language to locate positions and follow routes	123, 124, 125, 126, 175, 176, 177, 178, 179
	MA2-GM-02 measures and estimates lengths in metres, centimetres and millimetres	17, 18, 19, 24, 25, 158, 159, 160, 161, 164, 165
	MA2-GM-03 identifies angles and classifies them by comparing to a right angle	171, 172, 173
	Two-dimensional (2D) spatial structure	
	MA2-2DS-01 compares two-dimensional shapes and describes their features	85, 86
	MA2-2DS-02 performs transformations by combining and splitting two-dimensional shapes	130, 131
	MA2-2DS-03 estimates, measures and compares areas using square centimetres and square metres	162, 163
	Three-dimensional (3D) spatial structure	
	MA2-3DS-01 makes and sketches models and nets of three-dimensional objects including prisms and pyramids	36, 37, 38, 39, 40, 87, 88
	MA2-3DS-02 estimates, measures and compares capacities (internal volumes) using litres, millilitres and volumes using cubic centimetres	89, 90, 91
	Non-spatial measure	
	MA2-NSM-01 estimates, measures and compares the masses of objects using kilograms and grams	127, 128, 129
	MA2-NSM-02 represents and interprets analog and digital time in hours, minutes and seconds	32, 33, 34, 35, 132, 133, 134, 135, 174
Statistics & Probability	**Data**	
	MA2-DATA-01 collects discrete data and constructs graphs using a given scale	41, 43, 92, 93, 116, 117, 137, 138
	MA2-DATA-02 interprets data in tables, dot plots and column graphs	41, 42, 43, 92, 93, 116, 117, 136, 137
	Chance	
	MA2-CHAN-01 records and compares the results of chance experiments	44, 45, 139, 180, 181

	Australian Curriculum Content Descriptions *Students learn to:*	Student pages
Number & Algebra	**Number**	
	AC9M3N01 recognise, represent and order natural numbers using naming and writing conventions for numerals beyond 10 000	2, 3, 4, 5, 6, 7, 8, 10, 15, 56, 57, 58, 152, 154
	AC9M3N02 recognise and represent unit fractions including $\frac{1}{2}$, $\frac{1}{3}$, $\frac{1}{4}$, $\frac{1}{5}$ and $\frac{1}{10}$ and their multiples in different ways; combine fractions with the same denominator to complete the whole	20, 21, 22, 23, 71, 72, 73, 96, 108, 112, 113, 114, 115, 155
	AC9M3N03 add and subtract two- and three-digit numbers using place value to partition, rearrange and regroup numbers to assist in calculations without a calculator	7, 11, 12, 14, 15, 16, 56, 65, 66, 67, 68, 69, 97, 99, 100, 168
	AC9M3N04 multiply and divide one- and two-digit numbers, representing problems using number sentences, diagrams and arrays, and using a variety of calculation strategies	59, 61, 103, 106, 107, 108, 109, 110, 111, 144, 145, 147, 148, 149, 150, 151, 169
	AC9M3N05 estimate the quantity of objects in collections and make estimates when solving problems to determine the reasonableness of calculations	75, 89, 90, 91, 153
	AC9M3N06 use mathematical modelling to solve practical problems involving additive and multiplicative situations including financial contexts; formulate problems using number sentences and choose calculation strategies, using digital tools where appropriate; interpret and communicate solutions in terms of the situation	13, 23, 68, 70, 78, 80, 98, 100, 101, 104, 105, 106, 107, 108, 109, 111, 114, 142, 143, 148, 149, 150, 151
	AC9M3N07 follow and create algorithms involving a sequence of steps and decisions to investigate numbers; describe any emerging patterns	6, 8, 9, 28, 29, 30, 31, 60, 61, 62, 81, 82, 83, 84, 120, 121, 122, 146, 168, 170
	Algebra	
	AC9M3A01 recognise and explain the connection between addition and subtraction as inverse operations, apply to partition numbers and find unknown values in number sentences	63, 64, 69, 70, 122, 169
	AC9M3A02 extend and apply knowledge of addition and subtraction facts to 20 to develop efficient mental strategies for computation with larger numbers without a calculator	9, 10, 14, 16, 17, 63, 64, 65, 66, 67, 83
	AC9M3A03 recall and demonstrate proficiency with multiplication facts for 3, 4, 5 and 10; extend and apply facts to develop the related division facts	59, 60, 61, 84, 101, 102, 103, 104, 105, 142, 143, 144, 145, 146, 147
Measurement & Geometry	**Measurement**	
	AC9M3M01 identify which metric units are used to measure everyday items; use measurements of familiar items and known units to make estimates	18, 19, 24, 25, 128, 158
	AC9M3M02 measure and compare objects using familiar metric units of length, mass and capacity, and instruments with labelled markings	17, 18, 19, 24, 25, 75, 89, 90, 91, 127, 128, 129, 158, 159, 160, 164, 165
	AC9M3M03 recognise and use the relationship between formal units of time including days, hours, minutes and seconds to estimate and compare the duration of events	133, 134, 135, 174
	AC9M3M04 describe the relationship between the hours and minutes on analogue and digital clocks, and read the time to the nearest minute	32, 33, 34, 35, 40, 132, 134, 135, 174
	AC9M3M05 identify angles as measures of turn and compare angles with right angles in everyday situations	171, 172, 173
	AC9M3M06 recognise the relationships between dollars and cents and represent money values in different ways	11, 79, 80, 96, 99
	Space	
	AC9M3SP01 make, compare and classify objects, identifying key features and explaining why these features make them suited to their uses	36, 37, 38, 39, 40
	AC9M3SP02 interpret and create two-dimensional representations of familiar environments, locating key landmarks and objects relative to each other	123, 124, 125, 126, 175, 176, 177, 178, 179
Statistics & Probability	**Statistics**	
	AC9M3ST01 acquire data for categorical and discrete numerical variables to address a question of interest or purpose by observing, collecting and accessing data sets; record the data using appropriate methods including frequency tables and spreadsheets	41, 42, 92, 93, 116, 117, 136, 138
	AC9M3ST02 create and compare different graphical representations of data sets including using software where appropriate; interpret the data in terms of the context	41, 42, 93, 116, 117, 137, 138
	AC9M3ST03 conduct guided statistical investigations involving the collection, representation and interpretation of data for categorical and discrete numerical variables with respect to questions of interest	43, 116, 117, 137, 138
	Probability	
	AC9M3P01 identify practical activities and everyday events involving chance; describe possible outcomes and events as 'likely' or 'unlikely' and identify some events as 'certain' or 'impossible' explaining reasoning	44, 45, 139, 180, 181
	AC9M3P02 conduct repeated chance experiments; identify and describe possible outcomes, record the results, recognise and discuss the variation	45, 180, 181

How to Solve a Problem

Read • Plan • Work • Check

Read the problem carefully. Underline the question. Circle the facts.

Plan what you will do: +, –, × (multiply) or ÷ (divide).

Work Write or draw a diagram to work it out. Write the answer.

Check your answer! Make sure that your answer makes sense.

Draw a diagram

Draw a simple picture.
Use symbols if you can.

$12 - 5 = 7$

$3 \times 4 = 12$

Trial and Error

Make a guess and write it down. Check if it is right. If not, work out if your guess should be higher or lower. Make another guess and write it down. Check if it's right. Keep going until you have the correct answer.

Look for patterns

Study the numbers in the problem.
Write them down in a list.
Can you see a pattern?
What comes next in the pattern?
Write it as your answer.

Bundy runs 2 km, then 4 km, then 6 km on 3 days. How far should he run on the 4th day to keep to his pattern?

2, 4, 6, ? *2, 4, 6, 8*

Bundy should run 8 km.

Use a table

Put the information from the problem in columns. Can you see the pattern? The information is clearer in a table.

Use this to work out the answer.

Jerry	5 mins	10 cakes	2 in 1 min.
Cam	4 mins	8 cakes	2 in 1 min.
Tilly	3 mins	9 cakes	3 in 1 min.

Who eats the fastest?

Answer: Tilly eats fastest.

Work backwards

Read the problem all the way through. Find one piece of information. Write it down. Find another piece of information that relates and put them together. Write it down. Keep working backwards until you solve all the pieces of the problem.

Kell has $2 more than Greg, who has $3 less than Dee. Dee has $5. How much do they each have?

Dee = $5

Greg = $5 – $3 = $2

Kell = $2 + $2 = $4

Dictionary

am (ante meridiem)

The time from midnight to midday

angle

The amount of turning between two lines that meet at a point

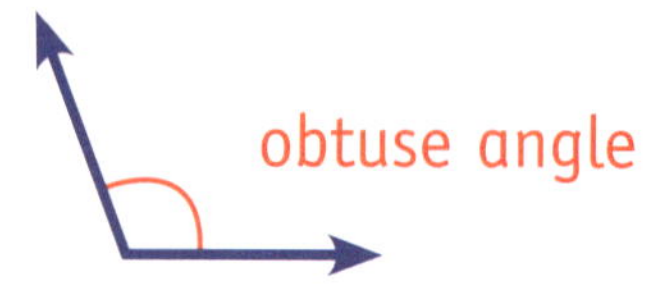

ascending order

In order from smallest to largest

1, 7, 11, 19, 32

capacity

The amount a container can hold

The capacity of this bottle is 1 litre.

centimetre (cm)

A unit of length

10 mm = 1 cm

100 cm = 1 m

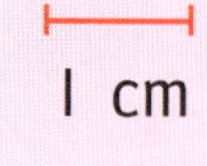

certain

Something that is definite. It will happen.

cone

A solid shape that tapers to a point and has a circular base

cube

A solid shape which has six square faces

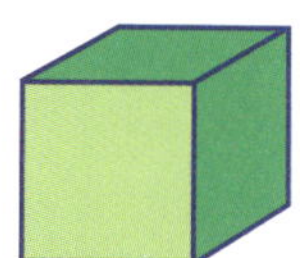

cylinder

A solid shape which has two circular ends and a curved surface

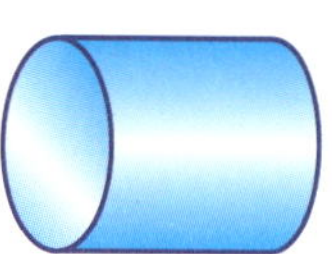

data

A collection of information

Favourite sports		
Sport	**Votes**	**Total**
Soccer		12
Netball		6
Football		8
Chess		11

decimal number

A number that has a decimal point

eg 0·3, 75·16

descending order

In order from largest to smallest

96, 84, 61, 37, 11

diagonal

A line that joins two corners in a polygon but does not make a side

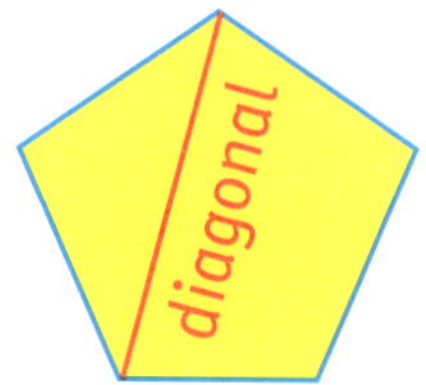

digit

The numerals that are used to write numbers: 0, 1, 2, 3, 4, 5, 6, 7, 8, 9

Dictionary

division (÷)

Sharing into equal groups

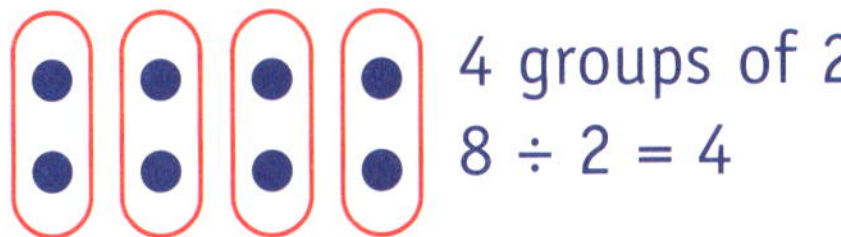

4 groups of 2
8 ÷ 2 = 4

edge

Where two surfaces meet

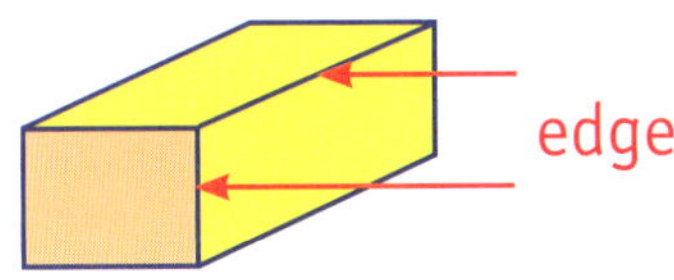

face

A flat surface of a solid shape

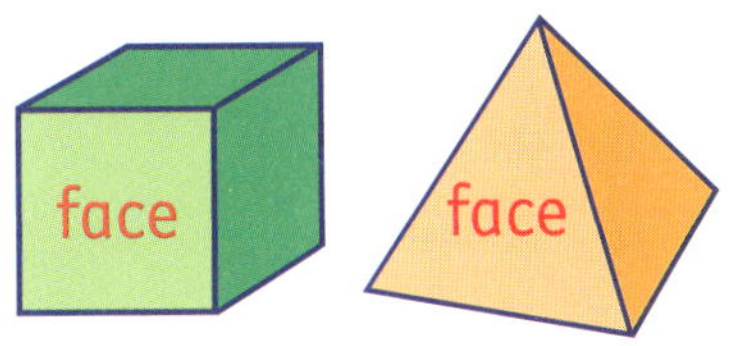

fraction

A part of a whole or a group

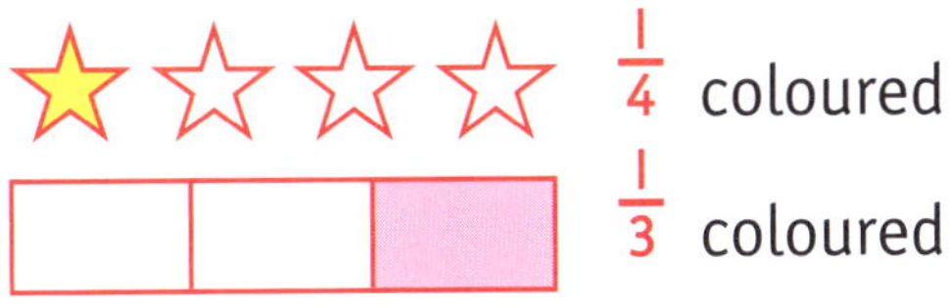

$\frac{1}{4}$ coloured

$\frac{1}{3}$ coloured

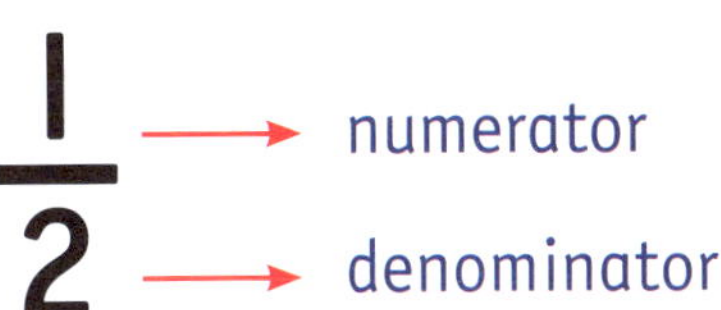

graph

A diagram that shows a collection of data

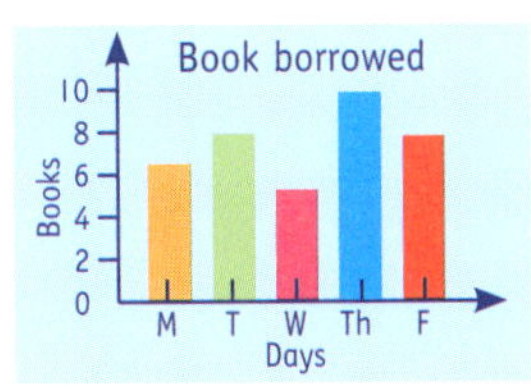

column graph

Money saved

Sam	$$$$$$
Mary	$$$
Jo	$$$$$

picture graph

hexagon

A 2D shape with 6 straight sides

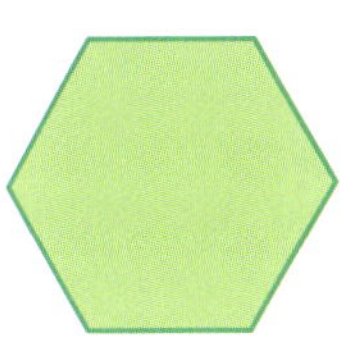

regular hexagon

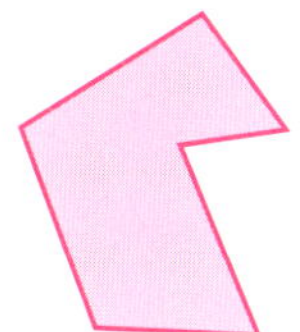

irregular hexagon

kilogram (kg)

A unit of mass for weighing things

1 kilogram = 1000 grams

1000 kilograms = 1 tonne

line

straight line

parallel lines

curved line

litre (L)

A unit of capacity

1 L = 1000 millilitres (mL)

mass

The amount of material that makes up an object. Measured in grams, kilograms and tonnes.

metre (m)

A unit of length

1 m = 100 cm

1000 m = 1 km

millimetre (mm)

A unit of length

10 mm = 1 cm

Dictionary

multiplication (×)
Find the total of a number of equal groups or equal rows

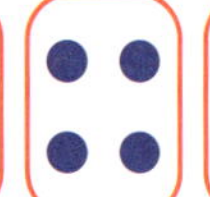
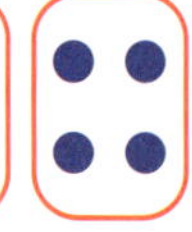

5 × 4 = 20

4 × 6 = 24

octagon
A 2D shape with 8 straight sides

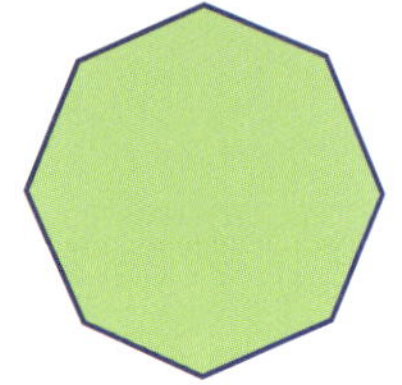
regular octagon

irregular octagon

parallelogram
A quadrilateral with opposite sides parallel

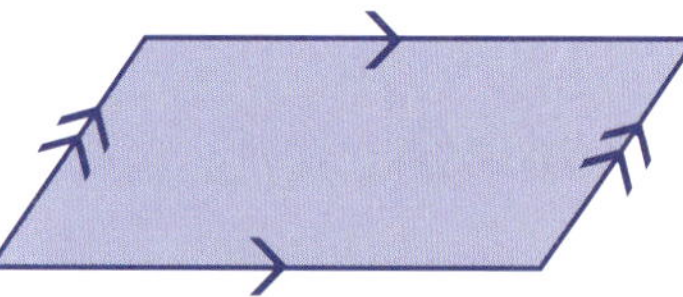

pentagon
A 2D shape with 5 straight sides

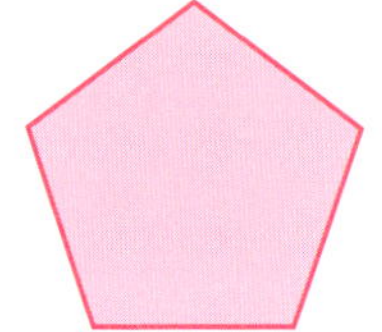
regular pentagon

irregular pentagon

place value
The value of a numeral depending on its position in a number

396 = 300 + 90 + 6

754 = 7 hundreds + 5 tens + 4 ones

8·57 = 8 ones + 5 tenths + 7 hundredths

pm (post meridiem)
The time from midday to midnight

polygon
A shape with 3 or more straight sides

eg

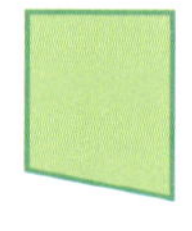

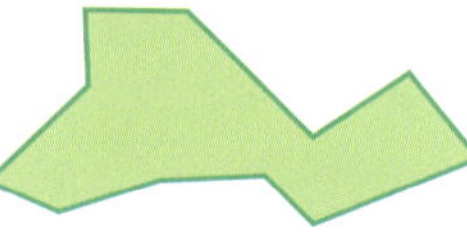

prism
A 3D shape with identical ends. All other faces are rectangles. The ends give a prism its name.

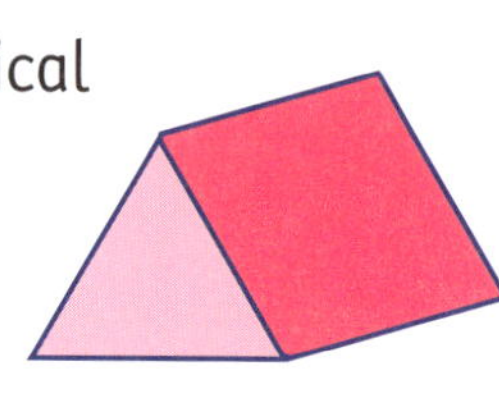
triangular prism

probability
The chance of something happening, eg certain, impossible, likely, unlikely.

product
When numbers are multiplied, the answer is called the product.

pyramid
A 3D object with one flat base. All other faces are triangles coming to a point at the apex. The base shape gives a pyramid its name.

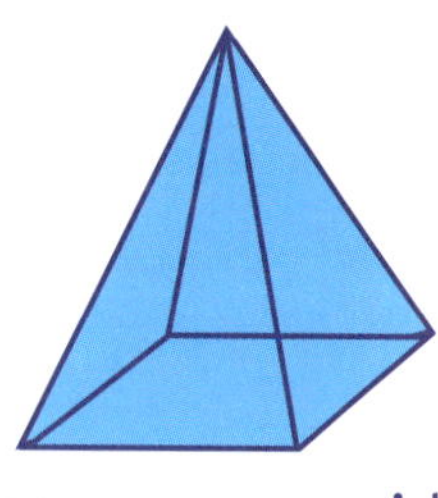
square pyramid

quadrilateral
A 2D shape with 4 straight sides

Dictionary

rhombus

A quadrilateral with all sides equal and opposite sides parallel. It is a special parallelogram.

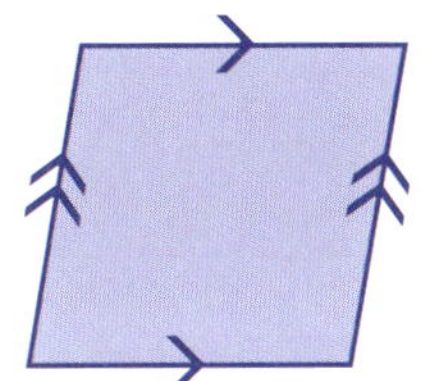

rounding (to nearest 10)

0 Round down ← 1 2 3 4 | Round up 0 → 5 6 7 8 9

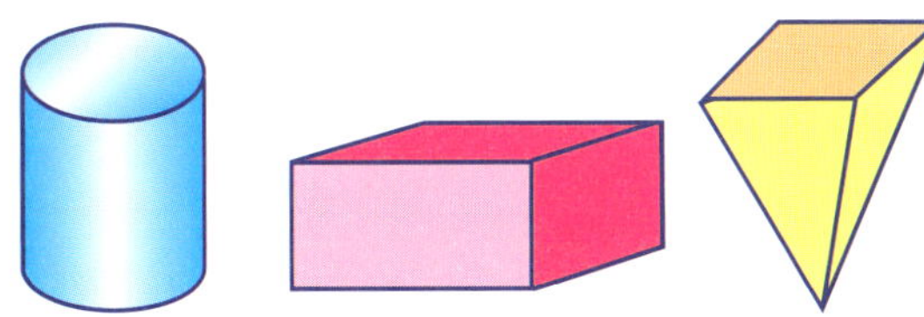

eg 675 ⟶ 700
(rounded to the nearest 100)
4492 ⟶ 4000
(rounded to the nearest 1000)

tally

Count and record in groups of 5

卌 = 5 卌 卌 || = 12

three-dimensional objects (3D)

Solid shapes that have length, width and height

time

analogue digital

1 hour = 60 minutes
1 minute = 60 seconds

trapezium

A quadrilateral that has one pair of parallel sides

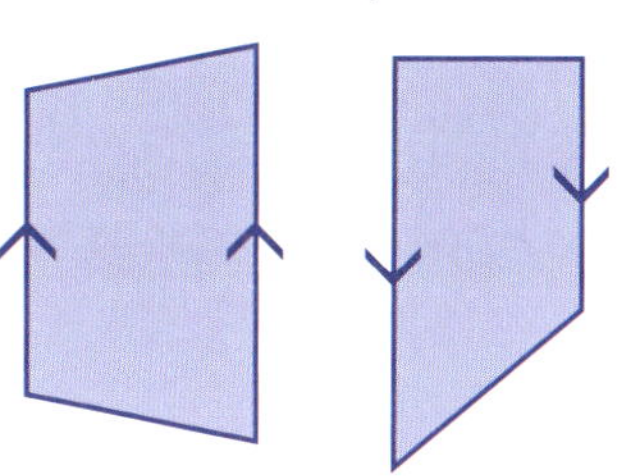

triangle

A 2D shape with 3 straight sides

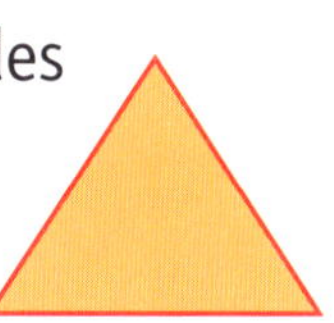

two-dimensional shapes (2D)

Shapes that only have length and width

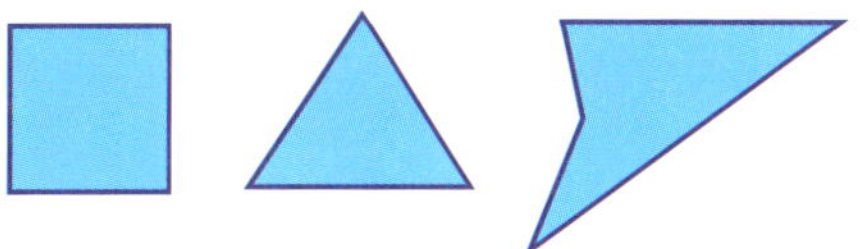

vertex

The point where the arms of an angle meet

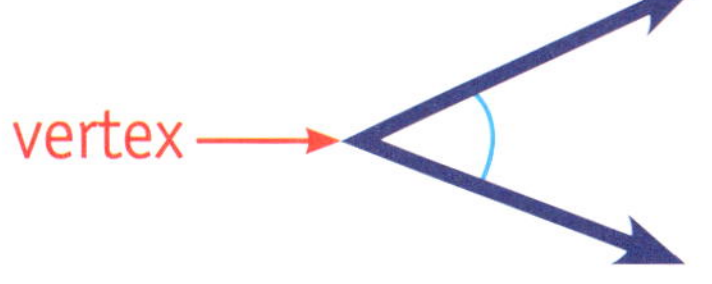

volume

The amount of space a solid object takes up

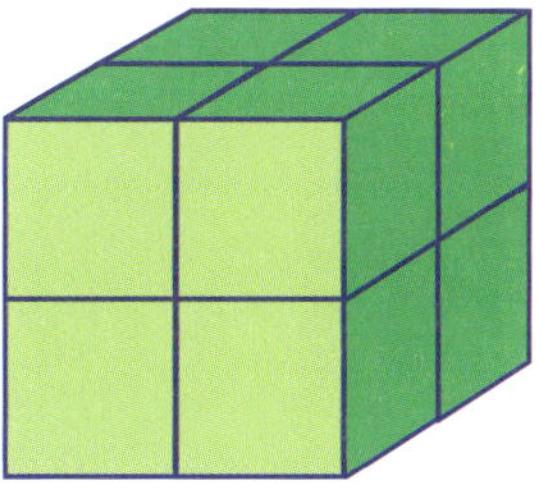

Unit 1 Numbers to 1000

10	20	30	40	50	60	70	80	90	100
110	120	130	140	150	160	170	180	190	200
210	220	230	240	250	260	270	280	290	300
310	320	330	340	350	360	370	380	390	400
410	420	430	440	450	460	470	480	490	500
510	520	530	540	550	560	570	580	590	600
610	620	630		650	660	670	680	690	700
710	720				760	770	780	790	800
810	820	830		850	860	870	880	890	900
910	920	930	940	950	960	970	980	990	1000

1 Write:

a the 5 missing numbers.

b the numbers between 360 and 370. 361, 362 ______

c 10 more than 160. ______ d 10 less than 700. ______

e 100 more than 180. ______ f 100 less than 910. ______

2 Count in 10s from 740 to 800. ______

3 Count in 100s from 440 to 840. ______

4 a Circle the numbers 10 more than 600, 770, 510, 850.

b Circle the numbers 100 less than 600, 770, 510, 850.

Unit 1 Counting in tens and hundreds

1 Complete.

a 196 197 198 ___ ___ ___ ___ ___

b 405 406 407 ___ ___ ___ ___ ___

c 770 769 768 ___ ___ ___ ___ ___

2 Complete the table.

Number	1 more	10 more	100 more
a 57			
b 300			
c 690			
d 799			
e 205			

3 Write the number 10 less than:

a 70 ________ b 330 ________ c 500 ________ d 405 ________

4 a 340 + 10 → ___ + 10 → ___ + 10 → ___

b 572 + 10 → ___ + 10 → ___ + 10 → ___

c 870 − 10 → ___ − 10 → ___ − 10 → ___

d 600 − 10 → ___ − 10 → ___ − 10 → ___

Challenge! Who will land on 850? ________

Flea jumps in tens, Grasshopper jumps in 20s, Frog jumps in 50s.

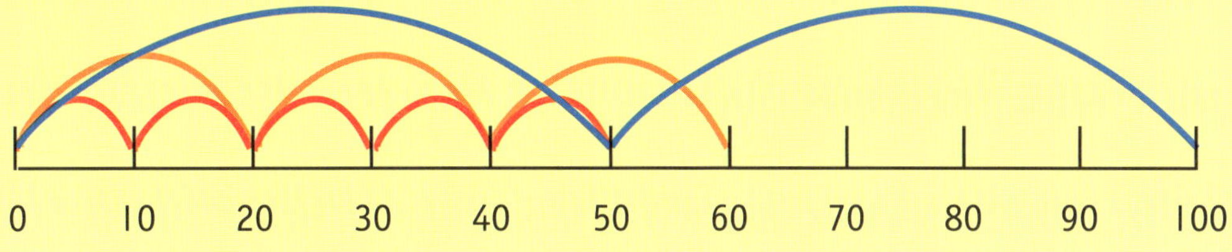

Unit 1 Place value

Place value

1 How many?

a

Hundreds	Tens	Ones
100 100 100 100 100	10 10 10 10 10 10	1 1 1

____

b

Hundreds	Tens	Ones
100 100 100 100 100 100		1 1 1 1 1 1 1

____

2 Complete: eg 549 = 5 hundreds, 4 tens and 9 ones

a 362 = _______ hundreds, _______ tens and _______ ones

b 791 = _______ hundreds, _______ tens and _______ ones

c _______ = 6 hundreds, 3 tens and 7 ones

d _______ = 8 hundreds and 4 tens

e 963 = _______ hundreds, _______ tens and _______ ones

f 602 = _______ hundreds, _______ tens and _______ ones

g _______ = 8 hundreds, 4 tens and 7 ones

3 Beware! These are not in place value order. Write the number:

a _______ = 2 hundreds, 4 ones and 3 tens

b _______ = 8 ones, 6 tens and 4 hundreds

c _______ = 9 ones and 7 hundreds

d _______ = 1 hundreds and 2 tens

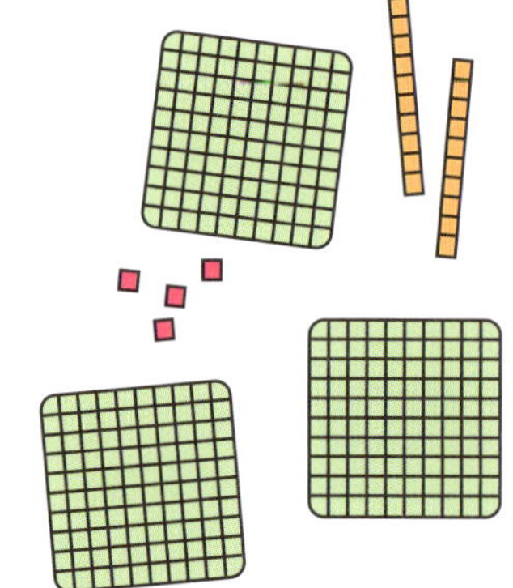

4 Complete.

a 264 = 200 + 60 + ☐

b 670 = ☐ + 70 + 0

c 712 = ☐ + 10 + ☐

d 354 = ☐ + ☐ + ☐

e 617 = 600 + ☐ + ☐

f 409 = ☐ + ☐ + 9

g 555 = ☐ + ☐ + ☐

h 830 = ☐ + ☐ + ☐

Challenge!

About how many marbles would fill the tray?

AC9M3N01 Number **MA2-RN-01** Representing numbers using place value A • Whole numbers: Apply place value to partition and regroup numbers up to 4 digits

Unit 1 Place value

1 Show the numbers on the numeral expanders.

a 679

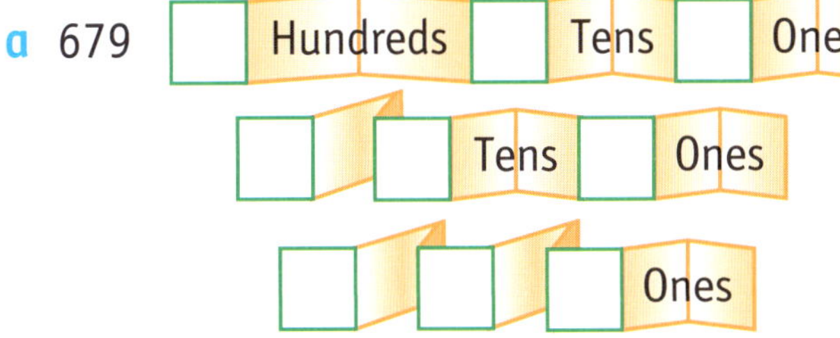

b 107

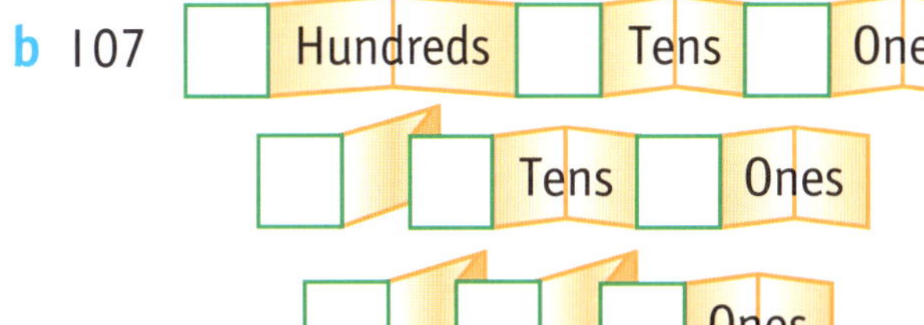

c 820

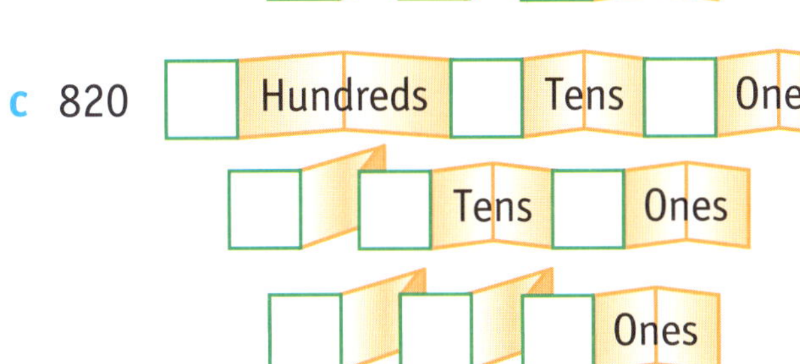

d 716

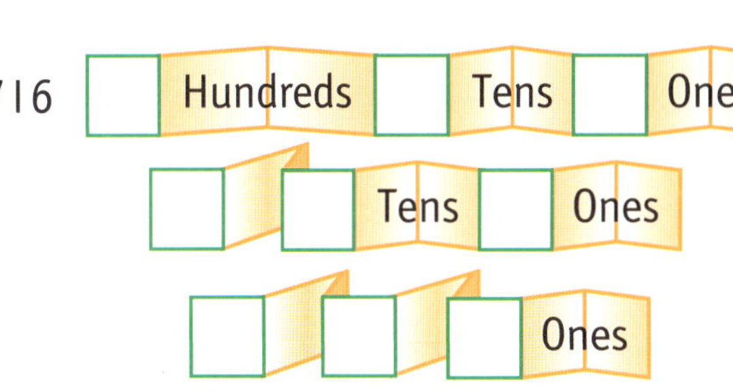

2 Write the hundreds, tens and ones.

a 642

__________ hundreds + __________ tens + __________ ones

__________ tens + __________ ones

__________ ones

b 495

__________ hundreds + __________ tens + __________ ones

__________ tens + __________ ones

__________ ones

c 281

__________ hundreds + __________ tens + __________ ones

__________ tens + __________ ones

__________ ones

d 95

__________ hundreds + __________ tens + __________ ones

__________ tens + __________ ones

__________ ones

AC9M3N01 Number **MA2-RN-01** Representing numbers using place value A • Whole numbers: Apply place value to partition and regroup numbers up to 4 digits

Unit 1 Write and order 3-digit numbers

1 Complete each counting pattern.

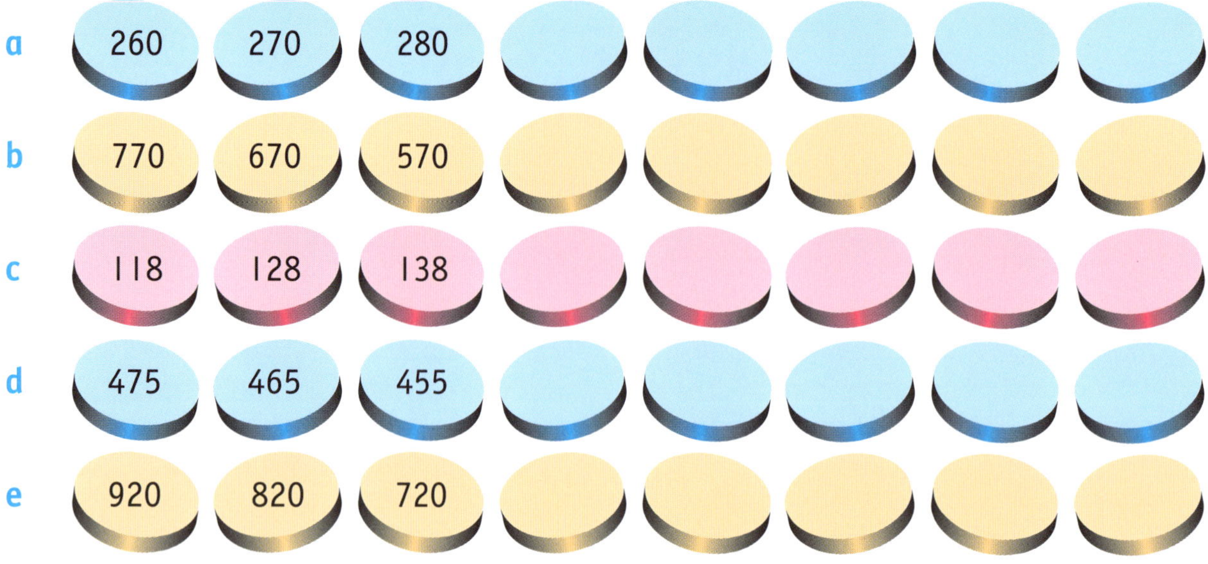

2 Write each number.

a three hundred and forty-two ________

b seven hundred and ten ________

c nine hundred and one ________

d four hundred and fourteen ________

3 Write in words.

a 509 ______________________________

b 213 ______________________________

4 Underline the larger number. Write **is less than** or **is greater than** to compare the two numbers.

a 269 ______________ 312

b 786 ______________ 867

c 499 ______________ 501

d 301 ______________ 199

e 614 ______________ 641

f 221 ______________ 212

Looking for patterns

Make different 3-digit numbers with these numbers. How many numbers can you make? How many are odd? How many are even? Repeat with 3 different numbers. Can you see a pattern?

Mastery Checklist I can:

- ☐ count in 10s and 100s to 1000
- ☐ find 1, 10 and 100 more or less
- ☐ understand place value to hundreds
- ☐ partition numbers into hundreds, tens and ones
- ☐ write and order 3-digit numbers.

Unit 2 Addition

0 10 20 30 40 50 60 70 80 90 100

1 Fill in the boxes.

2 Start at:

a 46 and go forward 8. ____ b 46 and go back 15. ____ c 46 and go forward 23. ____

3 Start at:

a 57 and go back 6. ____ b 57 and go forward 15. ____ c 57 and go forward 29. ____

4 Start at:

a 28 and go forward 2. ____ b 28 and go back 18. ____ c 28 and go forward 26. ____

5 This time keep hopping. Start at 81 and

a go back 5, ____ b now go forward 1, ____ c now go forward 9. ____

6 Start at 6 and

a go forward 14, ____ b now go back 6, ____ c now go forward 20. ____

Unit 2 Counting in 5s and 10s

1 Five more than:

a 20 ____	b 40 ____	c 75 ____	d 25 ____	e 10 ____
f 15 ____	g 35 ____	h 50 ____	i 11 ____	j 79 ____
k 17 ____	l 93 ____	m 44 ____	n 58 ____	o 86 ____

2 Ten less than:

a 60 ____	b 85 ____	c 30 ____	d 45 ____	e 95 ____
f 39 ____	g 91 ____	h 63 ____	i 13 ____	j 27 ____

3 Fill in the blanks and write a number sentence.

eg I start at 37, go forward 30 and stop at 67. [37] [+] [30] = 67

a I start at 48, go ____________ ____ and stop at 88. [ ] [ ] [ ] = 88

b I start at 64, go ____________ ____ and stop at 94. [ ] [ ] [ ] = 94

c I start at 22, go ____________ ____ and stop at 72. [ ] [ ] [ ] = 72

4 Fill in the missing numbers.

									Rule
a	14		24	29		39	44		+ 5
b	68		88			118			
c	65		55	50			35		
d	32	37		47		57			
e	129			114			99		

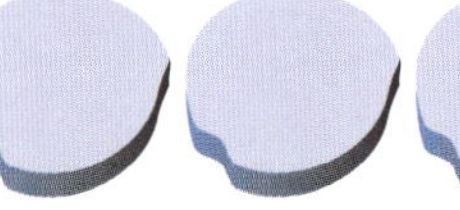

Challenge!

A springbok can leap 5 m.

If it travels 50 m, how many leaps does it make? 

A cougar can jump 10 m. If it jumps 7 times, how far does it travel? [ ]

Unit 2 Doubles and near doubles

1 a double 2 ☐ + ☐ = ☐ b double 8 ☐ + ☐ = ☐

c double 5 ☐ + ☐ = ☐ d double 10 ☐ + ☐ = ☐

e double 9 ☐ + ☐ = ☐ f double 16 ☐ + ☐ = ☐

2 a $\begin{array}{r} 4 \\ +\ 4 \\ \hline \end{array}$ b $\begin{array}{r} 7 \\ +\ 7 \\ \hline \end{array}$ c $\begin{array}{r} 11 \\ +\ 11 \\ \hline \end{array}$ d $\begin{array}{r} 13 \\ +\ 13 \\ \hline \end{array}$ e $\begin{array}{r} 0 \\ +\ 0 \\ \hline \end{array}$ f $\begin{array}{r} 9 \\ +\ 9 \\ \hline \end{array}$

Sometimes numbers are near doubles!

3 Show the near double you used.

a 4 + 5 = 4 + 4 + 1 = ____ b 10 + 9 = ____ = ____

c 3 + 2 = ____ = ____ d 8 + 9 = ____ = ____

e 7 + 6 = ____ = ____ f 6 + 5 = ____ = ____

g 12 + 13 = ____ = ____ h 17 + 16 = ____ = ____

i 15 + 14 = ____ = ____ j 19 + 18 = ____ = ____

4 a A cake costs $9. How much for 2 cakes? ____

b One puppy weighs 5 kg. What is the mass of two puppies? ____

c One bottle of cordial makes 18 drinks.
How many drinks will two bottles make? ____

d I bought two books. One book cost $14 and
the other cost $13. How much did I spend? ____

5 Keep doubling. a 2 4 8 ____ ____ ____

b 3 ____ ____ ____ ____ ____

c 5 ____ ____ ____ ____ ____

Challenge!

If one box holds 6 watermelons, how many watermelons will 8 boxes hold? ☐

Unit 2 Addition facts to 10 and 20

1 Look for the ten then find the total.

a | 7 | 5 | 3 | = 15 (handwritten: 10 above 7 and 3)

b | 5 | 5 | 1 | = ______

c | 9 | 6 | 4 | = ______

d | 6 | 8 | 2 | = ______

e | 1 | 3 | 9 | = ______

f | 9 | 1 | 7 | = ______

g | 4 | 6 | 2 | = ______

h | 2 | 4 | 8 | = ______

i | 3 | 8 | 7 | = ______

2

+	★★★	★★★ ★★★ ★★★	★★ ★★	★★★ ★ ★★★	★	★ ★ ★ ★ ★		★★★ ★★★	★★★ ★★ ★★★
●●● ●●●									
●●● ●									

3

a 6 + 7 = ______
16 + 7 = ______
26 + 7 = ______

b 5 + 8 = ______
15 + 8 = ______
25 + 8 = ______

c 9 + 4 = ______
9 + 14 = ______
9 + 24 = ______

d 5 + 6 = ______
25 + 6 = ______
65 + 6 = ______

e 8 + 7 = ______
8 + 37 = ______
8 + 57 = ______

f 3 + 8 = ______
43 + 8 = ______
83 + 8 = ______

4 Look for tens.

a 6 + 3 + 7 + 4 = ______

b 8 + 5 + 2 + 5 = ______

c 9 + 7 + 1 + 5 = ______

d 4 + 9 + 6 + 9 = ______

e 3 + 8 + 7 + 6 = ______

f 2 + 9 + 7 + 8 = ______

Mastery Checklist I can:
- ☐ count on to add
- ☐ count in 5s and 10s
- ☐ use doubles and near doubles to add
- ☐ make 10 to add
- ☐ use number patterns to add.

AC9M3N01 Number **AC9M3A02** Algebra **MA2-AR-01** Additive relations A • Select strategies flexibly to solve addition and subtraction problems of up to 3 digits

Unit 3 Subtraction

Change 

50c

75c

65c

45c

90c

25c

15c

80c

35c

John has $1 to spend at the fair. Draw two different combinations of change John could get if he buys these things.

1

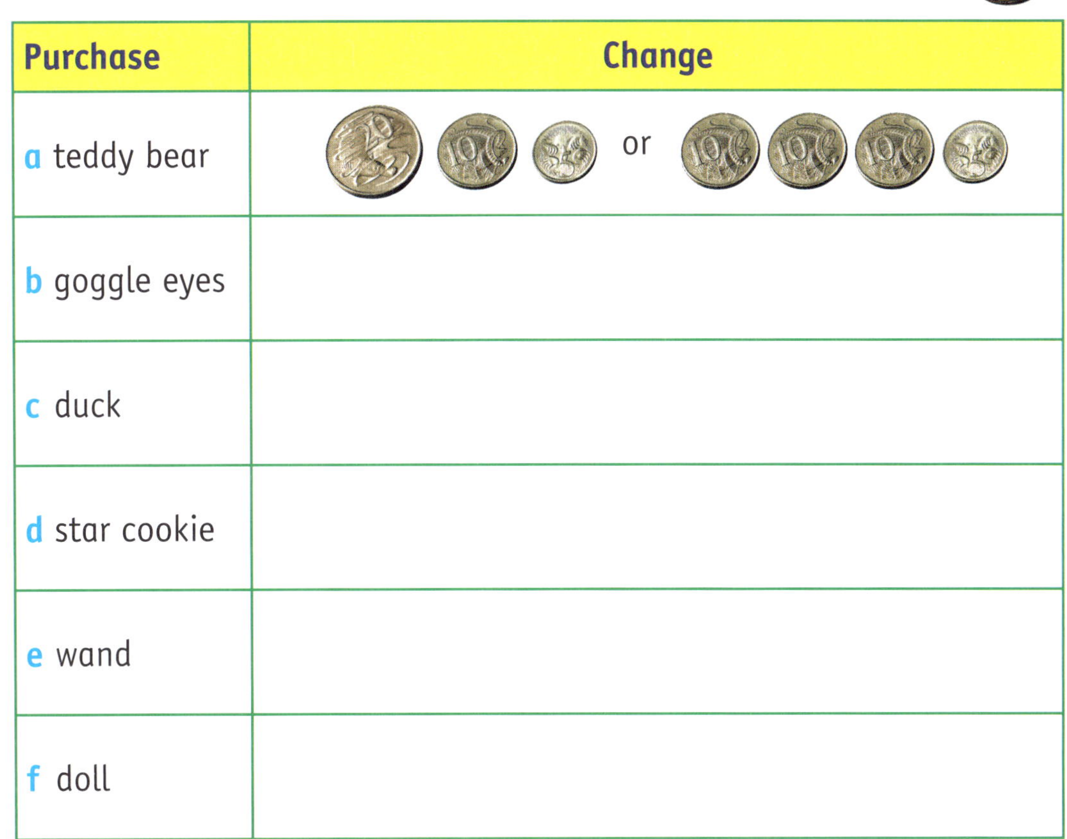

Purchase	Change
a teddy bear	or
b goggle eyes	
c duck	
d star cookie	
e wand	
f doll	

Unit 3 Use a number line

Look at this subtraction on the number line.

58 – 24 = ☐

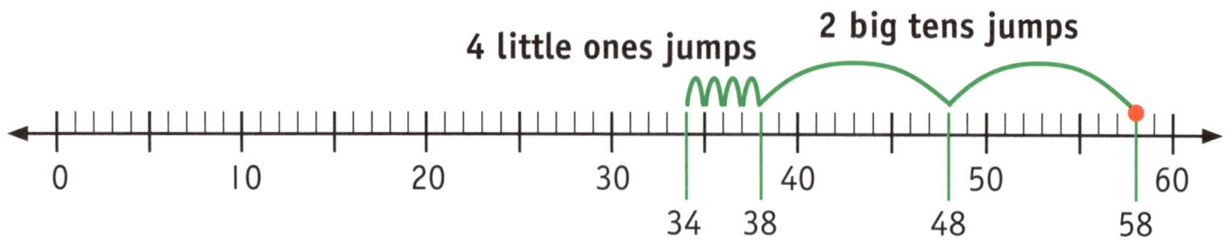

1 Use this number line to help you find the difference.

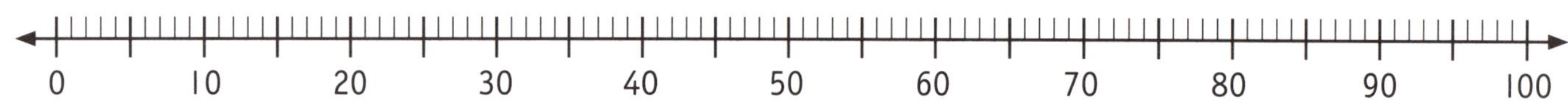

a 12 – 7 = ______	b 38 – 11 = ______	c 84 – 34 = ______
d 26 – 13 = ______	e 47 – 31 = ______	f 59 – 37 = ______
g 93 – 56 = ______	h 60 – 42 = ______	i 19 – 8 = ______
j 75 – 43 = ______	k 38 – 24 = ______	l 96 – 81 = ______
m 27 – 14 = ______	n 85 – 53 = ______	o 51 – 37 = ______

2 Write a story for each number line.

a

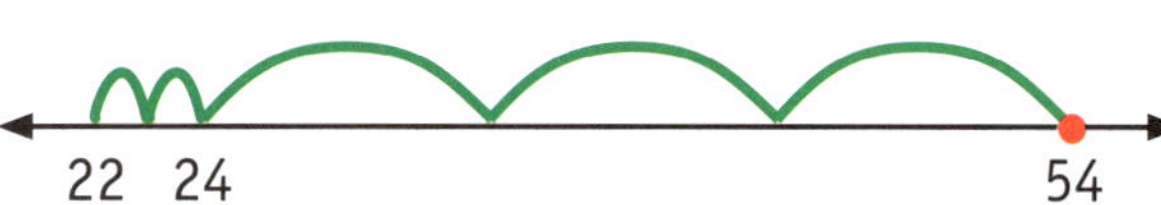

____

____

____

b

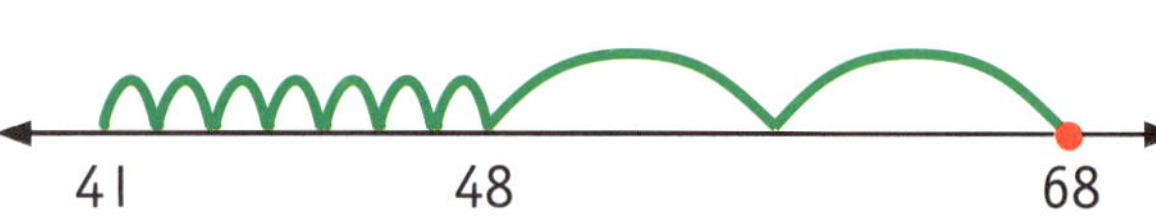

____

____

____

c

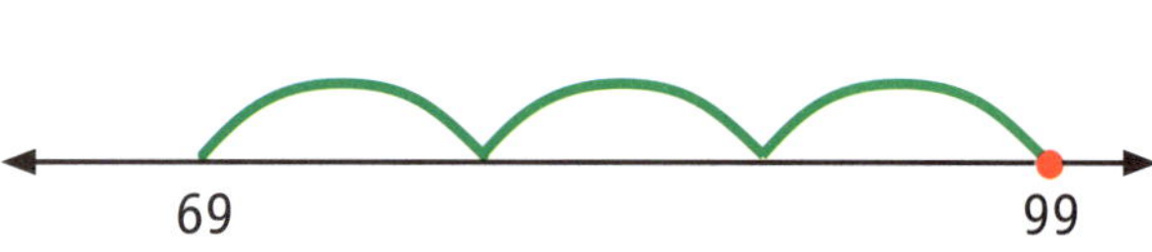

____

____

____

AC9M3N03 Number **MA2-AR-01 • MA2-AR-02** Additive relations A • Select strategies flexibly to solve addition and subtraction problems of up to 3 digits

Unit 3 Subtraction on a number line

Word problems

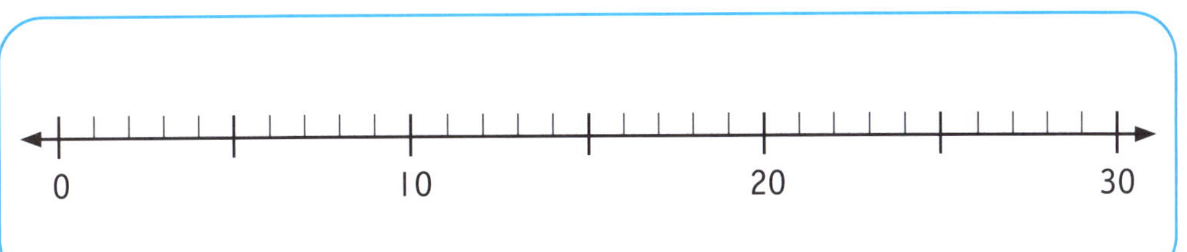

– is the take away sign. It means take away, subtract, difference between, minus or less.

1 Use the number line to find the difference.

a $17 - 9 =$ ____ b $12 - 4 =$ ____ c $10 - 3 =$ ____ d $16 - 7 =$ ____

e $15 - 8 =$ ____ f $26 - 9 =$ ____ g $18 - 12 =$ ____ h $23 - 5 =$ ____

i $19 - 7 =$ ____ j $29 - 17 =$ ____ k $15 - 9 =$ ____ l $21 - 7 =$ ____

2 a 15 pencils, 3 broke. How many not broken? ☐ – ☐ = ☐

b 29 jellybeans, 8 eaten. How many left? ☐ – ☐ = ☐

c 36 books, 5 torn. How many not torn? ☐ – ☐ = ☐

d 22 keys, 0 lost. How many keys? ☐ – ☐ = ☐

e 17 cakes, all eaten. How many left? ☐ – ☐ = ☐

f $48, $12 spent. How much left? ☐ – ☐ = ☐

3 Write a story for each. Then write a number sentence.

a

☐ – ☐ = ☐

b

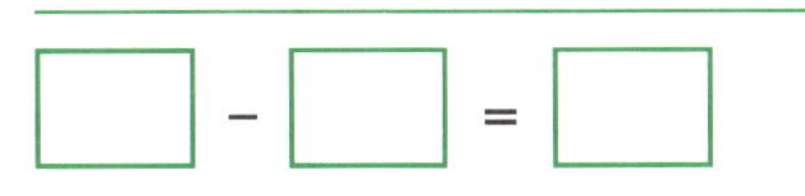

☐ – ☐ = ☐

Challenge! You have 36 lollies.

If you eat 3 every afternoon, how many days will they last? ☐

What if you ate 4 each night? ☐ Or 6 each night? ☐

Unit 3 Subtraction patterns

1 a 9 − 4 = 5
90 − 40 = 50
900 − 400 = 500

b 7 − 3 = ____
70 − 30 = ____
700 − 300 = ____

c 5 − 2 = ____
____ − ____ = ____
____ − ____ = ____

d 8 − 6 = ____
____ − ____ = ____
____ − ____ = ____

e 9 − 8 = ____
____ − ____ = ____
____ − ____ = ____

f 6 − 1 = ____
____ − ____ = ____
____ − ____ = ____

2 One addition fact tells us 4 things.

eg 5 + 3 = 8 3 + 5 = 8 8 − 5 = 3 8 − 3 = 5

a 7 + 2 = ____, ____ + ____ = ____, ____ − ____ = ____, ____ − ____ = ____
b 5 + 6 = ____, ____ + ____ = ____, ____ − ____ = ____, ____ − ____ = ____
c 8 + 5 = ____, ____ + ____ = ____, ____ − ____ = ____, ____ − ____ = ____
d 9 + 7 = ____, ____ + ____ = ____, ____ − ____ = ____, ____ − ____ = ____
e 6 + 7 = ____, ____ + ____ = ____, ____ − ____ = ____, ____ − ____ = ____
f 4 + 9 = ____, ____ + ____ = ____, ____ − ____ = ____, ____ − ____ = ____

3 a Cross out some dolls. Write a number story and a number sentence.

____ − ____ = ____

b Write the 3 other number facts.

Challenge! Zac had 14 marbles. He gave 2 away and had 16 left.

What is wrong with Zac's story? ____

How many did Zac give away if he had 2 left? ____

Unit 3 Two-digit subtraction

Subtract to 100

1 Use a number line.

eg 56 − 24 = 32

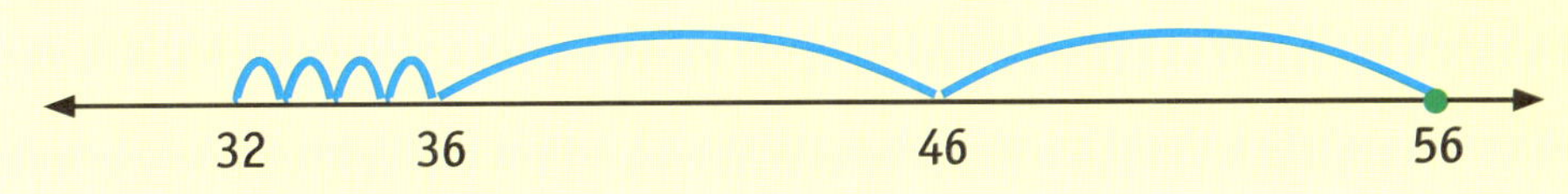

a 75 − 31 = ____

b 89 − 47 = ____

c 38 − 23 = ____

d 64 − 40 = ____

2 a 48 − 21 = ____

$$\begin{array}{r} 48 \\ -\ 21 \\ \hline \end{array}$$

b 66 − 36 = ____

$$\begin{array}{r} 66 \\ -\ 36 \\ \hline \end{array}$$

c 75 − 32 = ____

$$\begin{array}{r} 75 \\ -\ 32 \\ \hline \end{array}$$

d 99 − 61 = ____

$$\begin{array}{r} 99 \\ -\ 61 \\ \hline \end{array}$$

e 57 − 14 = ____

$$\begin{array}{r} 57 \\ -\ 14 \\ \hline \end{array}$$

f 83 − 70 = ____

$$\begin{array}{r} 83 \\ -\ 70 \\ \hline \end{array}$$

3 Jo had 38 baby mice. She sold 15. How many did she have left? ____

4 Ali picked 49 apples. He gave 23 to his friend. How many did he keep? ____

Trial and error

Look at page 11. If you had $3, what toys would you buy?

How much change would you get? ☐

Mastery Checklist I can:
- ☐ subtract money
- ☐ show change
- ☐ use a number line to subtract
- ☐ write subtraction stories
- ☐ write subtraction number sentences
- ☐ make patterns with subtraction
- ☐ use subtraction algorithms.

Problem solving

What's in a name?

Choose two friends and compare your names.

First name	Number of letters	Last name	Number of letters	Total

How many letters in: the longest name? _______ the shortest name? _______

What is the difference between the two totals? _______

Now score each name if you made them with Scrabble tiles.

Working out space

A 1, B 3, C 3, D 2, E 1, F 4
G 2, H 4, I 1, J 8, K 5, L 1
M 3, N 1, O 1, P 3, Q 10, R 1
S 1, T 1, U 1, V 4, W 4, X 8, Y 4, Z 10

First name	Number of letters	Last name	Number of letters	Total

What is the score for: the longest name? _______ the shortest name? _______

What is the difference between the two totals? _______

I can solve problems by:

☐ adding and subtracting numbers ☐ comparing my results with others.

AC9M3N03 Number **AC9M3A02** Algebra **MAO-WM-01** Working mathematically • communicating thinking and reasoning coherently and clearly **MA2-AR-01** Additive relations A • Select strategies flexibly to solve addition and subtraction problems of up to 3 digits

Unit 4 Metres

Length

12
11
10
9
8
7
6
5
4
3
2
1
0
Metres

Elephant Polar Bear Gorilla Giraffe Tom Dog Brachiosaurus

1 Which animal is the tallest? ______________________

2 Which animal is the shortest? ______________________

3 How tall is the giraffe? ______________________

4 How tall is the elephant? ______________________

5 How much taller is the polar bear than Tom? ______________________

6 How much shorter is the gorilla than the elephant? ______________________

7 If Tom stood on the elephant's back how high would he be? ______________________

8 Are all dogs the same height? ______________________

9 Name a tall dog ______________________ and a short dog. ______________________

10 Write the animals in order from shortest to tallest.

____

____

____

Unit 4 Measuring in metres and centimetres

measure length in cm and m

Estimate then measure the length of each item.

	Estimate	Measure
1 a length of your table	about ________ m	________ m
b length of classroom	about ________ m	________ m
c length of school corridor	about ________ m	________ m

	Estimate	Measure
2 a length of this book	about ________ cm	________ cm
b length of your pencil	about ________ cm	________ cm
c length of your desk	about ________ cm	________ cm

3

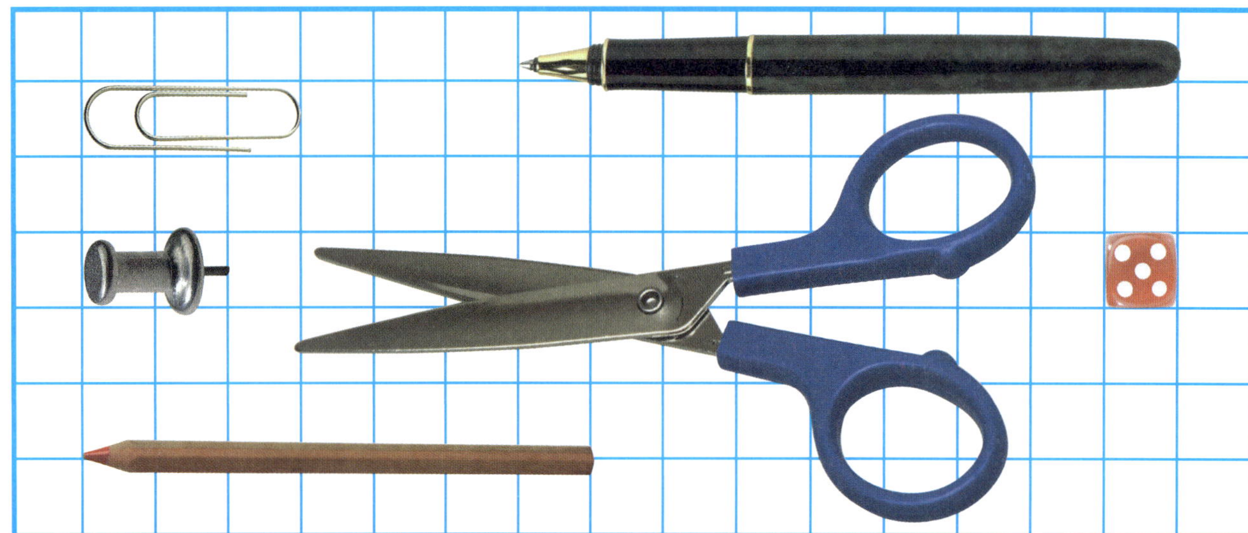

a What is the longest? __________

b What is the shortest? __________

c How long is the pen? __________

d How long is the paperclip? __________

e Which two items together are 5 cm? ______________________________

f The pushpin is __________ cm longer than the die.

g The paperclip is __________ cm shorter than the scissors.

4 Find something in your classroom that is:

a 1 m ______________

b 30 cm ______________

c 2 m ______________

d 10 cm ______________

e 50 cm ______________

f 80 cm ______________

AC9M3M01 • AC9M3M02 Measurement MA2-GM-02 Geometric measure A • Length: Measure and compare objects using metres, centimetres and millimetres • Geometric measure B • Length: Use scaled instruments to measure and compare lengths

Unit 4 Measuring and estimating length

m = metre
cm = centimetre

1 Use the number bank to complete each sentence.

Number Bank 1 2 4 10 30 180

a The door is ______ m high.

b The globe is ______ cm long.

c The man is ______ cm tall.

d The hen is ______ cm tall.

e The car is ______ m long.

f The wheelbarrow is ______ m long.

2

The bus stop sign is 1 m high.

a How high is the bus? __________

b How long is the bus? __________

3 Use a ruler to measure these lines to the nearest cm.

a ____ b ____ c ____ d ____

a [ ] b [ ] c [ ] d [ ]

measure cm with a ruler

Mastery Checklist I can:
- ☐ compare heights in metres
- ☐ measure lengths in m and cm
- ☐ estimate lengths in m and cm
- ☐ find the difference in lengths.

Unit 5 Fractions

A

B

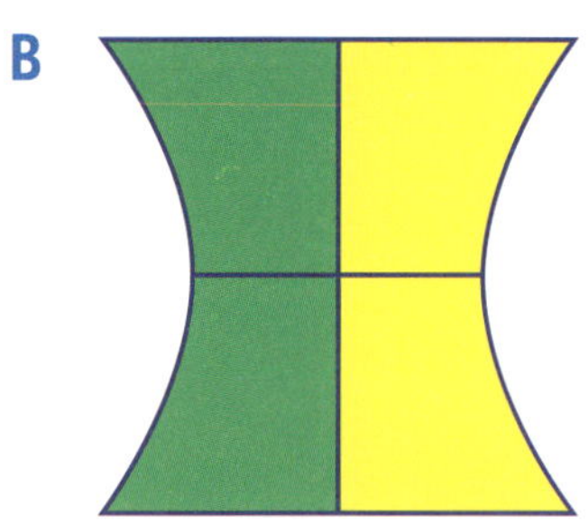

C

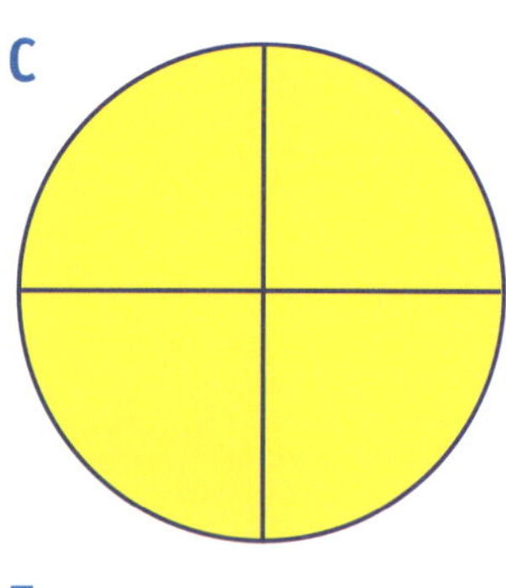

D

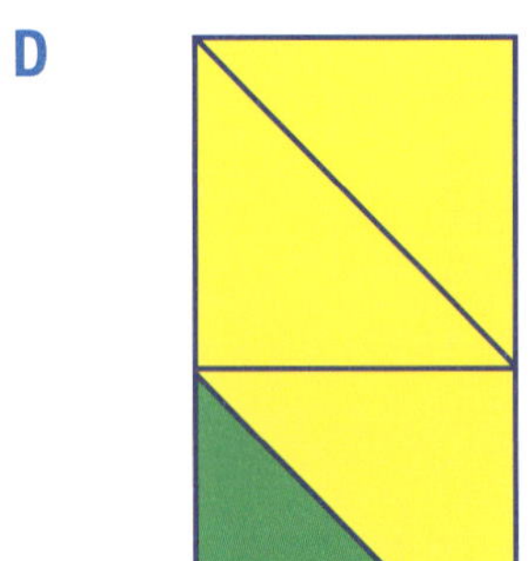

E

F

G

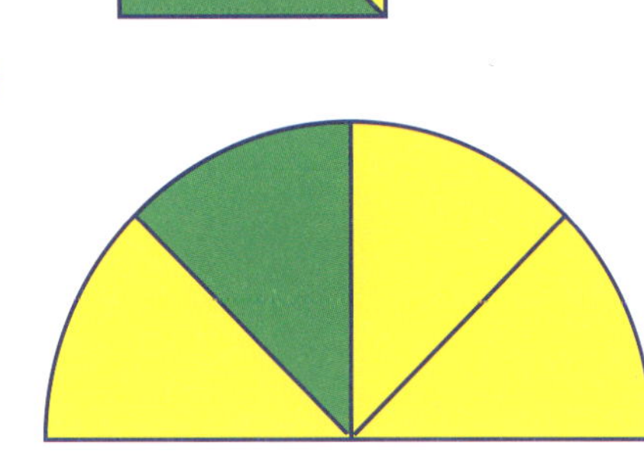

H

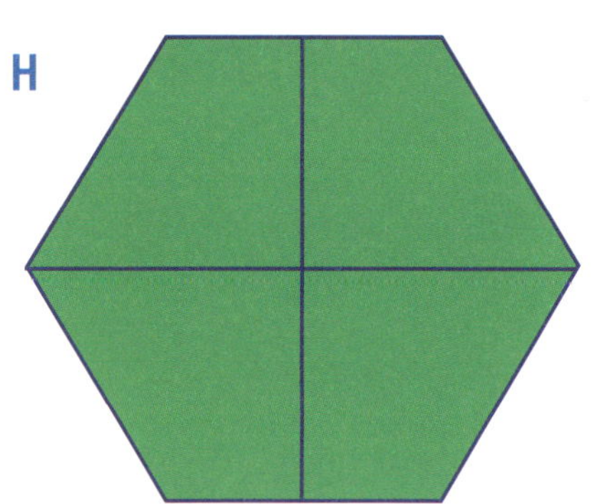

I

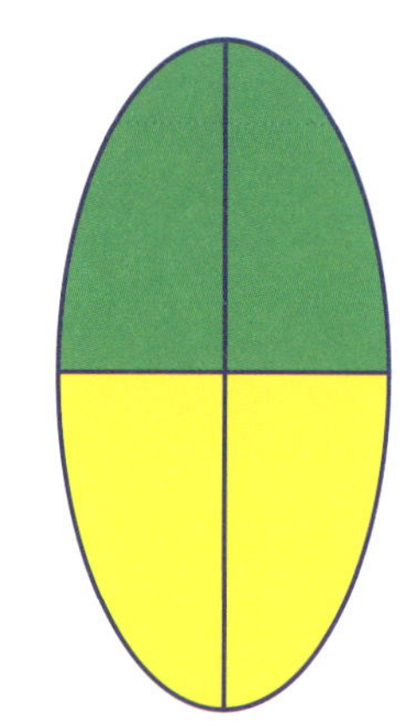

1 Which shapes are one quarter green? D and ______

2 Which shapes are one half yellow? ______

3 Which shapes show one whole? ______

4 Which shapes are one half green? ______

5 In F what fraction is yellow? ______

6 In G what fraction is green? ______

7 How many quarters are in one whole? ______

8 How many halves are in one whole? ______

9 How many quarters are in one half? ______

10 How many halves are in 2 wholes? ______

3 wholes? ______

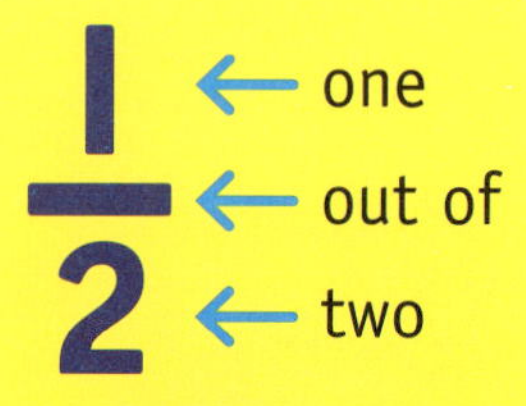

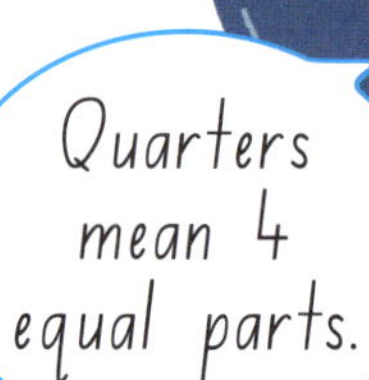

Unit 5 Halves and quarters

1 Colour the letters that are cut in half.

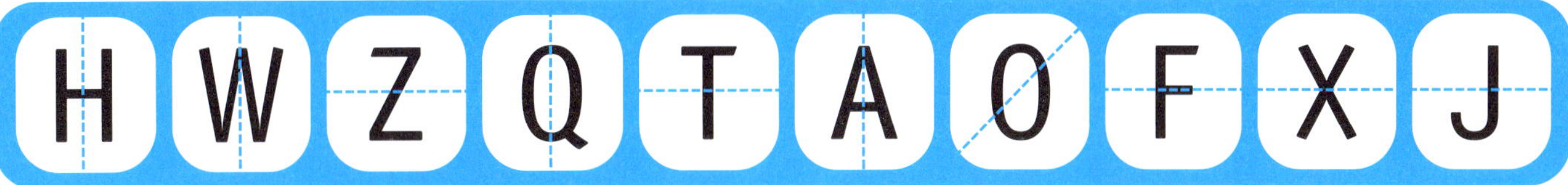

2 Draw a line to cut these letters in half.

3 Circle the halves. Tick the quarters.

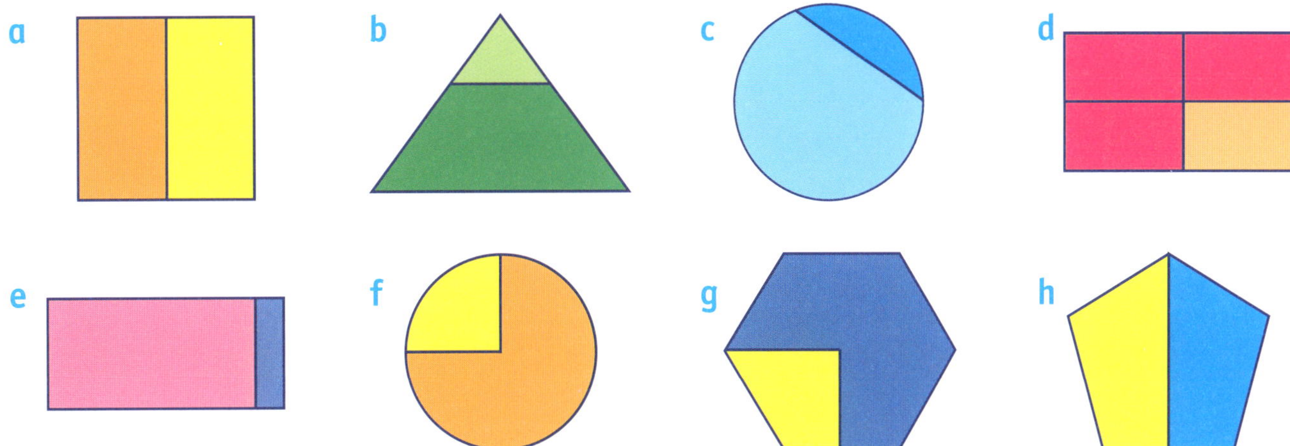

4 Use red to circle the objects that have been cut in half. Use blue to circle the objects that have been cut into quarters.

Unit 5 Fractions as part of a whole

1 Colour part of each shape to match the fraction.

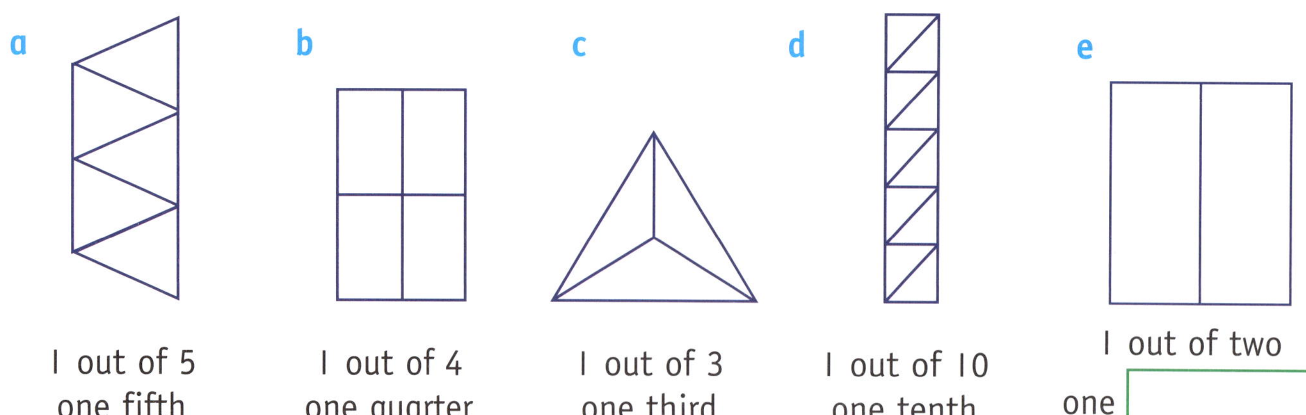

a 1 out of 5
one fifth

b 1 out of 4
one quarter

c 1 out of 3
one third

d 1 out of 10
one tenth

e 1 out of two
one

2 Write the fraction for the part coloured.

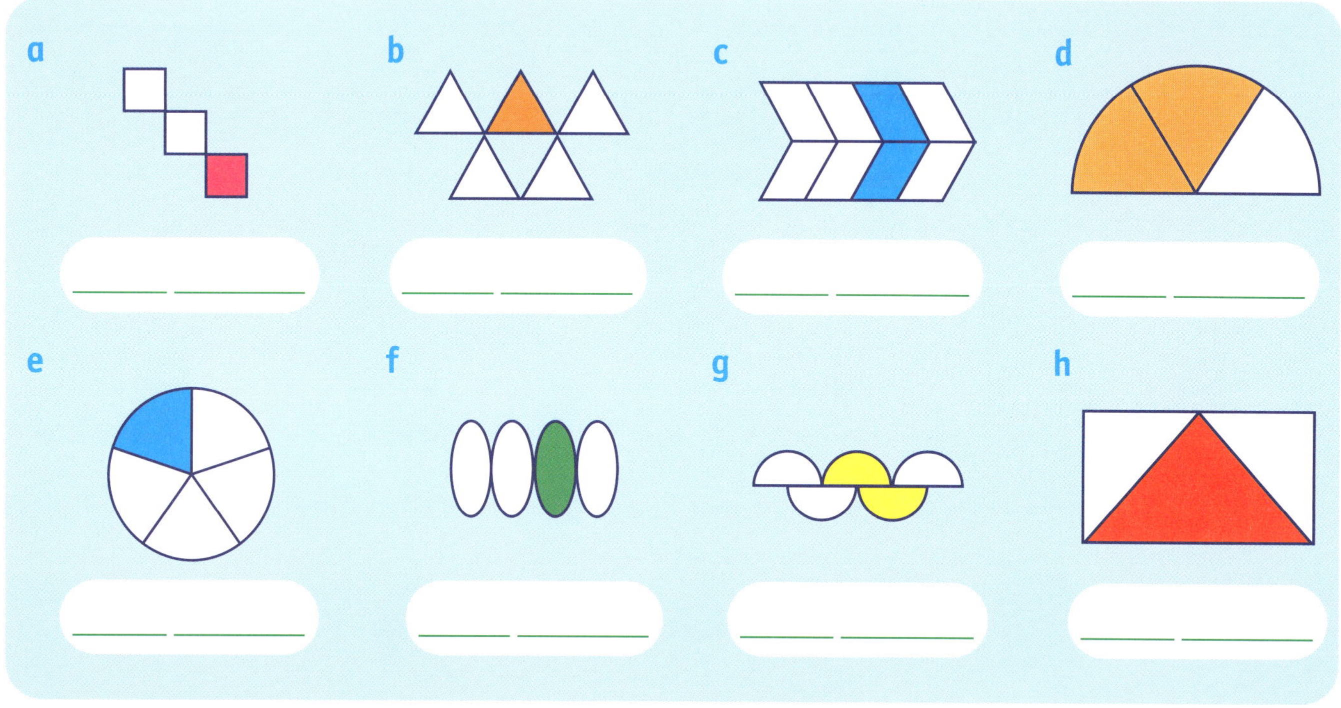

3 Draw lines to make equal parts. Colour and name a fraction you like.

a 

b 

Mastery Checklist I can:
- ☐ understand that fractions are equal parts
- ☐ recognise diagrams of halves and quarters
- ☐ divide letters into halves
- ☐ recognise halves and quarters in the real world
- ☐ recognise unit fractions as one part of a whole.

Problem solving

Fraction rewards

1 As a reward each person in the red team got one piece of a Jolly Chew Bar. Colour the pieces each child received.

a Nelly got one piece of a four piece bar.

b Feng got one piece of a three piece bar.

c Sara got one piece of an eight piece bar.

d Mei got one piece of a six piece bar.

2 Write the names in order from smallest piece to largest piece.

________ ________ ________ ________

3 a Are these rewards fair? Why? ________________

b What would you have done? ________________

____

4 How many different ways can you divide this Jolly Chew Bar into quarters to share with three other people and yourself?

I can solve problems by:

☐ dividing in equal shares ☐ using drawings and diagrams.

Measure length with people measures Investigation 1

Your classroom is getting new carpet. The principal needs the measurements of your room.

Estimate first. The room is ______________ long and ______________ wide.

How could you measure the room without using a tape measure?

____

measure without a tape measure

Draw your room here and show the different measurement tools you used.

Write what you found out.

____

____

____

____

Measure length with people measures

Investigation 1

Your teacher says you could rearrange the furniture in your classroom, so you have to measure it too. Do this with parts of your body: feet, hands, arms, forearms. Make a table to record the measurements. Explain how you measured the objects.

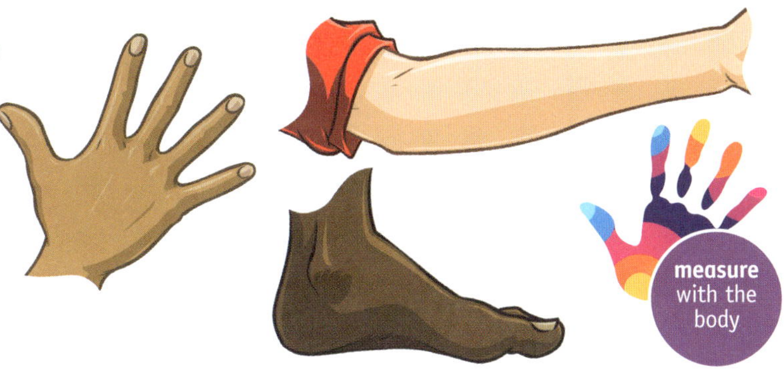

Why are people measures useful?

____

____

____

To carry out these tasks I need to:

- ☐ estimate lengths
- ☐ measure lengths with parts of my body
- ☐ explain how I measure lengths
- ☐ use a table to record lengths of different objects
- ☐ work well in a group.

I enjoyed this task!

☆☆☆☆☆

Revision

Shade one bubble.

1 Which number completes the pattern?

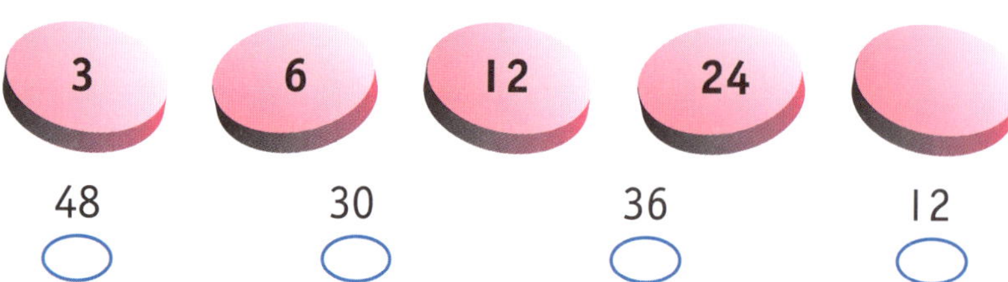

48 ◯ 30 ◯ 36 ◯ 12 ◯

2 Which group shows 54?

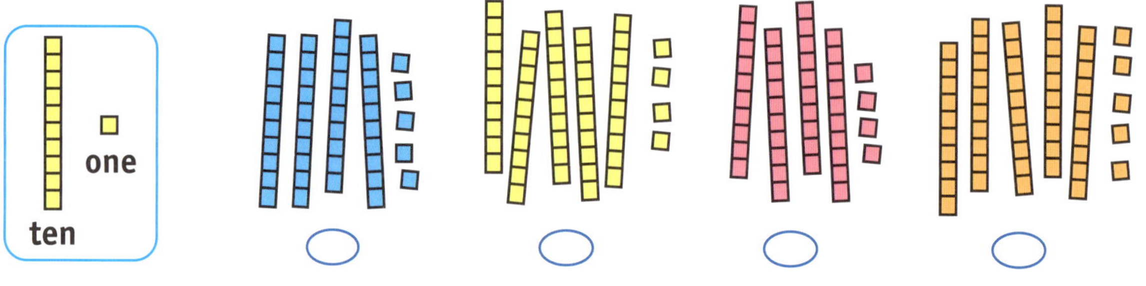

3 Huey had $1 to spend and bought this toy.

How much change did he get? 5c ◯ 25c ◯ $1.15 ◯ 15c ◯

4 A cake costs $13. How much for two cakes?

$15 ◯ $23 ◯ $26 ◯ $25 ◯

5 How much altogether?

$100 $100 $10 $100

$523 ◯ $532 ◯ $343 ◯ $432 ◯

Revision

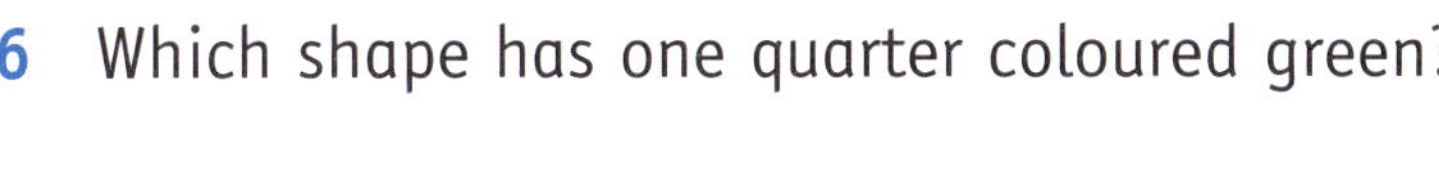

6 Which shape has one quarter coloured green?

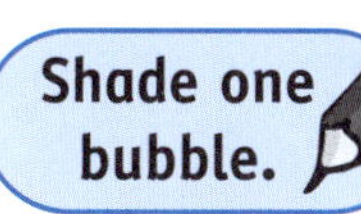

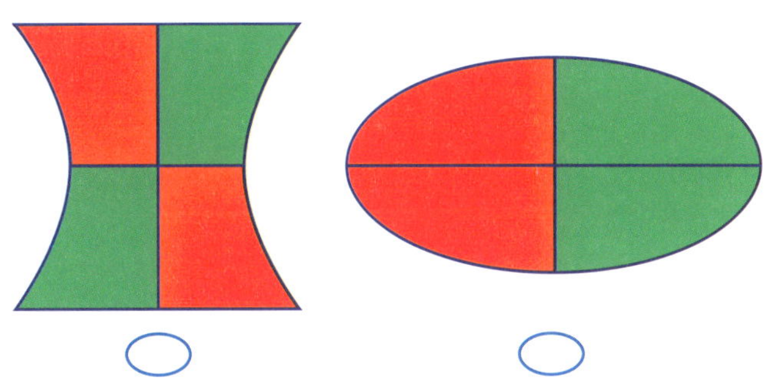

7 Which shape has been cut in half?

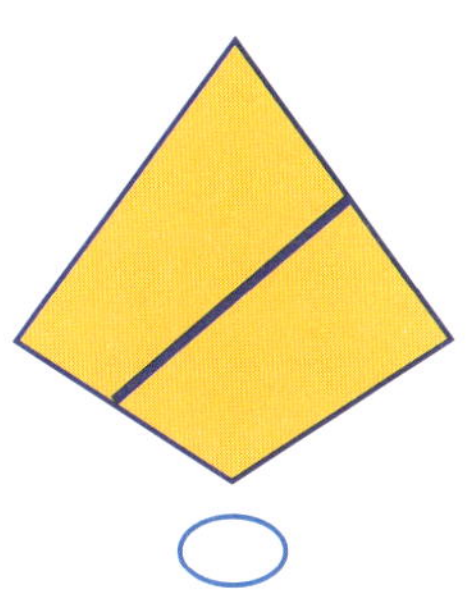

8 Which number is closest to 500?

475 520 560 490

9 Which snake is 5 m long?

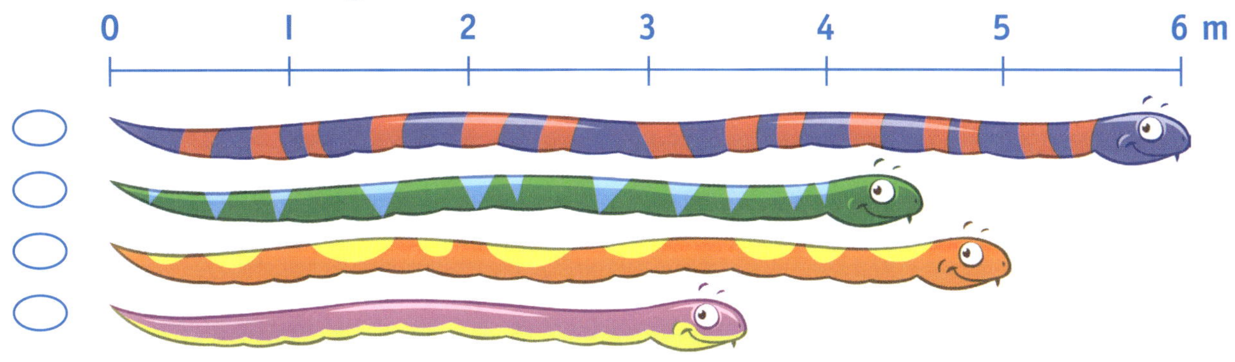

10 Write the number sentence to match.

Write your answer in the box.

Unit 6 Patterns

A

0 4 8 12 16 20

B

C

2 5 8 11 14 17

D

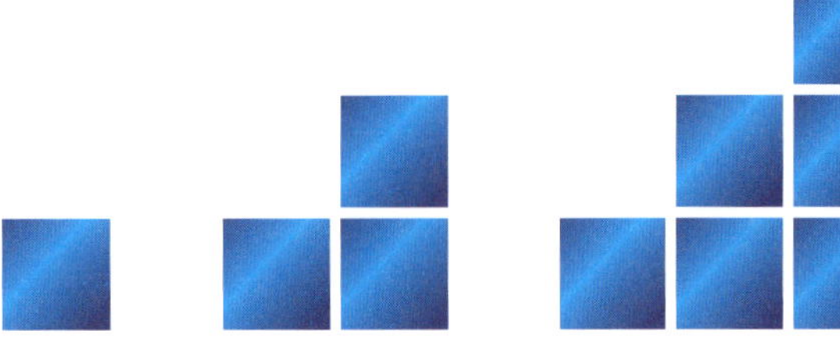

1 a How is pattern **A** made? ______

b What are the next three numbers? ______ ______ ______

c What will the 12th number be? ______

2 Draw the next term for **B**.

3 a What is the next number in **C**? ______

b What is the pattern for **C**? ______

c Will 27 be in **C**? ______ Why? ______

4 a How many squares will be in the next term for **D**? ______

b Draw it.

Unit 6 Patterns using shapes and numbers

Patterns

1 a Start at 2. Make a pattern by adding four.

b Start at 1. Make a pattern by adding four.

c 3 7 11 15 19 23

How was this pattern made? ______________________________

d Each pattern rule is add 4. Why are the patterns different? ______________________________

____

Look at page 28.

2 a What is happening to change the terms in **B**? ______________________________

b Write the pattern in numbers. ______ ______ ______ ______

c How many spots will there be in the 10th term? ______ 14th term? ______

d Draw another pattern like **B** using triangles.

3 a What shape is used for **D**? ______________

b Will the next term use a circle? ______________

Why? ______________________________

Challenge!

How many squares will be in the 10th shape for **D**? ☐

Unit 6 Patterns with numbers

1 Finish each pattern and write the rule.

a 2, 4, 6, 8, ____, ____, ____ Rule ____________

b 10, 13, 16, 19, ____, ____, ____ Rule ____________

c 30c, 25c, 20c, 15c, ____, ____, ____ Rule ____________

d 20 cm, 30 cm, 40 cm, 50 cm, ____, ____, ____ Rule ____________

e 1, 10, 19, 28, ____, ____, ____ Rule ____________

f 1, 2, 4, 8, ____, ____, ____ Rule ____________

g 48, 42, 36, 30, ____, ____, ____ Rule ____________

h 2, 9, 16, 23, ____, ____, ____ Rule ____________

i $\frac{1}{5}$, $\frac{2}{5}$, $\frac{3}{5}$, $\frac{4}{5}$, ____, ____, ____ Rule ____________

j 39, 35, 31, 27, ____, ____, ____ Rule ____________

2 a Start with 20. Make a pattern by adding 4.

b Start with 86. Make a pattern by taking away 10.

c Write the instructions for this pattern. ____________

____

Looking for patterns

Finish this pattern. 1, 3, 7, 15, ☐, ☐

What did you do? ☐

Mastery Checklist I can:
- ☐ work out the rule for a number pattern
- ☐ continue patterns
- ☐ follow a rule to make a number pattern
- ☐ make my own patterns with numbers and shapes.

Problem solving

Frog jumps

Froggy jumps by **twos** to visit Ducky. He jumps to lily pad **2**, then **4** and so on until he gets there.

Froggy's jumps: **2, 4, 6** ______________________ How many jumps? ______

Next, Froggy jumps by **fours** from Ducky to the flies for a snack, starting at **12**.

Froggy's jumps: **12** ______________________ How many jumps? ______

Now Froggy jumps by **fives** from the flies to visit his mum, starting at **5**.

Froggy's jumps: **5** ______________________ How many jumps? ______

Make up your own pattern for Froggy's next set of jumps.

____

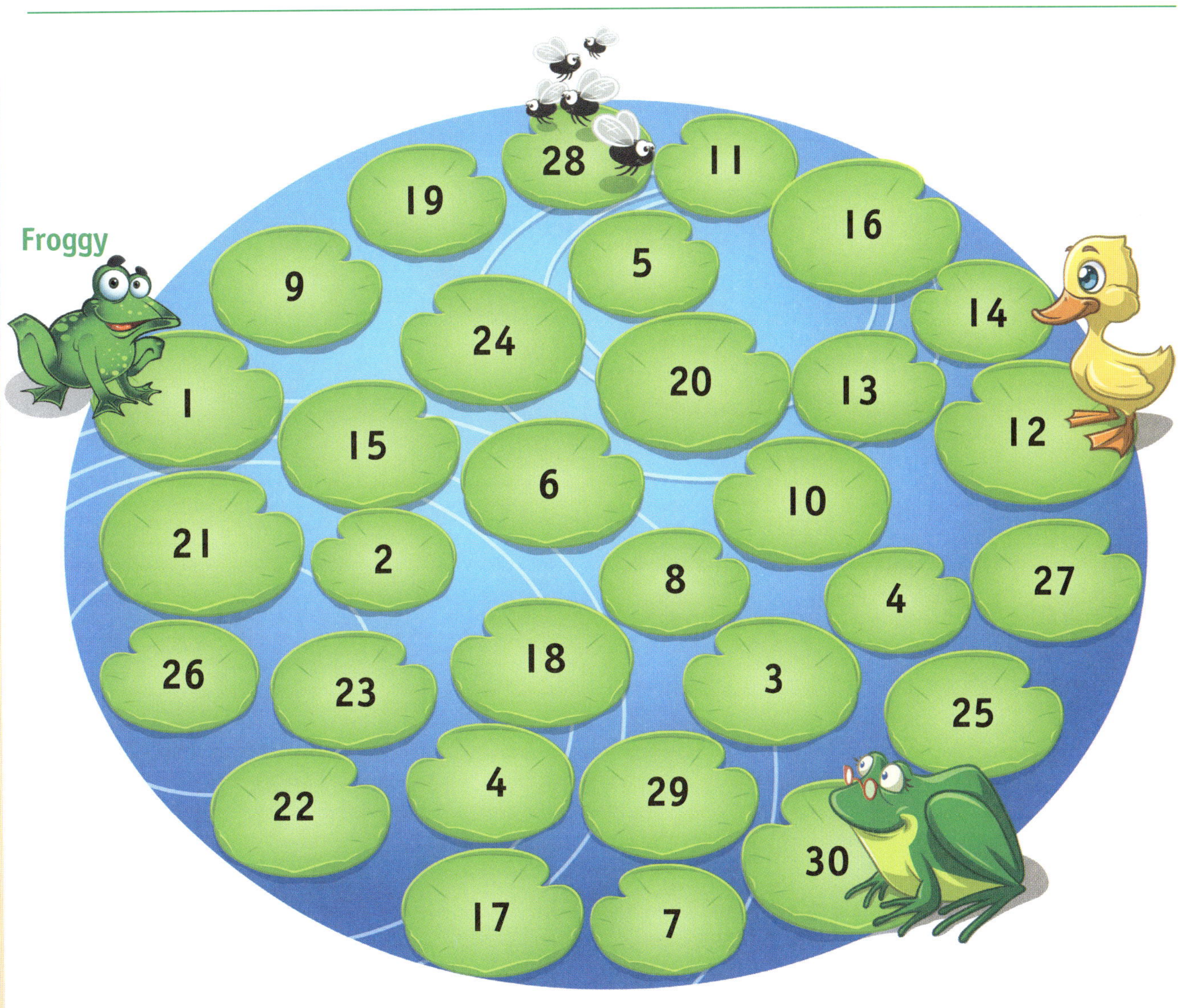

I can solve problems by:

☐ completing patterns by adding ☐ describing the patterns I see.

Unit 7 Half hours and quarter hours

Get two craft sticks: a shorter one for the hour hand and a longer one for the minute hand.

use sticks to show the time

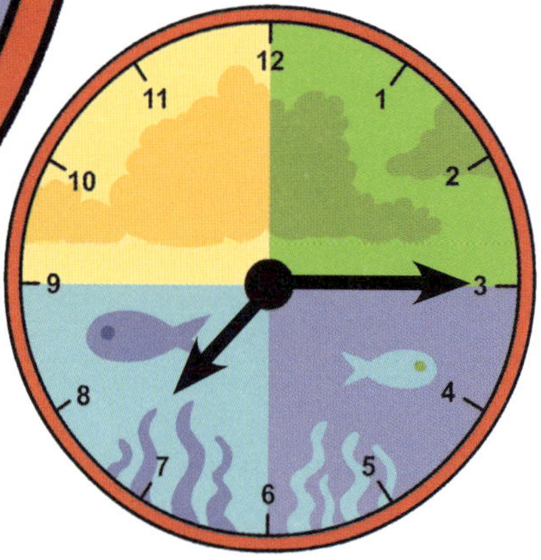

1 With your craft sticks show: a 4 o'clock b 7 o'clock c 10 o'clock

d Where is the minute hand each time? ______

e Where is the hour hand at 4 o'clock? ______

2 With your craft sticks show: a $\frac{1}{2}$ past 8 b $\frac{1}{2}$ past 11 c $\frac{1}{2}$ past 5

d Where is the minute hand each time? ______

e Where is the hour hand at $\frac{1}{2}$ past 8? ______

3 a What is the time on the small clock? ______

b Why is the minute hand on 3? ______

c Where is the hour hand? ______

4 With your craft sticks show: a $\frac{1}{4}$ past 9 b $\frac{1}{4}$ past 2 c $\frac{1}{4}$ past 10

d $\frac{1}{4}$ to 5 e $\frac{1}{4}$ to 3 f $\frac{1}{4}$ to 12

Unit 7 Five-minute intervals

1 How many minutes pass as the minute hand moves from:

a 12 to 1 ______ b 12 to 3 ______ c 12 to 6 ______

d 12 to 9 ______ e 12 to 7 ______ f 12 to 2 ______

g 12 to 12 ______ h 12 to 11 ______ i 12 to 4 ______

j 12 to 10 ______ k 12 to 5 ______ l 12 to 8 ______

2

a 3:25 b ______ c ______ d ______ e ______

3 Use 'past' and 'to' to tell these times, eg $\frac{1}{4}$ to 5.

a ______ b ______ c ______

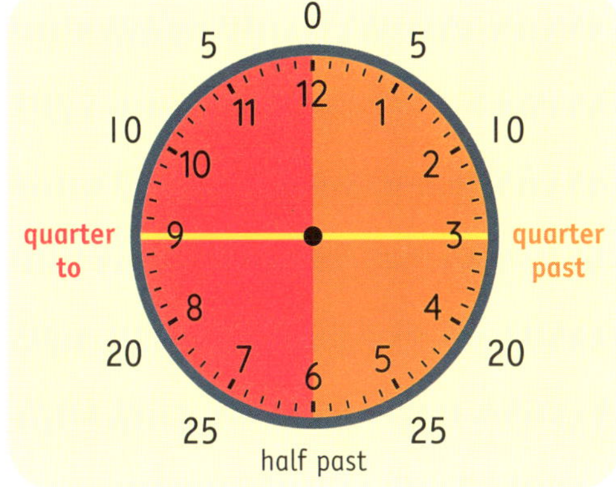

4 Draw these times.

a 25 to 5

b 5 past 10

c $\frac{1}{4}$ to 5

d 20 past 12

e 10 past 7

Unit 7 Analogue and digital times

1

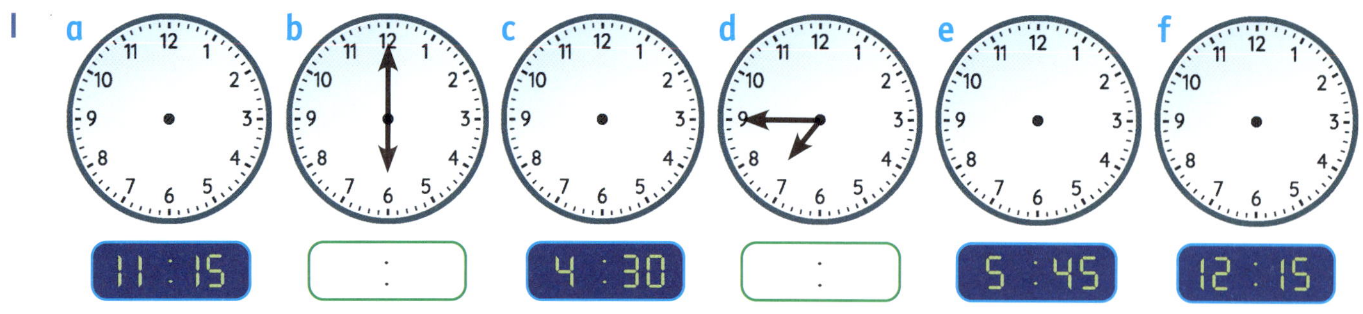

2 a 7 : 05 b 11 : 15 c 3 : 45 d 9 : 05 e 5 : 30

	Read	Means
a	seven-oh-five	5 minutes past 7
b		
c		
d		
e		

3 Match the time to the correct clock.

 AC9M3M04 Measurement **MA2-NSM-02** Non-spatial measure A • Time: Represent and read analog time • Non-spatial measure B • Time: Represent and interpret digital time displays

Unit 7 Time to the minute

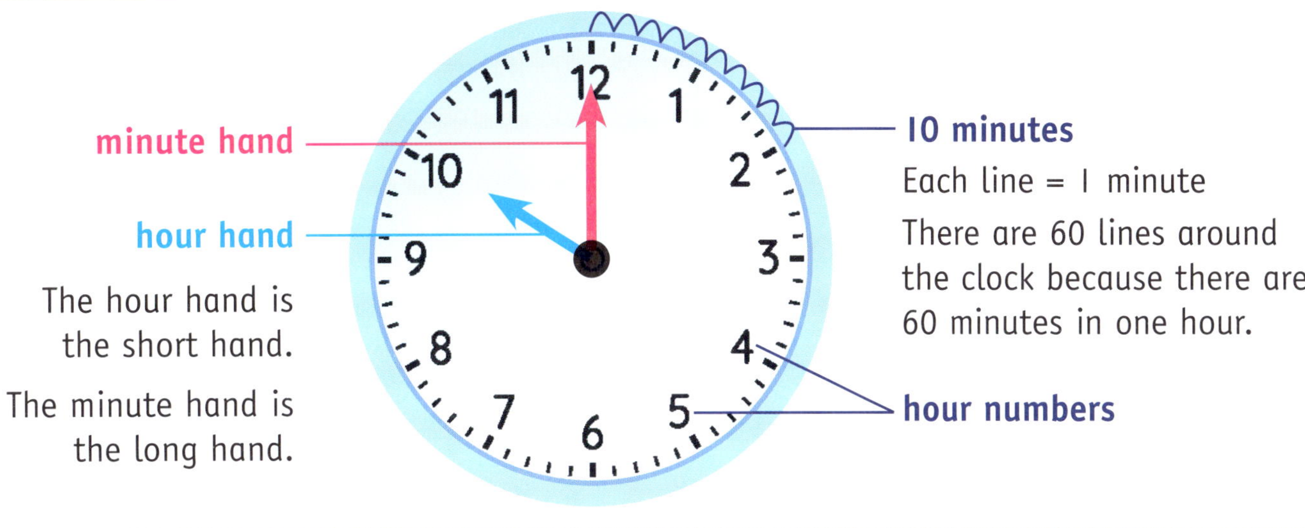

1 Write the minutes past the hour time. Then show the digital time.

2 Draw these times.

26 to 5 | 6 past 11 | 14 to 4 | 21 past 1 | 9 past 6

Mastery Checklist I can:
- ☐ show half hours and quarter hours on a clock
- ☐ recognise and show times to the nearest 5 minutes
- ☐ match analogue and digital times
- ☐ recognise and show times to the minute.

Unit 8 Prisms

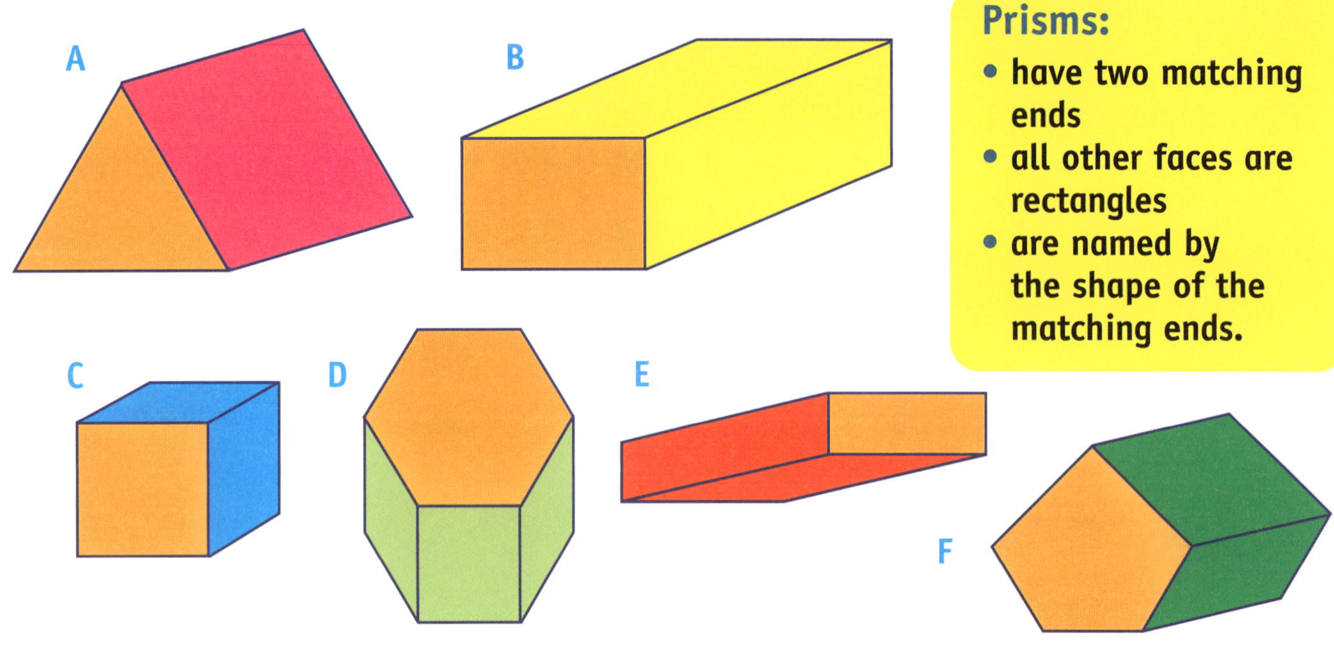

Prisms:
- **have two matching ends**
- **all other faces are rectangles**
- **are named by the shape of the matching ends.**

1 Name the shape of each orange face (end).

A ______________________ B ______________________

C ______________________ D ______________________

E ______________________ F ______________________

2 Use the orange face name (end) to name each prism.

A Triangular prism______ B ______________________

C ______________________ D ______________________

E ______________________ F ______________________

3 How many faces and ends altogether does each prism have? Remember that you can't see them all.

A ________ B ________ C ________ D ________ E ________ F ________

4 What shape are all the faces that aren't ends? ______________________

5 What is a prism? ____

____

6 Draw these prisms.

a rectangular prism | b triangular prism | c hexagonal prism

 AC9M3SP01 Space **MA2-3DS-01** Three-dimensional spatial structure B • 3D objects: Connect three-dimensional objects and two-dimensional representations

Unit 8 Pyramids

Pyramids:
- **have one base and all other faces are triangles**
- **are named by the shape of the base.**

1 Name these pyramids.

a 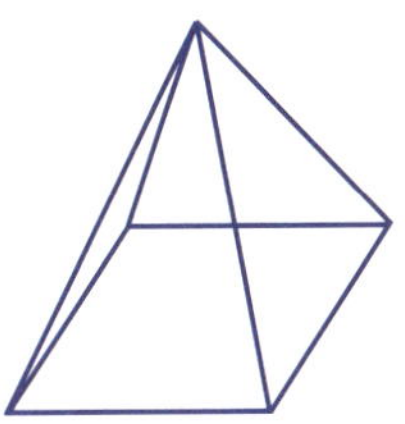

____

____

b 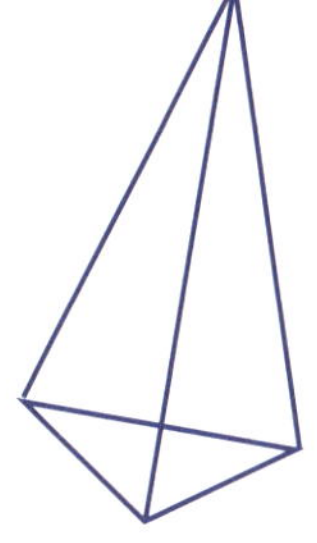

____

____

c 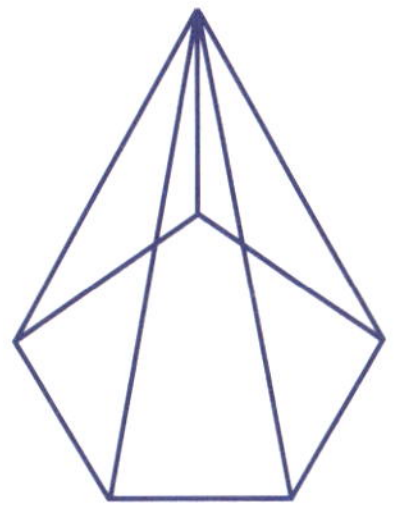

____

____

2 Circle the pyramids. Draw a square around the prisms.

A 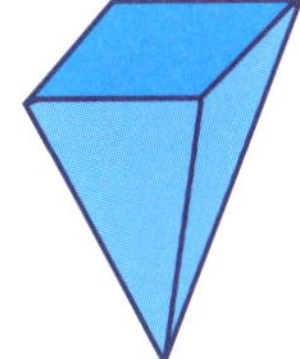

B 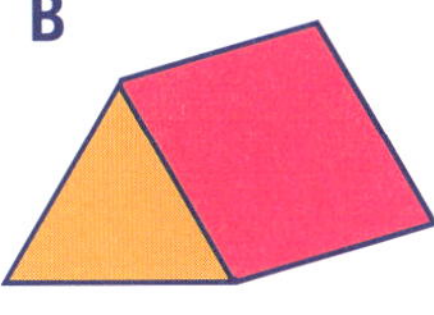

C 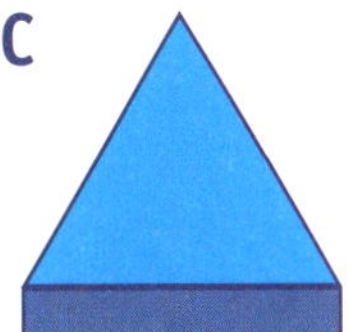

D 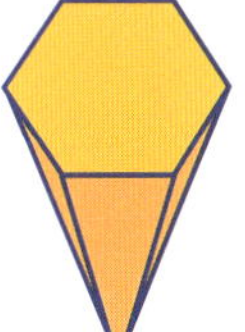

E 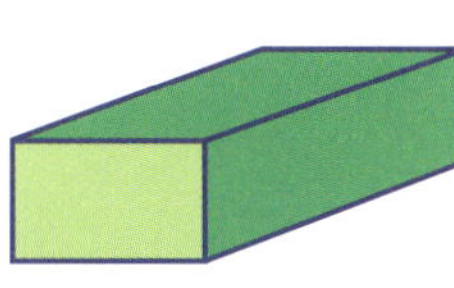

a How many faces has object **D**? ______________

b How many faces has object **A**? ______________

c Which picture shows a square pyramid? ______________

d Which picture shows a rectangular prism? ______________

3 Draw each face.

4 Draw these pyramids.

a pentagonal pyramid

b rectangular pyramid

c triangular pyramid

Challenge! How many everyday items can you name that are pyramid-shaped or triangular prisms?

____

____

Unit 8 Constructing 3D objects

build 3D objects

Use clay and small pieces of sticks or straws to construct the 3D objects. Then write how many faces, edges and corners.

Prism	Faces	Edges	Corners
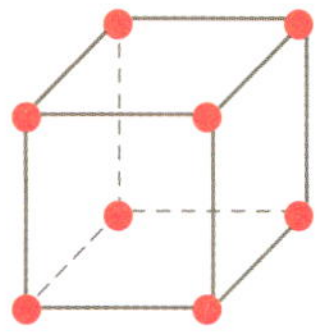	6	12	8
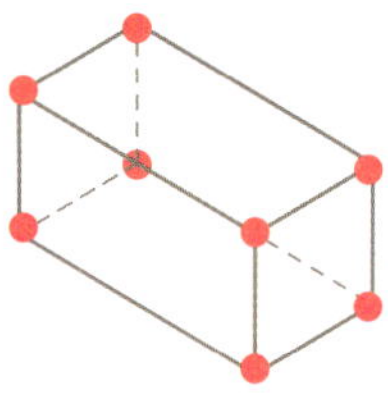			
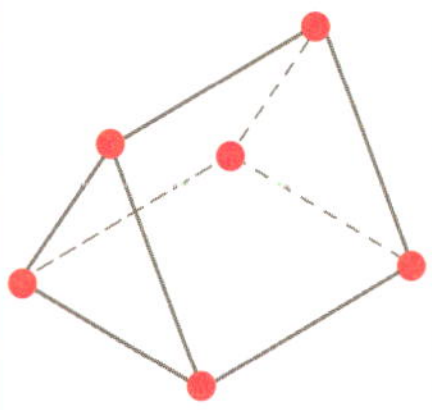			
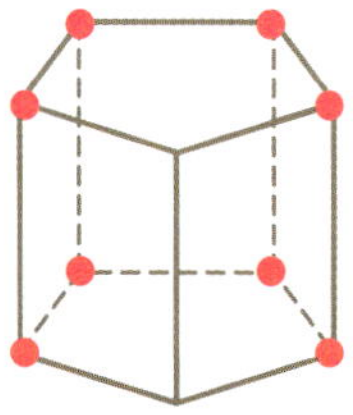			
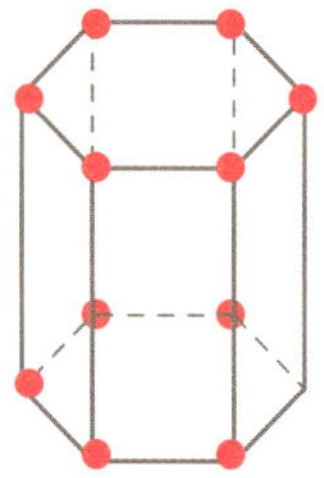			
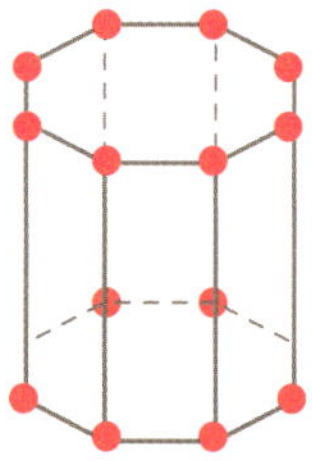			

Pyramid	Faces	Edges	Corners
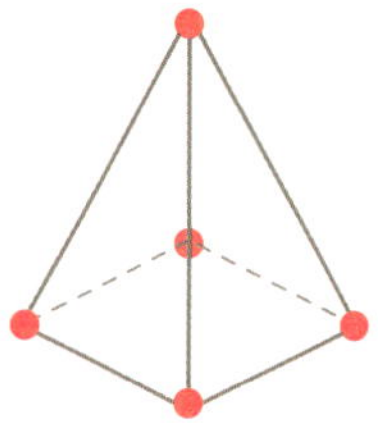	5	8	5
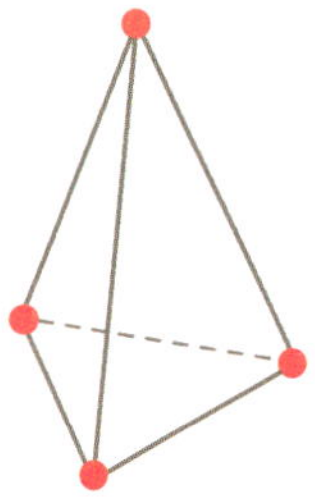			
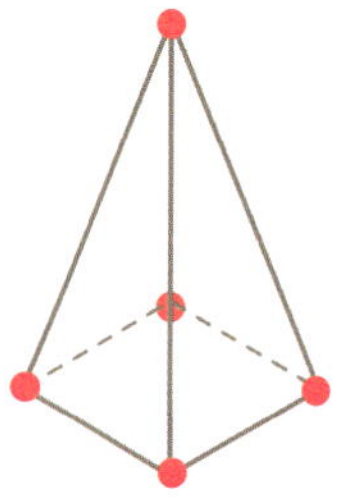			
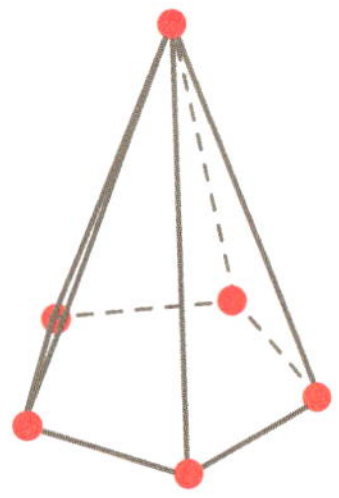			
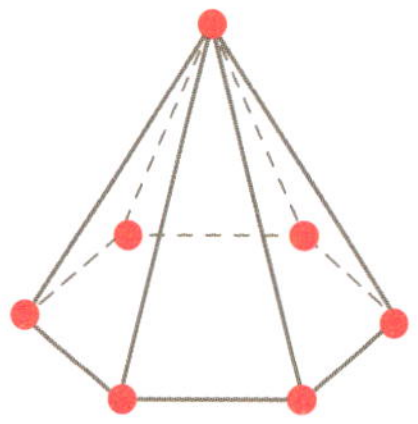			
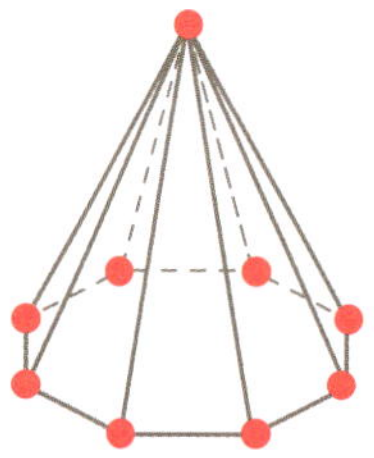			

Unit 8 Cones, cylinders and spheres

3D objects 

cylinder

cone

sphere

1 Name three things that are cylinders.

a ______________ b ______________ c ______________

2 Name three things that are cones.

a ______________ b ______________ c ______________

3 Name three things that are spheres.

a ______________ b ______________ c ______________

4 Which object above can be most easily stacked? ______________

Why? ______________

5

A 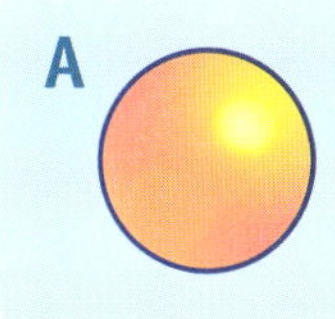 B 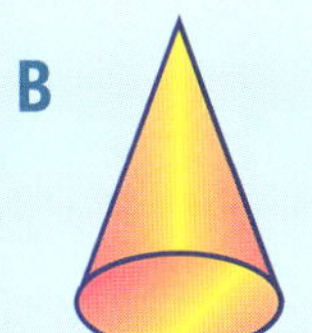 C 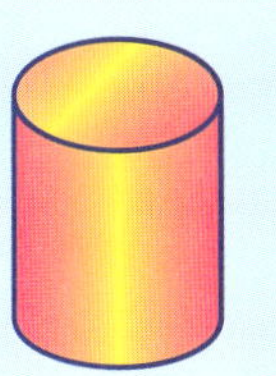

Am I **A**, **B** or **C**?

a I have 1 curved surface and 1 flat surface. ______________

b I have only 1 surface. ______________

c I have 2 flat surfaces and 1 curved surface. ______________

6 How many surfaces has **A**? ________ **B**? ________ **C**? ________

Mastery Checklist I can:
- ☐ describe the features of prisms
- ☐ describe the features of pyramids
- ☐ make prisms and pyramids
- ☐ describe the features of cones, cylinders and spheres.

Problem solving

How can you make prisms?

1 Write the time when you start this page, using 'to' or 'past'. ______________

2 Make a prism. Choose from the following ways.
Use pattern blocks.
Use paper.
Use clay or another solid material.

build
a prism

3 Describe what you did and how you did it. Draw it.

____
____
____
____
____
____
____

4 Draw your prism from a different view.

5 What did you find out about prisms?

____
____

6 Write the time when you finished working on this page. ______________
How long were you working on this page? ______________

I can solve problems by:

☐ understanding properties of prisms ☐ drawing prisms from different views.

 AC9M3SP01 Space **MAO-WM-01** Working mathematically • choosing and applying mathematical techniques to solve problems • communicating thinking and reasoning coherently and clearly • **MA2-3DS-01** Three-dimensional spatial structure A • 3D objects: Make models of three-dimensional objects to compare and describe key features

Unit 9 Graphs

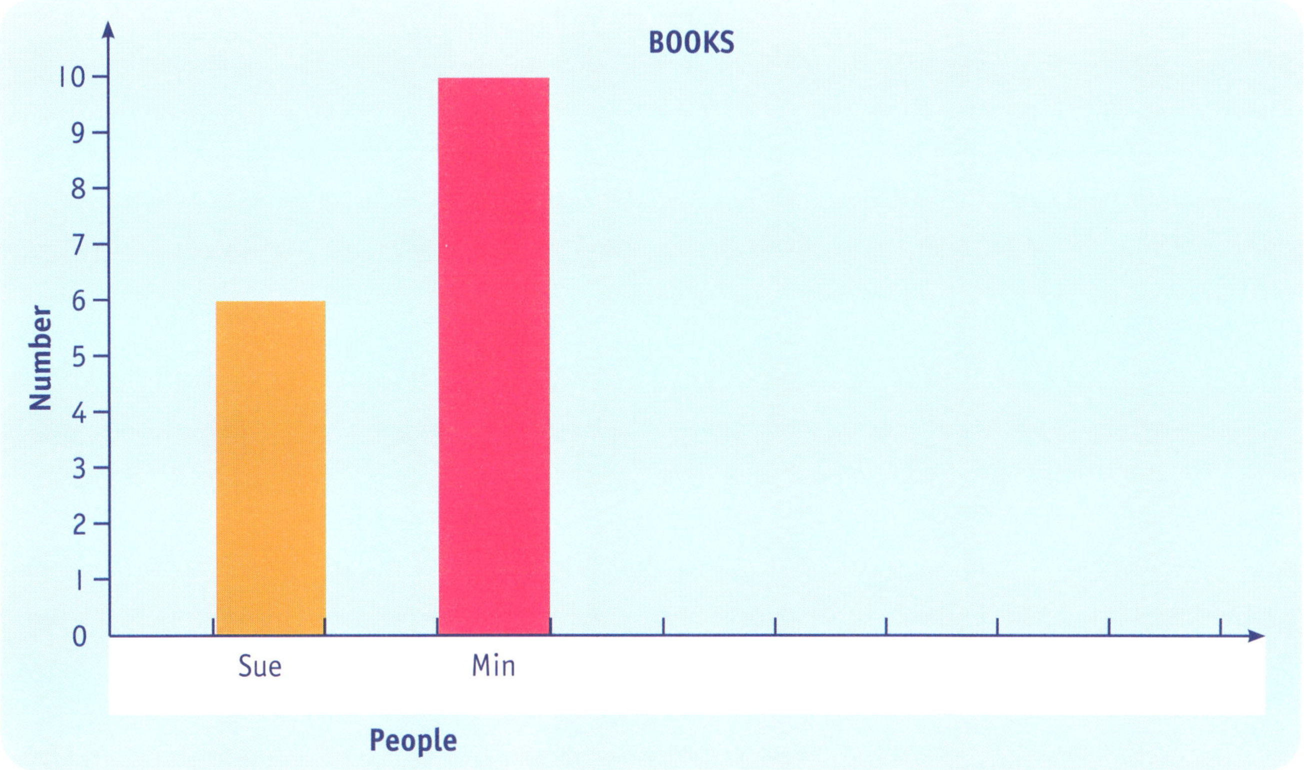

1 Complete the column graph. Write the children's names under the columns.

2 What is this graph telling us? ______________________

3 Who has: a the most books? ____________ b the least books? ____________

4 Who has two less books than Amy? ____________

5 Which two children together have 9 books? ____________

6 How many books do the children have altogether? ____________

7 If John gives half his books to Min, how many will he now have? ____________

8 Does the graph tell us who likes reading most? Why or why not?

____

____

____

Unit 9 Column graph

At the beginning of the year Mr Wright gave the students in his class new pencils.

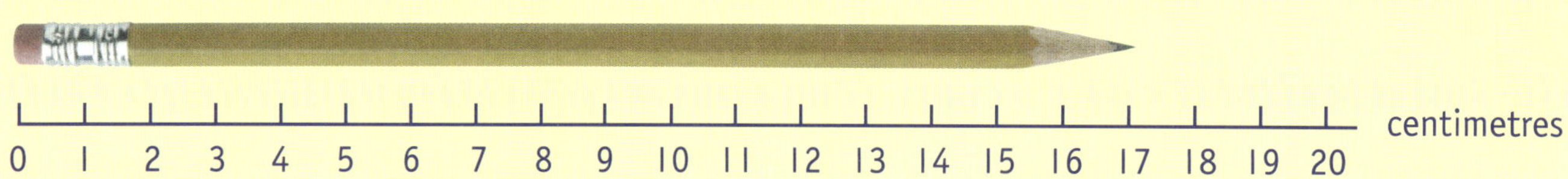

1 How long were the pencils? ____________

One month later Mr Wright asked some students how long their pencils were now. He graphed the results.

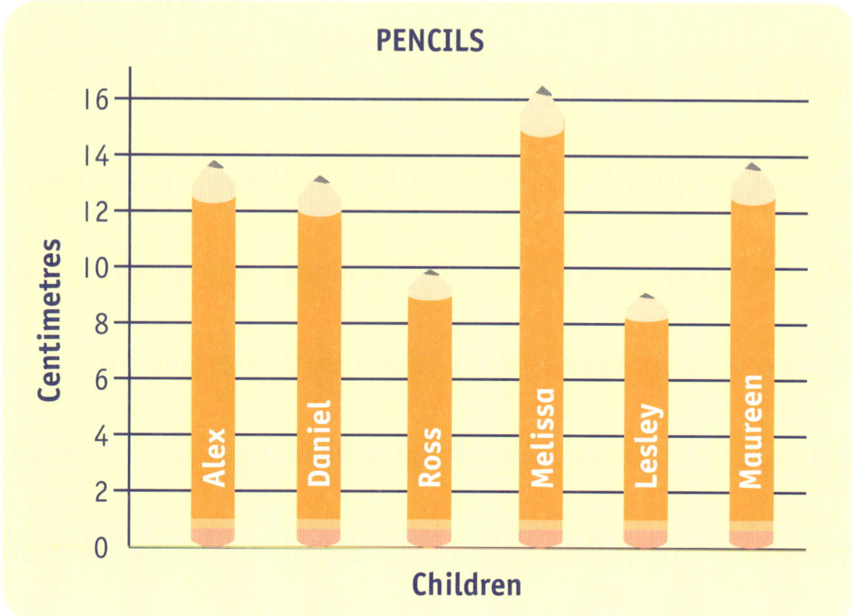

2 How long is Alex's pencil? ____________

3 How long is Daniel's pencil? ____________

4 Who has the longest pencil? ____________

5 Whose pencil is the shortest? ____________

6 a How long is Lesley's pencil? ____________

b How much shorter is it now than when she got it? ____________

7 How much shorter is Ross's pencil now than when Mr Wright gave it to him? ____________

8 Give one reason why Lesley's pencil is so short.

____

____

9 Why do you think Melissa's pencil is so long?

____

____

10 Why did Mr Wright measure pencils? ____________

____

Problem solving

Class favourites survey

Find out about your class. Survey the class about a topic: Sports, Food or Games.
What question will you ask?

Carry out a survey.

Tally

Show your results as a picture graph or column graph.

What did you find out?

I can solve problems by:

☐ understanding data and data displays ☐ collecting and organising data.

Unit 9 Certain, likely, unlikely, impossible

1 Write *certain*, *likely*, *unlikely* or *impossible*.

a The sky will be green tomorrow. ____________

b The sun will rise in the morning. ____________

c I may not be able to go to the party. ____________

d I will grow taller than a giraffe. ____________

e It might rain tonight. ____________

f We will have a holiday this year. ____________

2 There are 6 red, 4 green and 2 yellow balls in the bag.

Without looking, what is your chance of choosing a:

a	red ball?	50-50	likely	unlikely	impossible
b	yellow ball?	50-50	likely	unlikely	impossible
c	green ball?	50-50	likely	unlikely	impossible
d	purple ball?	50-50	likely	unlikely	impossible
e	ball?	50-50	likely	unlikely	impossible

3 Colour the flowers so that it would be likely you choose purple, unlikely you choose orange, impossible to choose white.

4 Colour the marbles so you have an equal chance of choosing red or blue.

Unit 9 Chance outcomes

> **The different ways a thing can happen are called outcomes.**

1 A coin is tossed.

a What two ways can it fall? __________ __________

b How many outcomes can there be? __________

2 a What colours show on traffic lights? ____________________

b How many are there? __________

c How many possible outcomes are there? __________

3 a How many faces are on this die? __________

b If you toss the die, what are the possible outcomes?

________ ________ ________ ________ ________ ________

c How many possible outcomes are there? __________

4 This basket contains two apples and two oranges.
Without looking, you pick out one piece of fruit.

a What could it be? ____________________

b How many possible outcomes are there? __________

5 Write something where:

a the outcome is certain. ____________________

b the outcome is impossible. ____________________

c the outcome is likely. ____________________

d the outcome is unlikely. ____________________

Challenge!

Work with a partner. Throw a die 10 times.
Record the outcomes. There are 6 possible outcomes.
Does each outcome occur the same number of times?
Why or why not?

chance experiment

Mastery Checklist I can:

- ☐ complete a column graph
- ☐ answer questions about a column graph
- ☐ carry out a survey and present the results
- ☐ identify events as certain, likely, unlikely or impossible
- ☐ show an equal chance
- ☐ work out possible outcomes.

Revision Term 1

1 Write the number: p 2

a 10 more than 115 ______

b 100 less than 810 ______

c 10 less than 370 ______

d 100 more than 370 ______

2 Write in numerals: p 6

a three hundred and seventy-one ______

b five hundred and six ______

c two hundred and forty ______

3 Write in words: p 6

a 98 ______

b 613 ______

c 480 ______

4 Write in the missing numbers. p 8

a 95 90 ______ 80 75 ______

b 59 ______ 39 ______ 19

c 19 17 ______ ______ 11 9

5 Double: a 7 ______ b 19 ______ p 9

6 Use the number lines. p 12

a 32 − 17 = ______

b 53 − 25 = ______

p 13

7 a 17 − 9 = ______ b 15 − 8 = ______

c 20 − 13 = ______ d 16 − 7 = ______

8 p 13

Write a story and a number sentence.

______

______

______

9 Circle the correct answer. p 18

a A door is about 2 cm 2 m high.

b A book cover is about 20 cm 1 m wide.

c A bedroom is about 50 m 4 m long.

p 19

10 Measure the lines to the nearest cm.

a ______ b ______

11 What part has been shaded? p 22

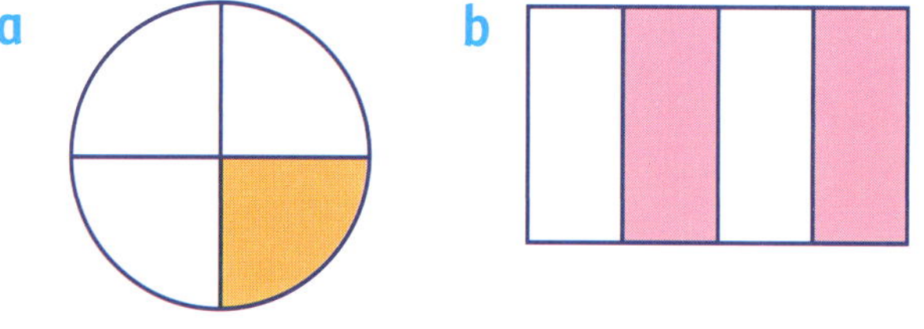

a ______

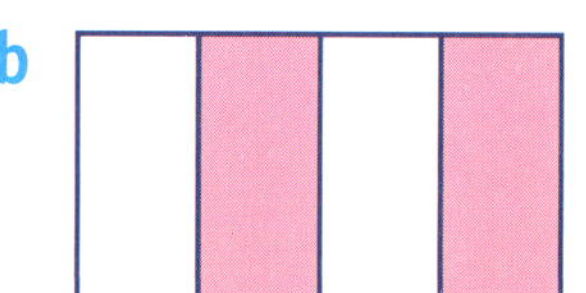

b ______

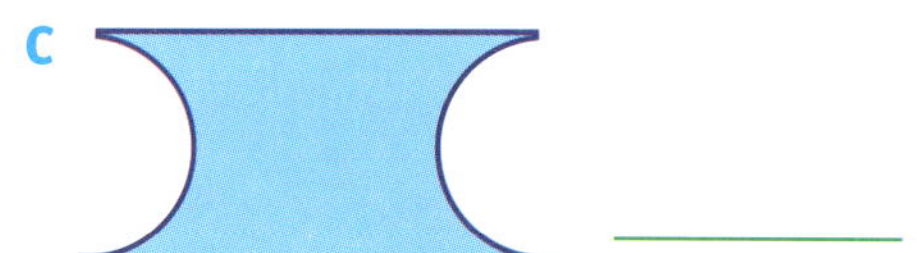

c ______

12 Draw lines to cut this into quarters. Shade $\frac{1}{2}$. p 22

Revision Term 1

13 Write a fraction for the part coloured. p 22

a 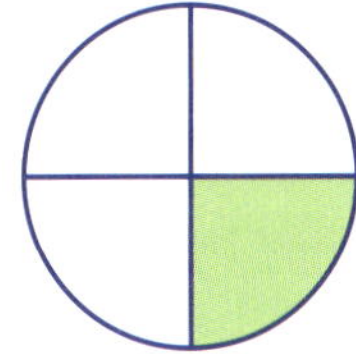 ______

b 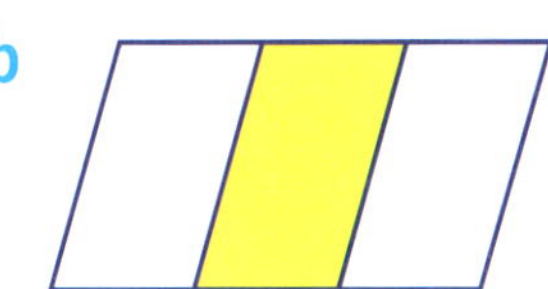 ______

c 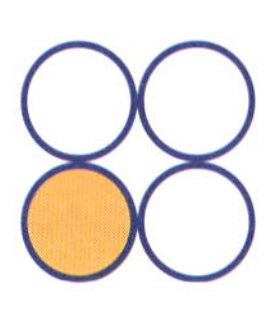 ______

d  ______

14 Write the next two terms and the rule. p 30

a 5 8 11 14 17 ______ ______

Rule ______

b 20 25 30 35 ______ ______

Rule ______

c 63 58 53 48 ______ ______

Rule ______

15 Make your own pattern on the grid. Write the rule. p 30

1	2	3	4	5
6	7	8	9	10
11	12	13	14	15
16	17	18	19	20
21	22	23	24	25

______

16 What is the time? p 33

a 

b 

______ ______

17 Name these 3D objects. p 36

a 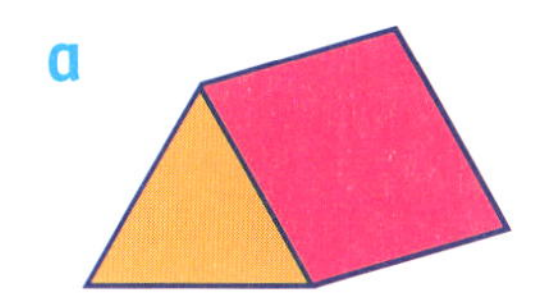

b

______ ______

18 How many faces has: p 38

a a cube? ______

b a triangular pyramid? ______

19 Draw: p 39

a cone	a cylinder

20 What am I? p 39

a I have 1 curved surface only. ______

b I have 4 triangular faces. ______

21 Write one thing for tomorrow: p 44

a that is certain to happen. ______

b that is unlikely to happen. ______

c that is impossible. ______

22 a How many possible outcomes are there if you throw a die? ______ p 45

b What are they? ______

NAPLAN* practice

This is a test to see how well you understand what you have learnt.

Instructions

Read each question carefully. There are three different ways to show your answer:

- Shade the bubble next to the correct answer.
- Write a word in a box.
- Write a number in a box.

Use a pencil. DO NOT use a pen. If you make a mistake, rub it out and try again.

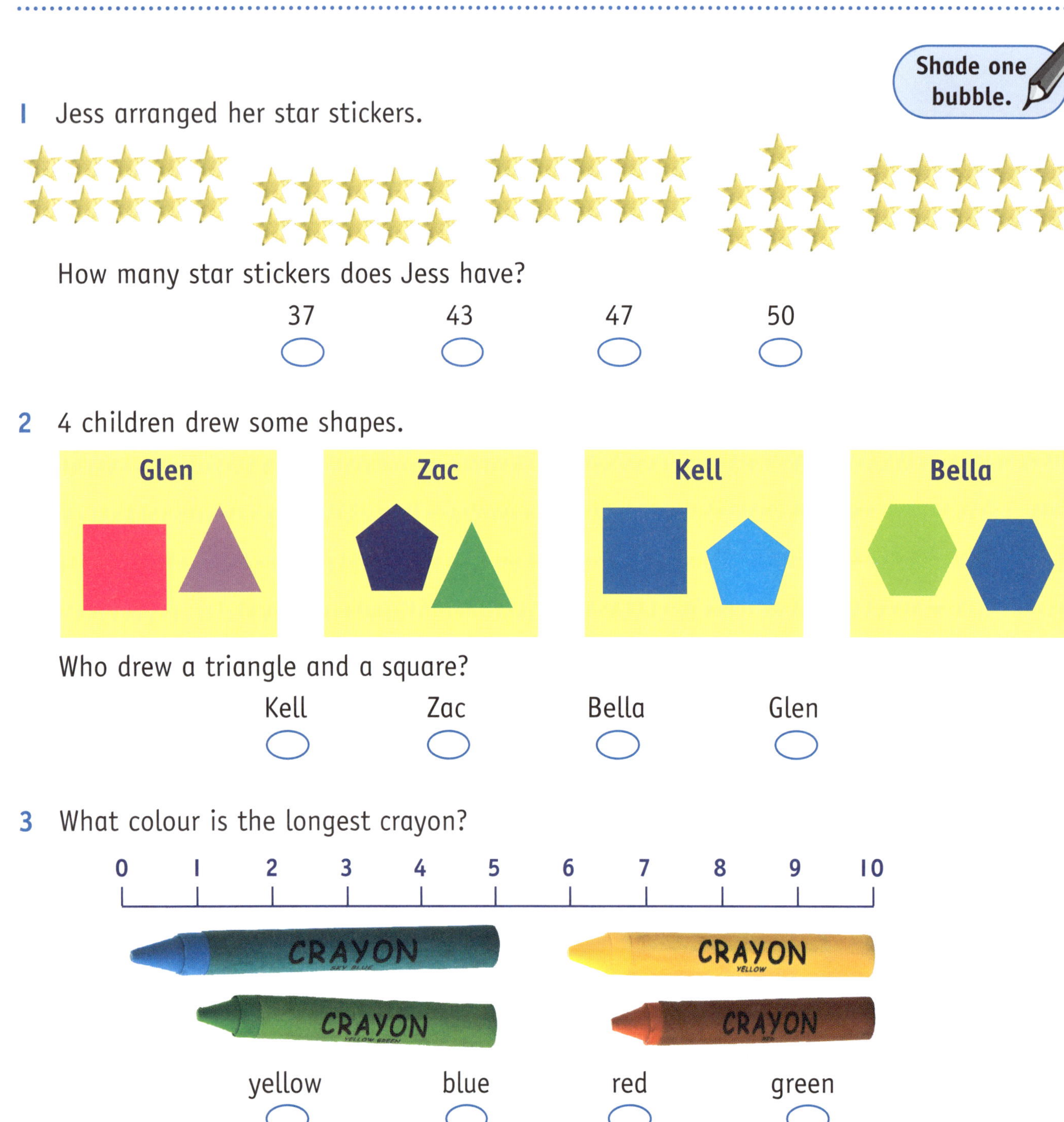

1 Jess arranged her star stickers.

How many star stickers does Jess have?

37 43 47 50

2 4 children drew some shapes.

Who drew a triangle and a square?

Kell Zac Bella Glen

3 What colour is the longest crayon?

yellow blue red green

* This is not an officially endorsed publication of the NAPLAN program and is produced independently of Australian governments.

Test practice

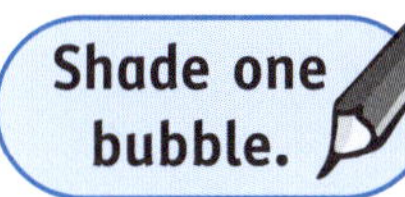

4 Here are four numbers.

What is the second largest number?

85 ◯ 805 ◯ 588 ◯ 815 ◯

Write your answer in the box.

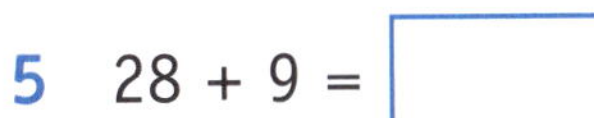

6 Double 9 and add 4. ☐

Shade one bubble.

7 Which letter can be cut into halves?

◯

◯

◯

◯

8 If we count by threes, what will we say after 24?

25 ◯ 26 ◯ 27 ◯ 28 ◯

9 How many wheels on 4 cars?

5 + 4 + 4 + 4 = ◯ 5 × 4 = ◯ 4 + 4 + 4 + 4 = ◯ 5 + 4 = ◯

10 Jimmy's shape has a right angle. Which is Jimmy's shape?

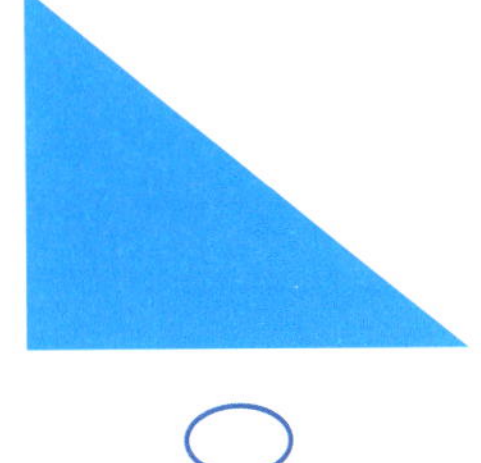
◯

◯

◯

◯

Test practice

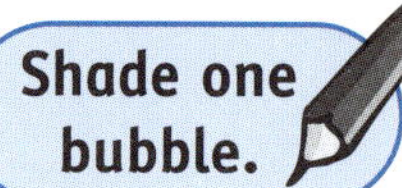

11 Gary has 8 more fish than mice. Which statement is true?

There are less mice than fish. ◯

There are the same numbers of fish and mice. ◯

There are less fish than mice. ◯

Mice plus fish is more than fish plus mice. ◯

Write your answer in the box.

12 Nan has 20 metres of ribbon and cuts off 5 metres for Nadeem, then another 5 metres for Stacey.

How much does she have left? ☐

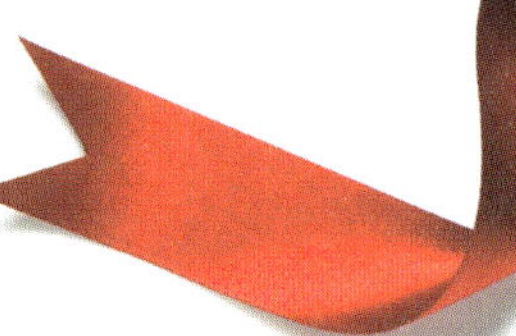

13 47 − 34 = ☐

14 There was 2 L of juice in this bottle. How much did I pour out?

◯ one litre

◯ half a litre

◯ 750 mL

◯ 2 litres

Write your answer in the box.

15 If this Friday is 9th April, what is the date next Friday? ☐

Test practice

16 This is a counting pattern.

38, 35, 32, , 26, 23, 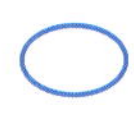

What numbers go in the shapes?

26 and 23 ○ | 30 and 29 ○ | 31 and 30 ○ | 29 and 20 ○

17 Which pattern has one quarter coloured?

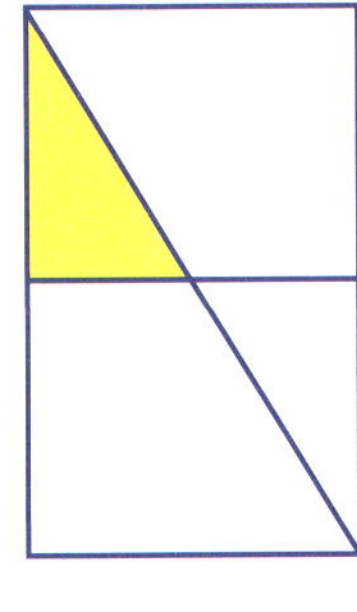 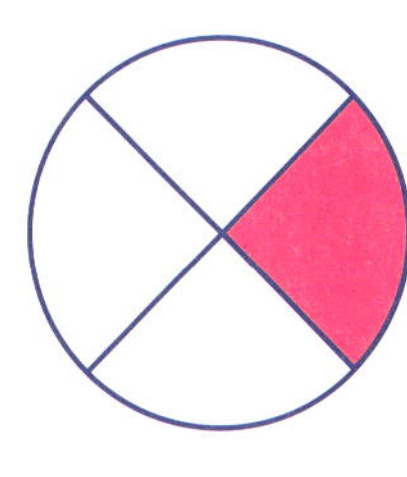  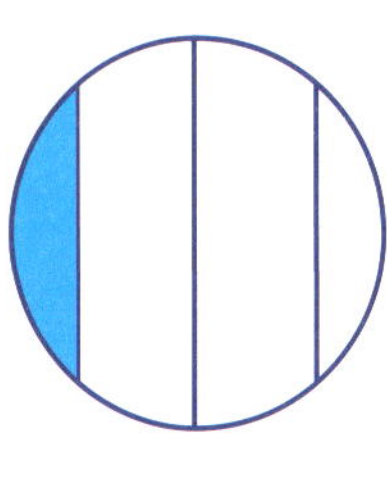

18 Which object is a cylinder?

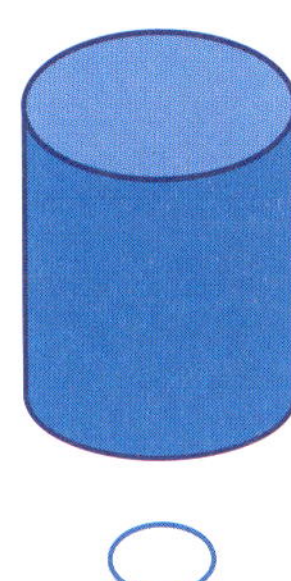   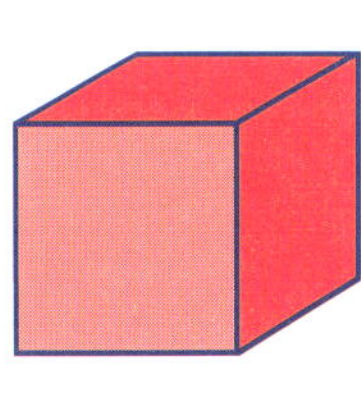

○ ○ ○ ○

19 Which object is a triangular pyramid?

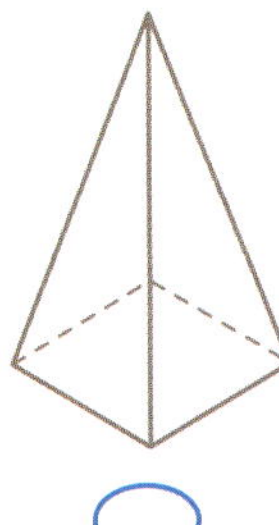 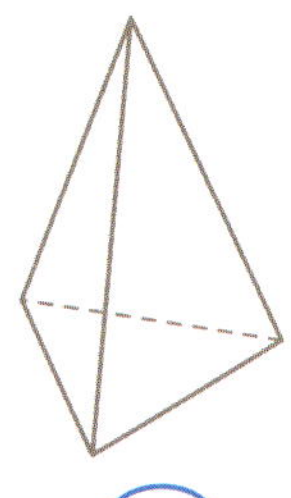 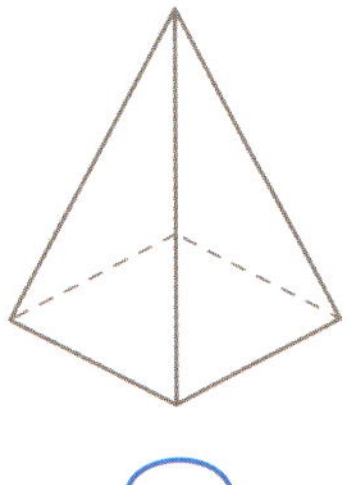 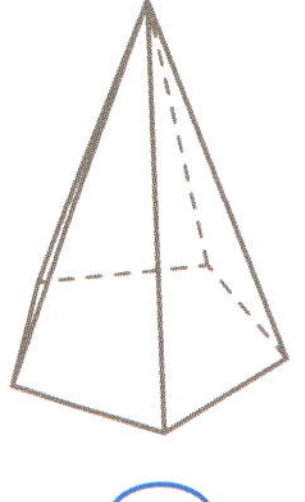

○ ○ ○ ○

Test practice

20 How many faces, edges and corners does a triangular prism have?

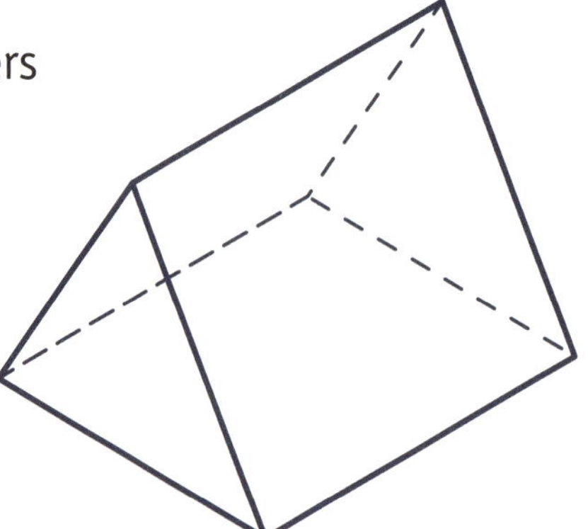

◯ 6 faces, 5 edges, 9 corners

◯ 5 faces, 6 edges, 9 corners

◯ 9 faces, 5 edges, 6 corners

◯ 5 faces, 9 edges, 6 corners

21 This graph shows runs scored by 5 children.

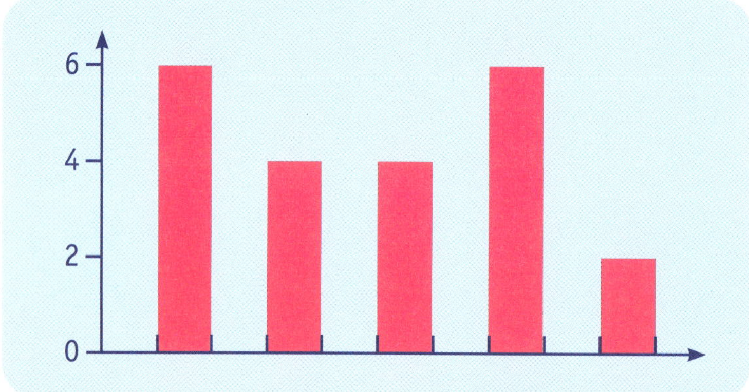

How many children scored 6 runs?

1	6	2	5
◯	◯	◯	◯

22 This arrow shows how many metres a snail has travelled.

200 ←——————————————↓———→ 300 m

How many metres has the snail travelled?

250	280	207	290
◯		◯	◯

Test practice

23 Which clock is showing a quarter to 4?

24 Talya has 24 stickers to share equally. If she has 8 friends, how many stickers can she give each friend?

Write your answer in the box.

25 To be certain of pulling out a red ball from a bag of six balls, what should be in the bag?

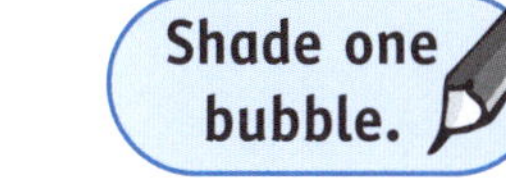

3 red 3 blue   5 red 1 blue   4 red 2 blue   6 red

26 Cow needs 25 squares. Horse needs 30 squares.
Pig needs 18 squares. Sheep needs 17 squares.
Which paddock does the sheep live in?

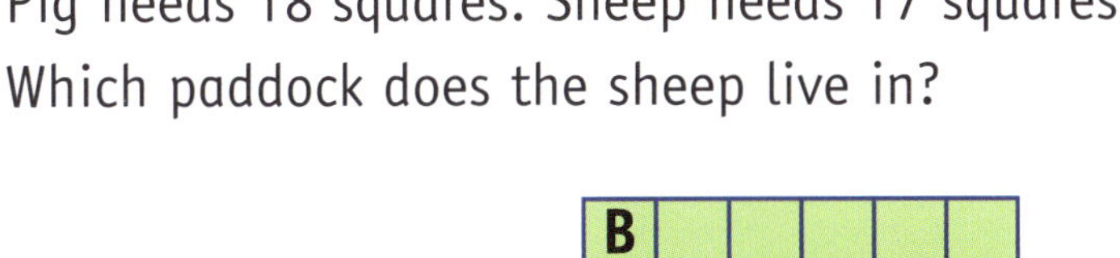

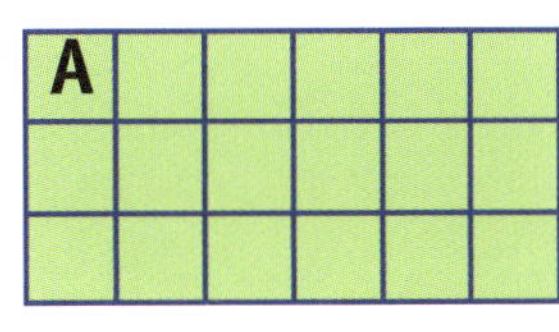

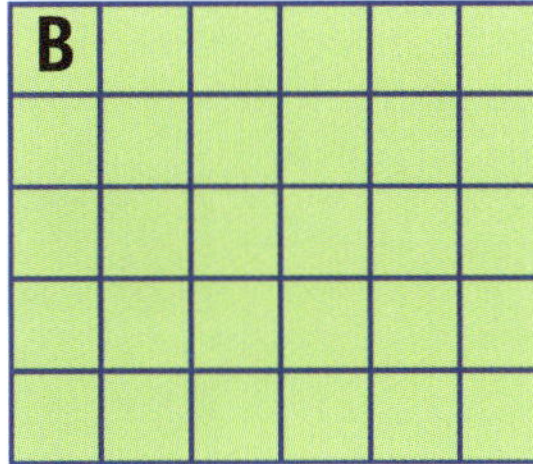

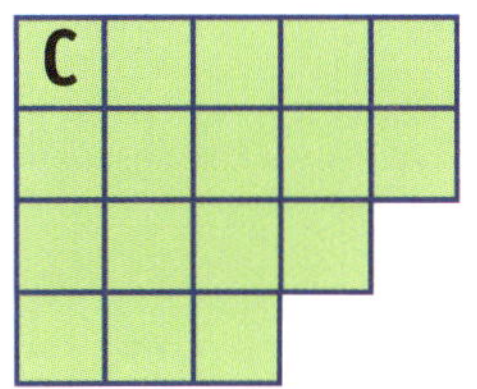

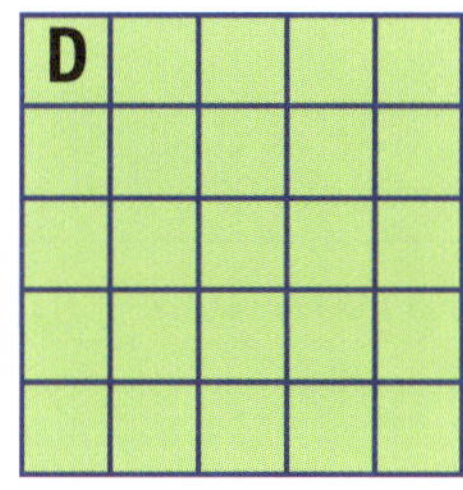

A   B   C   D

27 We spent $4.80 on biscuits and $3.95 on drinks.
How much more did we spend on biscuits than drinks?

$0.85 $1.05 $0.90 $1.15

Test practice

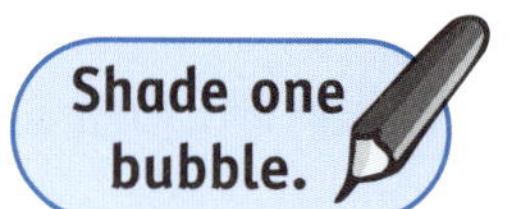

28 The cow is heavier than the pig, the pig is heavier than the cat, but the cat is lighter than the dog. Which animal is lightest?

the dog ◯ the cow ◯ the cat ◯ the pig ◯

29

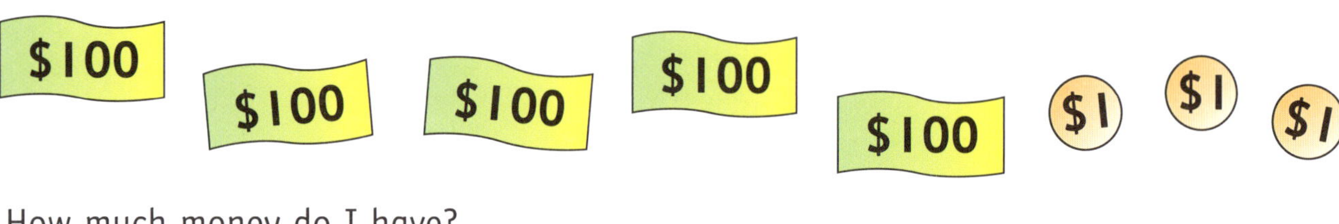

How much money do I have?

$530 ◯ $511 ◯ $503 ◯ $500 ◯

30 Kerry built a cube from straws. She used one straw for each edge. How many straws did she use?

12 ◯ 8 ◯ 21 ◯ 24 ◯

31 This is a train timetable.

Train to:	Time leaving:
Banker	10:00
Havely	10:10
Spickle	10:15
Kenso	10:40

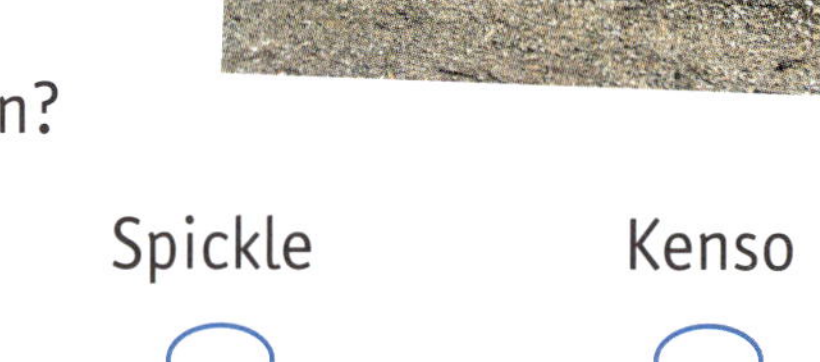

Which train is leaving at a quarter past ten?

Banker ◯ Havely ◯ Spickle ◯ Kenso ◯

Test practice

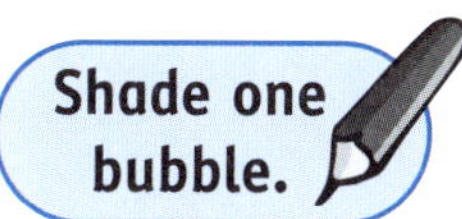

32 Some friends had 10 strawberries to share equally. There was 1 left over. How many friends were there?

3	4	5	2
◯	◯	◯	◯

33 This is a map of Jackie's town.

On her way to the Library after school, what does Jackie walk past?

- ◯ the Café and home
- ◯ the field and the Police Station
- ◯ the Café and the Church
- ◯ the field and the Mall

34 To make this number pattern, what is the rule?

7, 11, 15, 19, 23

- ◯ add all numbers to 20
- ◯ double and add 1
- ◯ add 5
- ◯ add 4

Unit 10 Thousands

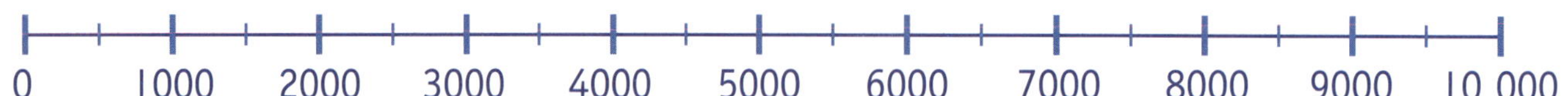

1 Write the number 1000 more than:

a 2000. ________ b 5000. ________ c 7000. ________ d 3000. ________

2 Write the number 1000 less than:

a 10 000. ________ b 5000. ________ c 9000. ________ d 2000. ________

3 What number is halfway between:

a 0 and 1000? ________ b 6000 and 7000? ________

c 3000 and 4000? ________ d 9000 and 10 000? ________

e 1000 and 2000? ________ f 8000 and 9000? ________

4 Add.

a 

Add 10

b 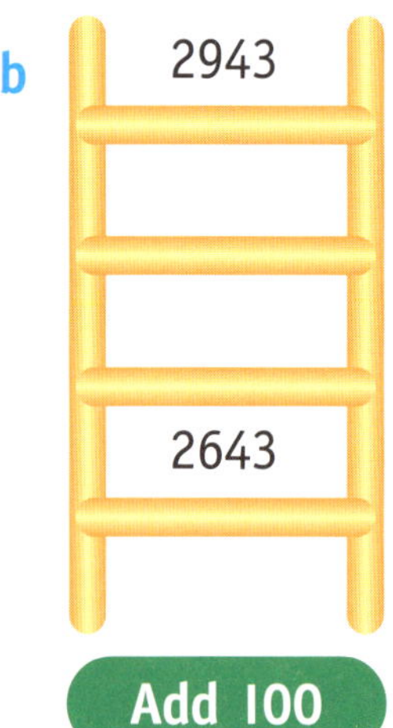

Add 100

c 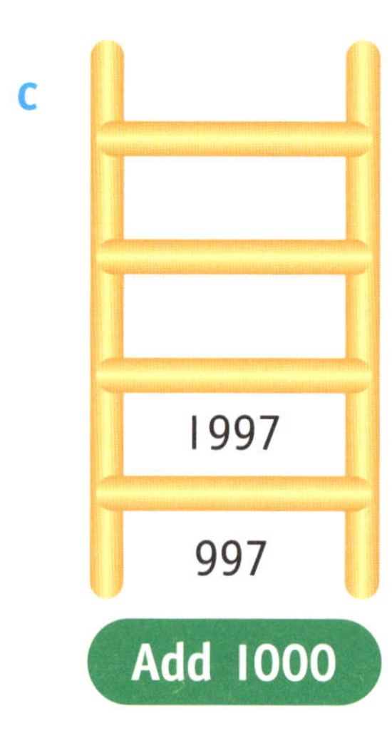

Add 1000

d 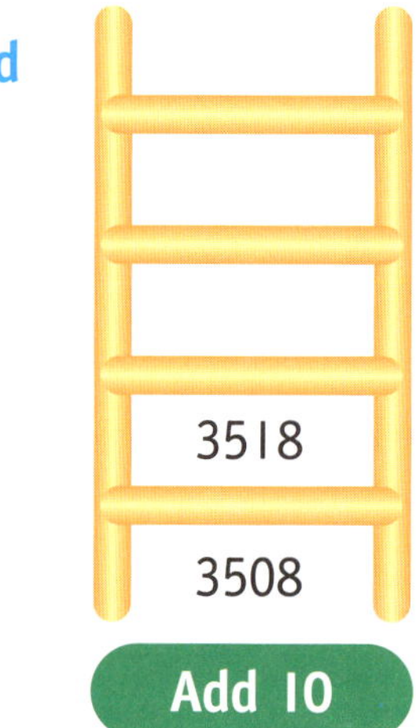

Add 10

5 Write the number for:

a two hundred and forty-eight. ________ b eight hundred and eleven. ________

c four hundred and fifty. ________ d seven hundred and nine. ________

e one thousand three hundred and sixty-five. ________

f two thousand one hundred and ninety-seven. ________

g four thousand five hundred and eighteen. ________

h seven thousand six hundred and twenty. ________

Challenge! What is my number?

a My ones digit is 4, my hundreds digit is 7, my tens digit is 5 and my thousands digit is 9. ☐

b My tens digit is 8 and my thousands digit is 2. ☐

Unit 10 Numbers to 10 000

1 Write the number shown.

a

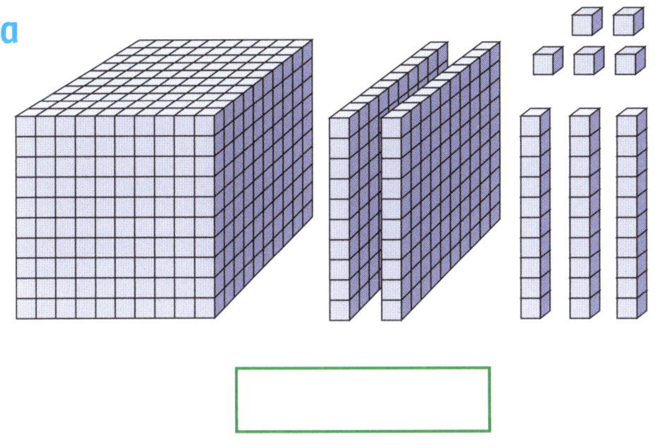

b

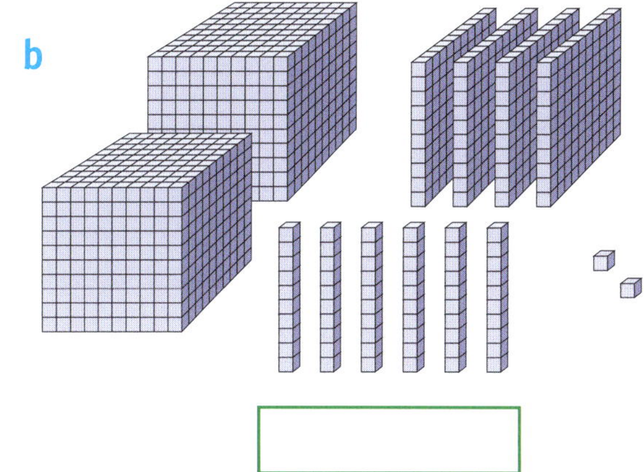

c

d

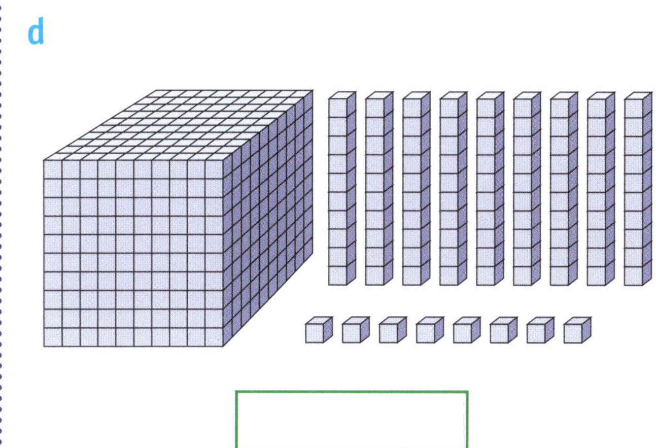

2 Write the numbers from question 1 in words.

a ______________________

b ______________________

c ______________________

d ______________________

3 Circle the larger number.

a 690 609

b 937 793

c 2985 2002

d 4157 5147

e 8061 6810

f 2594 2954

4 Join the numeral to its name.

one thousand and one

one thousand one hundred and ten

one thousand and ten

one thousand one hundred

Unit 10 Place value

1 Complete.

a 9526 = 9000 + 500 + ______ + ______

b 3749 = ______ + ______ + ______ + ______

c 5618 = ______ + ______ + ______ + ______

d 7293 = ______ + ______ + ______ + ______

e 6054 = ______ + ______ + ______ + ______

3648
3000 + 600 + 40 + 8
The value
of the 3 is 3000
of the 6 is 600
of the 4 is 40
of the 8 is 8

2 Write the number.

a 2000 + 800 + 10 + 7 = ______

b 8000 + 400 + 60 + 1 = ______

c 4000 + 900 + 70 + 2 = ______

d 1000 + 300 + 80 + 5 = ______

e 3000 + 40 + 8 = ______

f 7000 + 200 + 6 = ______

3 What is the value of the underlined numeral?

a $26\underline{1}8$ ______ b $15\underline{8}4$ ______ c $\underline{6}372$ ______ d $949\underline{3}$ ______

e $\underline{3}265$ ______ f $\underline{7}726$ ______ g $1\underline{5}9$ ______ h $50\underline{8}7$ ______

i $4\underline{9}03$ ______ j $26\underline{0}0$ ______ k $\underline{7}008$ ______ l $30\underline{4}$ ______

4 Write these in ascending order.

a 8420 2048 3915 ______ ______ ______

b 7506 983 9375 ______ ______ ______

c 5130 5301 5013 ______ ______ ______

d 4142 1244 4214 ______ ______ ______

e 8080 8800 8008 ______ ______ ______

Challenge!

Use these numerals to write as many different four-digit numbers as you can.

How many could you find? ☐

3

Mastery Checklist I can:
- ☐ add 10, 100 and 1000 to 4-digit numbers
- ☐ order 4-digit numbers
- ☐ find the number halfway between
- ☐ recognise numbers in base 10 blocks
- ☐ expand 4-digit numbers to show place value.

AC9M3N01 Number **MA2-RN-01** Representing numbers using place value A • Whole numbers: Read, represent and order numbers to thousands • Whole numbers: Apply place value to partition and regroup numbers up to 4 digits

Unit 11 Number facts 3×

1

0	a	0 × 3 = 3 × 0 = 0
3	b	1 × 3 = 3 × 1 = 3
6	c	2 × 3 = 3 × 2 = ☐
9	d	3 × 3 = 3 × 3 = ☐
12	e	4 × 3 = 3 × ☐ = ☐
15	f	☐ × 3 = 3 × 5 = ☐
18	g	6 × 3 = 3 × ☐ = ☐
21	h	7 × 3 = 3 × ☐ = ☐
24	i	☐ × 3 = 3 × ☐ = 24
27	j	☐ × 3 = 3 × ☐ = ☐
30	k	10 × 3 = 3 × 10 = ☐

NOTICE!
Memorise the 3× table.

2 30 – ☐ – 24 – ☐ – ☐ – 15 – 12 – ☐ – 6 – ☐ – ☐

3 Pick (3) and another number from the bag. Multiply them.
Colour the two numbers in the bag and the answer in the rhombus the same colour.

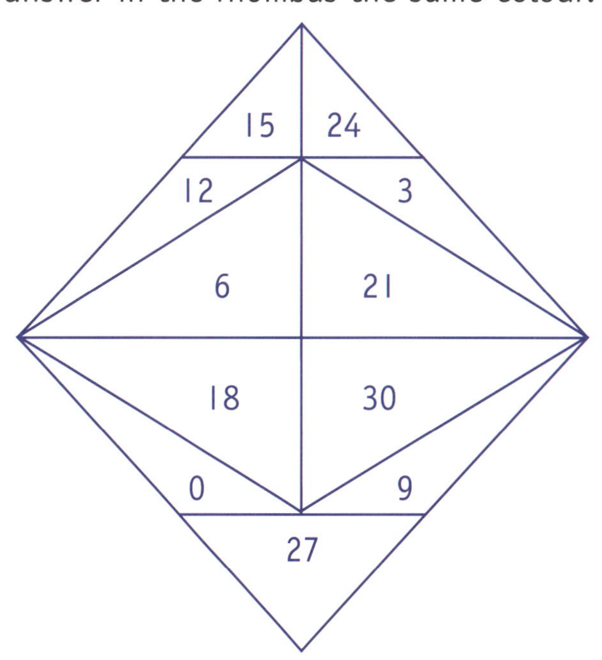

Unit 11 Number facts 0×, 6×

0, 6 tables

1 How many petals on:

a 1 flower? ____ b 7 flowers? ____

c 3 flowers? ____ d 10 flowers? ____

e 2 flowers? ____ f 4 flowers? ____

g 9 flowers? ____ h 6 flowers? ____

i 5 flowers? ____ j 8 flowers? ____

k How many petals on no flowers? ____

l $11 \times 6 =$ ____ m $12 \times 6 =$ ____

Any number times zero is always equal to zero.

2 a $0 \times 6 =$ ☐ b $3 \times 0 =$ ☐ c $2 \times 0 =$ ☐ d $0 \times 8 =$ ☐

e $9 \times 0 =$ ☐ f $0 \times 4 =$ ☐ g $66 \times 0 =$ ☐ h $999 \times 0 =$ ☐

3 Count by 6s.

4

1	2	3	4	5	6	7	8	9	10
11	12	13	14	15	16	17	18	19	20
21	22	23	24	25	26	27	28	29	30
31	32	33	34	35	36	37	38	39	40
41	42	43	44	45	46	47	48	49	50
51	52	53	54	55	56	57	58	59	60

a Colour the ×3 numbers yellow.

b Colour the ×6 numbers blue.

c Which numbers turn green?

____

____

____

____

____

 AC9M3A03 Algebra • **AC9M3N07** Number **MA2-MR-01** Multiplicative relations A • Generate and describe patterns • Multiplicative relations B • Use known number facts and strategies • Use number properties to find related multiplication facts

Unit 11 Number facts 3×, 4×, 5×, 10×

0×
0 × 3 = 0
0 × 5 = 0
0 × 10 = 0

1 Count backwards in:

a 3s from 21, ____, ____, ____, ____, ____, ____

b 4s from 38, ____, ____, ____, ____, ____, ____

c 5s from 50, ____, ____, ____, ____, ____, ____

d 6s from 60, ____, ____, ____, ____, ____, ____

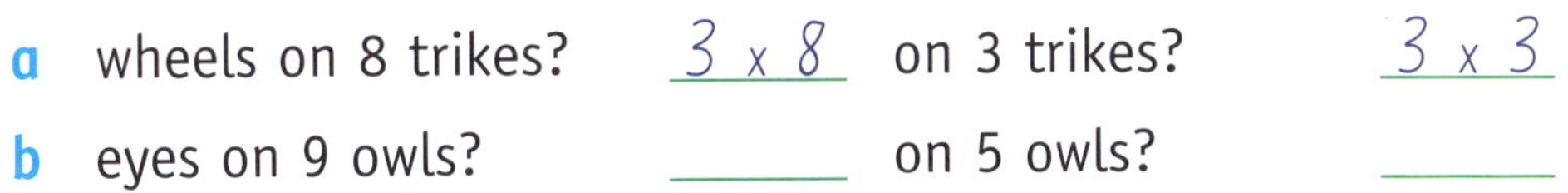

2 Write the number sentence. How many:

a	wheels on 8 trikes?	3 x 8	on 3 trikes?	3 x 3
b	eyes on 9 owls?	____	on 5 owls?	____
c	10c coins in $7?	____	in $4?	____
d	toes on 6 feet?	____	on 8 feet?	____
e	hands on 5 clocks?	____	on 10 clocks?	____
f	arms on 4 starfish?	____	on 9 starfish?	____
g	corners on 7 squares?	____	on 4 squares?	____
h	ears on 10 horses?	____	tails on 10 horses?	____
i	feet on 1 dog?	____	feet on 3 dogs?	____

3 a One ticket to a show costs $10. What is the cost of 6 tickets? ☐

b Ten children get 5 lollies each. How many lollies altogether? ☐

4 Complete these from memory.

a

×	0	1	2	3	4	5	6	7	8	9	10
5											

b

×	0	1	2	3	4	5	6	7	8	9	10
10											

Unit 11 Odds and evens

1 Show by pairing circles that:

a 14 is an even number.

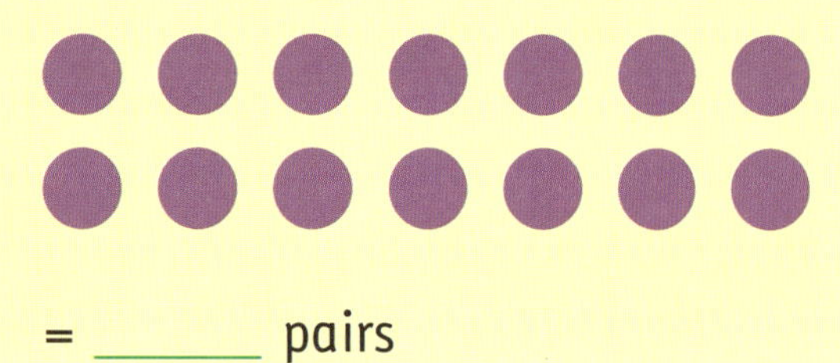

= ______ pairs

b 17 is an odd number.

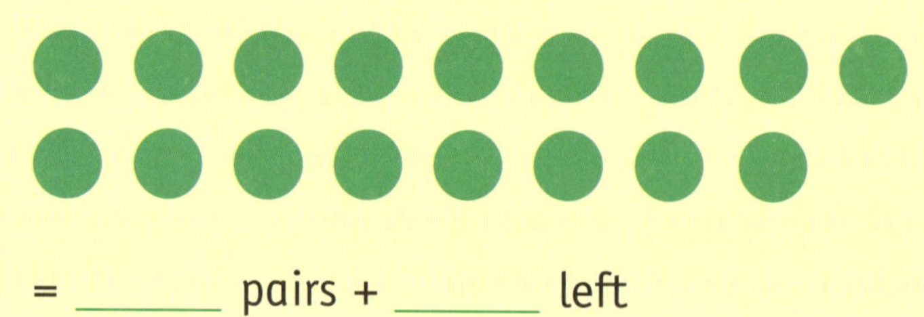

= ______ pairs + ______ left

2 Circle the odd numbers.

9, 15, 22, 100, 51, 352, 249, 150, 791

3 Write the next three numbers in the pattern.

a 91, 89, 87 ______ ______ ______ odd or even? ____________

b 240, 242, 244 ______ ______ ______ odd or even? ____________

4 a Odd numbers all end in ______, ______, ______, ______ or 9.

b Even numbers all end in 2, ______, ______, ______ or ______.

5 Write 5 even numbers between 500 and 1000.

____

6 Circle all the sums with an odd number answer.

5 + 14	3 + 9	17 + 2	11 + 6	1 + 14
2 + 6	9 + 12	12 + 4	7 + 13	6 + 8
5 + 5	8 + 13	12 + 12	9 + 15	16 + 3

7 Answer odd or even.

odd + odd = ____________

even + even = ____________

odd + even = ____________

8 True or false?

Numbers are odd or even. ____________

Only the ones digit tells us odd or even. ____________

Challenge!

Odd or even?

odd × odd = [ ]

even × even = [ ]

odd × even = [ ]

Mastery Checklist

I can:

- ☐ remember the 3×, 4×, 5×, 6×, 10× tables
- ☐ write number sentences
- ☐ complete number facts from memory
- ☐ understand odd and even numbers.

AC9M3N07 Number

Unit 12 Subtraction facts to 20

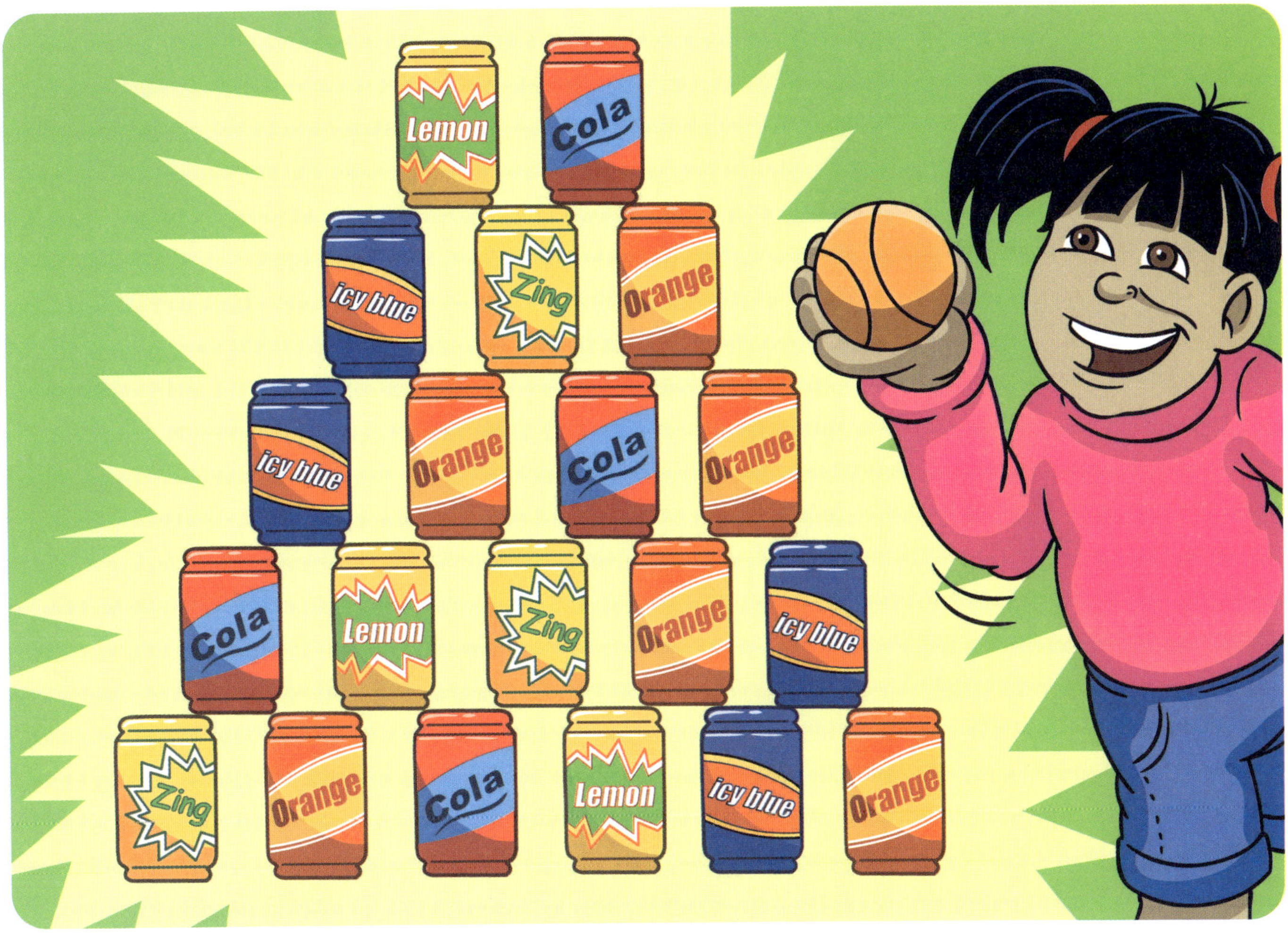

1 Ronnie made a pile of cans for target practice.

a How many cans are there? ______

How many would be left if she knocked down:

b 6? ______ c 11? ______ d 15? ______ e 2? ______ f 13? ______

g the top row? ______ h the top two rows? ______

i the top three rows? ______ j the top four rows? ______

k all the cans? ______

2 How many would she need to rebuild if these were left?

a 7 ______ b 12 ______ c 19 ______ d 4 ______ e 9 ______

3 She rebuilds only the bottom three rows. How many are left if she knocks down:

a 6? ______ b 9? ______ c 13? ______ d 7? ______ e 3? ______

4 She doesn't put up the top row. How many are left if she knocks down:

a 18? ______ b 11? ______ c 6? ______ d 13? ______ e 4? ______

Unit 12 Subtraction linked with addition

1 Write three more related facts.

a	20 – 6 = 14	20 – 14 = 6	6 + 14 = 20	14 + 6 = 20
b	20 – 13 = ______	______	______	______
c	20 – 9 = ______	______	______	______
d	20 – 16 = ______	______	______	______
e	20 – 5 = ______	______	______	______
f	20 – 12 = ______	______	______	______

2 Complete these puzzles.

–		
18	6	
14	3	
		☐

–		
20	9	
15	7	
		☐

–		
19	7	
11	4	
		☐

–		
16	8	
9	5	
		☐

3 Jay has $20. How much change would she get if she bought the:

a top? ______ b teddy bear? ______ c robot? ______ d goggles? ______

e top and chocolates? ______ f table tennis bat and goggles? ______

4 Vinny has $16. What item can't he buy? ______

5 True or false?

a Jay could buy three items. ______

b Why? ______

c Vinny bought the goggles and has $8 left. ______

d Why? ______

AC9M3A01 • AC9M3A02 Algebra MA2-AR-01 Additive relations A • Recognise and explain the connection between addition and subtraction • Additive relations B • Apply addition and subtraction to familiar contexts, including money and budgeting

Unit 12 Counting on

subtract
minus
less than
take from
take away
difference

1
a 16 take away 9 ______ b 11 minus 7 ______
c 19 subtract 12 ______ d take 8 from 12 ______
e 80 subtract 10 ______ f 7 less than 47 ______
g 15 minus 10 ______ h take 0 from 18 ______

We sometimes find the difference by counting on.

20, 21, 22, 23, 24, 25. That's 6 more!

2 Count on to complete.

a

	39	43	40	42	46	45
−37						

b

	62	68	60	66	64	61
−59						

c

	26	21	25	20	23	28
−18						

d

	80	87	89	83	90	84
−76						

3 Count on to find the answers. Then write the subtraction.

a Carl had 19 marbles.
Ingrid had 24 marbles.
How many more did Ingrid have? ______

b Bella had 37 Smarties.
Bill had 29 Smarties.
How many more did Bella have? ______

☐ − ☐ = ☐

c Shona ate 53 cherries.
Seb ate 61 cherries.
How many more did Seb eat? ______

☐ − ☐ = ☐

d Nicole read 48 pages.
Ned read 39 pages.
How many more did Nicole read? ______

☐ − ☐ = ☐

Looking for patterns

What is the pattern? Make up another subtraction pattern.

	11	61	81	31	51	91	21	71
−7								

Unit 12 Two-digit subtraction

1 Quick practice.

a	b	c	d	e	f	g
16 − 7	20 − 12	18 − 13	14 − 9	13 − 6	15 − 8	12 − 5

2 Use the number line.

a 37 minus 23 — number line: 14, 17, 27, 37 — 37 − 23

b 52 take away 34 — number line: 52 — 52 −

c subtract 15 from 61 — number line: 61 — 61 −

d 94 less 47 — number line: 94 — −

e difference between 72 and 23 — −

Draw a diagram

Jay's ant farm had 96 ants. 47 escaped and 25 died.

How many are left? 

Hint: Draw a number line.

Mastery Checklist

I can:
- ☐ use subtraction facts to 20
- ☐ connect addition and subtraction
- ☐ work out change from $20
- ☐ count on to subtract
- ☐ use algorithms to subtract
- ☐ use number lines to subtract.

AC9M3N03 Number **AC9M3A02** Algebra **MA2-AR-01** Additive relations A • Select strategies flexibly to solve addition and subtraction problems of up to 3 digits

Unit 13 Subtraction strategies

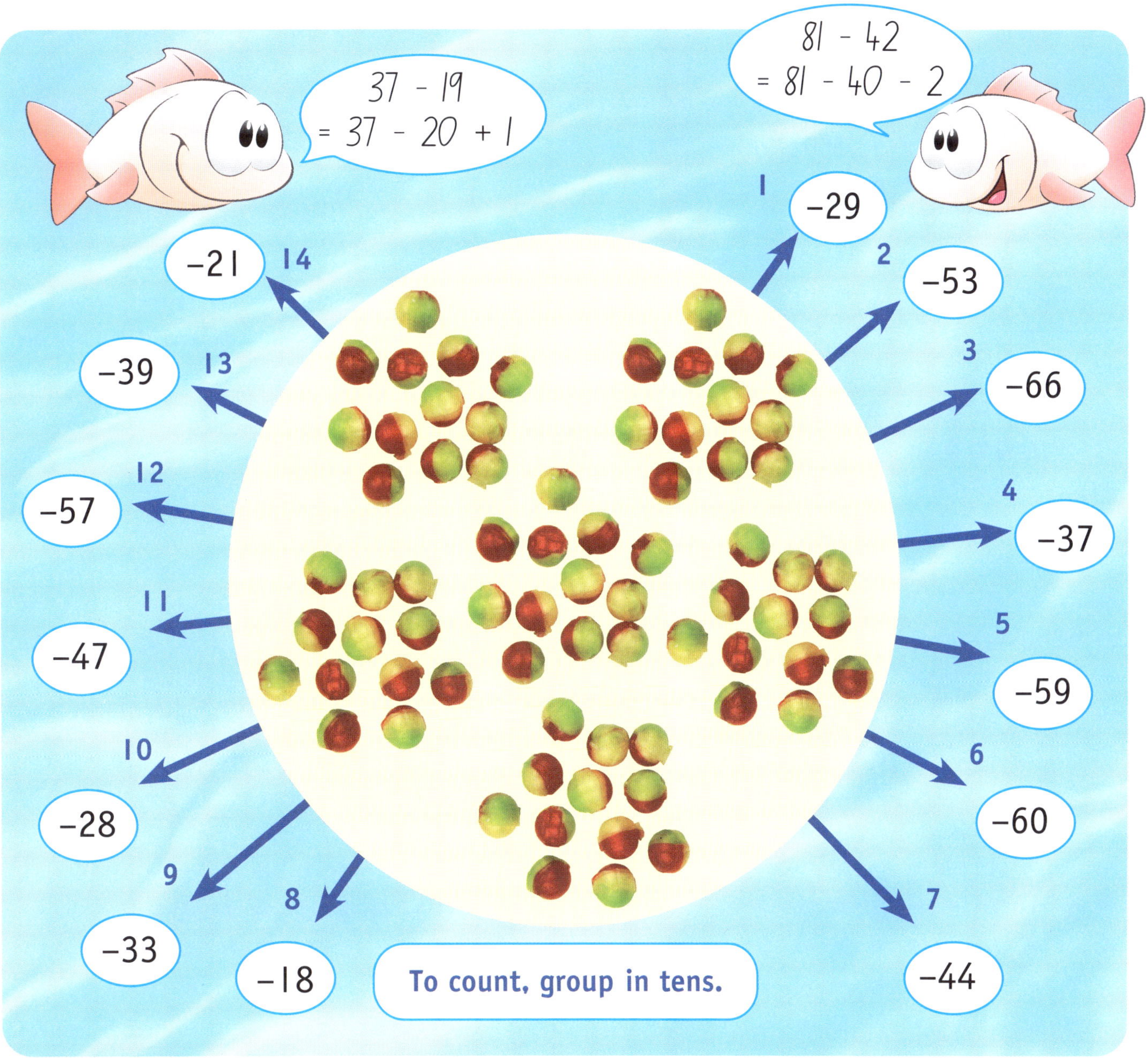

37 − 19
= 37 − 20 + 1

81 − 42
= 81 − 40 − 2

1 −29
2 −53
3 −66
4 −37
5 −59
6 −60
7 −44
8 −18
9 −33
10 −28
11 −47
12 −57
13 −39
14 −21

To count, group in tens.

1 72 − 30 + 1 = ____ ☐ − ☐ = ☐

2 72 − 50 − 3 = ____ ☐ − ☐ = ☐

3 ________ = ____ ☐ − ☐ = ☐

4 ________ = ____ ☐ − ☐ = ☐

5 ________ = ____ ☐ − ☐ = ☐

6 ________ = ____ ☐ − ☐ = ☐

7 ________ = ____ ☐ − ☐ = ☐

8 ________ = ____ ☐ − ☐ = ☐

9 ________ = ____ ☐ − ☐ = ☐

10 ________ = ____ ☐ − ☐ = ☐

11 ________ = ____ ☐ − ☐ = ☐

12 ________ = ____ ☐ − ☐ = ☐

13 ________ = ____ ☐ − ☐ = ☐

14 ________ = ____ ☐ − ☐ = ☐

Unit 13 Two-digit subtraction

Subtract to 100

1 Write stories.

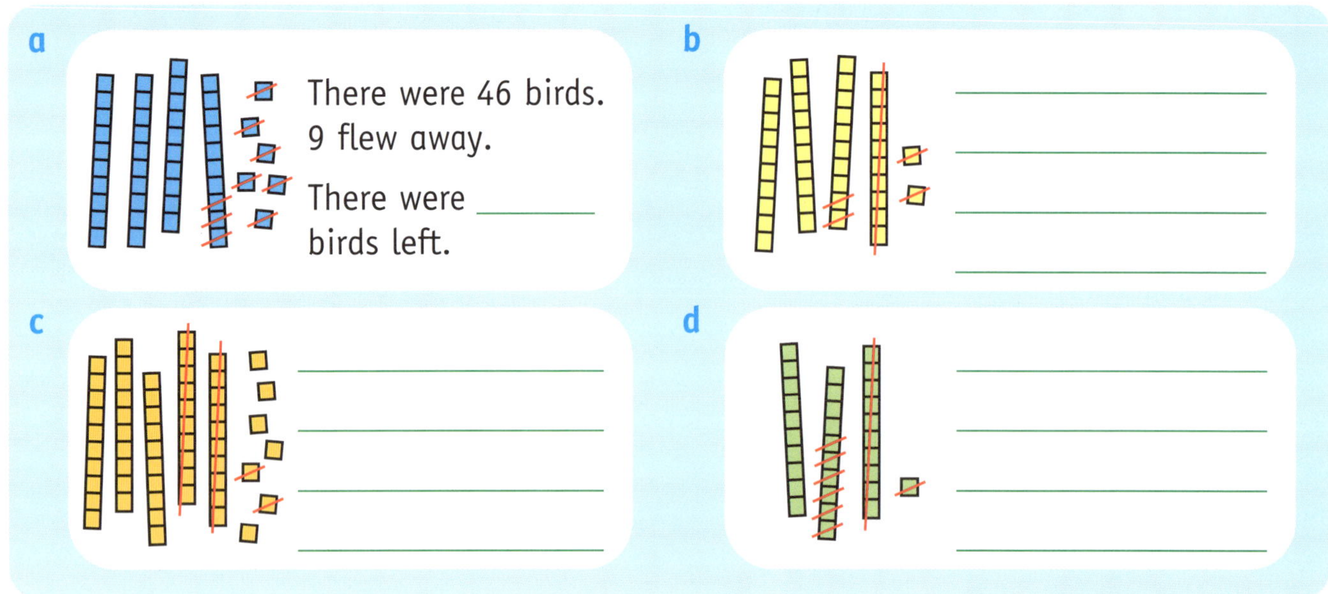

2 Use the blocks to find the answers.

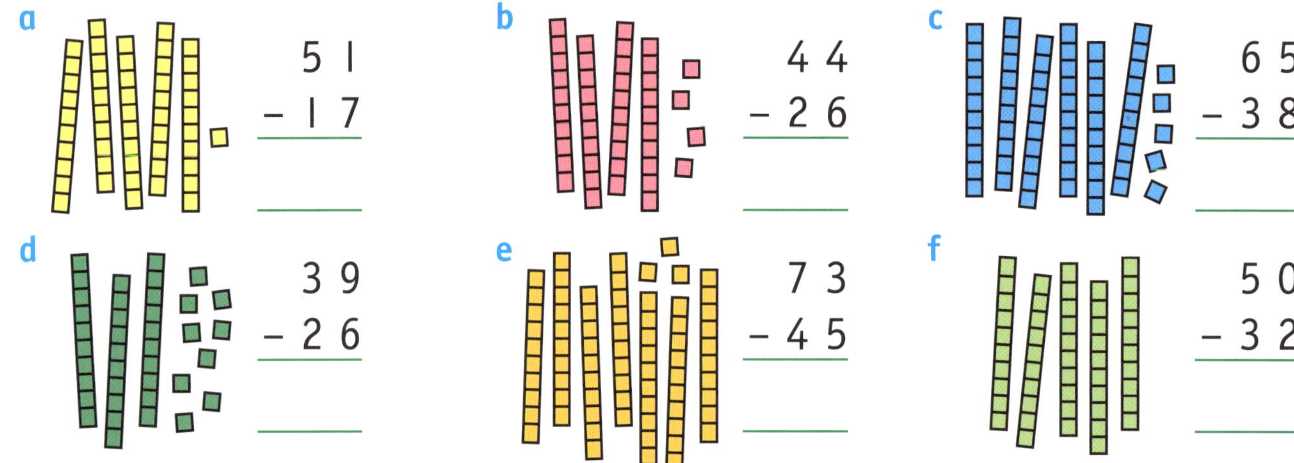

3 Use Base 10 blocks if you need help.

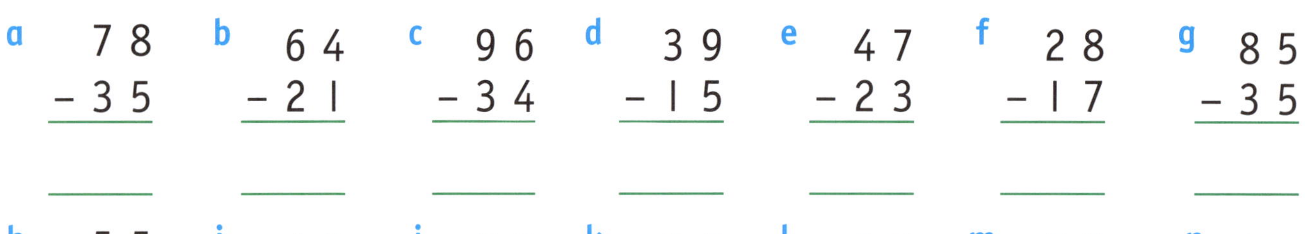

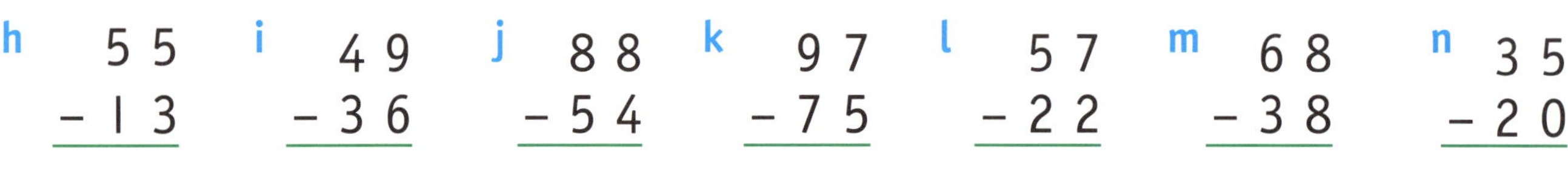

Challenge! Find 4 pairs of numbers with a difference of 27.

Unit 13 Subtraction stories

Related facts

1	2	3	4	5	6	7	8	9	10
11	12	13	14	15	16	17	18	19	20
21	22	23	24	25	26	27	28	29	30
31	32	33	34	35	36	37	38	39	40
41	42	43	44	45	46	47	48	49	50
51	52	53	54	55	56	57	58	59	60
61	62	63	64	65	66	67	68	69	70
71	72	73	74	75	76	77	78	79	80
81	82	83	84	85	86	87	88	89	90
91	92	93	94	95	96	97	98	99	100

1 a Find pairs of numbers the same colour.

b Work out the difference for each pair.

c Write one subtraction sentence and one addition sentence for each pair.

74 – 3 = ☐
☐ + ☐ = ☐

☐ – ☐ = ☐
☐ + ☐ = ☐

☐ – ☐ = ☐
☐ + ☐ = ☐

☐ – ☐ = ☐
☐ + ☐ = ☐

☐ – ☐ = ☐
☐ + ☐ = ☐

☐ – ☐ = ☐
☐ + ☐ = ☐

☐ – ☐ = ☐
☐ + ☐ = ☐

☐ – ☐ = ☐
☐ + ☐ = ☐

2 a Tom threw the basketball 25 m and kicked the soccerball 67 m. Write the difference in metres. ☐

b 

The red balloon drifted 39 m and the blue balloon drifted 24 m. Write the difference in metres. ☐

c 

Sal jumped 44 cm and Sue jumped 66 cm. Write the difference in centimetres. ☐

Mastery Checklist

I can:
- ☐ regroup numbers to subtract
- ☐ write subtraction stories
- ☐ use blocks to subtract
- ☐ use algorithms to subtract
- ☐ connect addition and subtraction
- ☐ solve subtraction stories.

Problem solving

Work backwards

1 Three children ran a race. Jack ran the race 3 seconds faster than Dave. Dave ran 2 seconds slower than Jerry. Jerry took 14 seconds. What was Jack's time?

Working:

Jerry 14 secs   Dave 14 + 2 = 16   Jack 16 − 3 = 13

Dave 16 secs   Jack's time was ________

2 Four children joined the 'Read-a-thon' to improve their reading rate. Toby read 4 books more than Koli. Koli read 5 books less than Troy, who read 16. How many books did Toby read?

Working:

Troy ____________   Koli ____________   Toby ____________

Troy read ________   Koli read ________   Toby read ________

Write your own *work backwards* problems and show the solution.

3 The answer is 50 stickers. What might the problem be?

____

____

____

____

Working: ____

____

4 Write your own.

____

____

____

____

Working: ____

____

I can solve problems by:

☐ using addition facts and related subtractions ☐ working backwards.

AC9M3N06 Number **AC9M3A01** Algebra **MAO-WM-01** Working mathematically • choosing and applying mathematical techniques to solve problems • communicating thinking and reasoning coherently and clearly **MA2-AR-01** Additive relations A • Select strategies flexibly to solve addition and subtraction problems of up to 3 digits

Unit 14 Fractions in a line

1 Write each set of fractions in order, smallest to largest.

a $\frac{1}{4}, \frac{3}{4}, \frac{2}{4}, \frac{4}{4}$ ______

b $\frac{3}{3}, \frac{1}{3}, \frac{2}{3}$ ______

c $\frac{1}{6}, \frac{5}{6}, \frac{3}{6}, \frac{6}{6}, \frac{2}{6}, \frac{4}{6}$ ______

d $\frac{1}{8}, \frac{7}{8}, \frac{3}{8}, \frac{2}{8}, \frac{4}{8}, \frac{6}{8}, \frac{8}{8}, \frac{5}{8}$ ______

e $\frac{7}{8}, \frac{2}{8}, \frac{6}{8}, \frac{8}{8}, \frac{5}{8}, \frac{3}{8}, \frac{1}{8}, \frac{4}{8}$ ______

f $\frac{2}{2}, \frac{1}{2}$ ______

2 Colour the fraction. Then write and colour a smaller fraction.

a $\frac{3}{4}$

b $\frac{4}{8}$

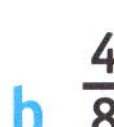

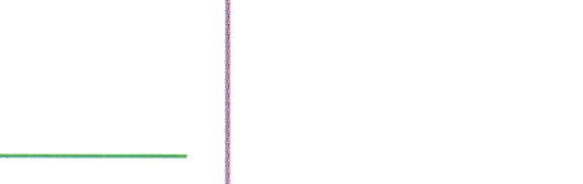

c $\frac{2}{3}$

d $\frac{2}{6}$

Unit 14 Count with fractions

1 Count by halves up to 1.

0 ______ ______

2 Count by thirds up to 1.

0 ______ ______ ______

3 Count by quarters up to 1.

0 ______ ______ ______ ______

4 Count by fifths up to 1.

0 ______ ______ ______ ______ ______

5 Count by tenths up to 1.

0 $\frac{1}{10}$ ______ ______ ______ ______ ______ ______ ______ ______ ______

6 a Five boys get 1 slice each.

How much pizza did each boy get? ______

b Two girls get 2 slices each.

How much pizza did each girl get? ______

Challenge! I cut a pizza into ten slices to share between five people.
How many pieces does each person get? ______
What fraction of the pizza is that? ______

Unit 14 Fractions of a group

$\frac{1}{4}$ means one of four equal parts. We can make a fractional part of a group.
Find $\frac{1}{4}$ of a group by dividing it into 4.
eg $\frac{1}{4}$ of 8 is the same as 8 divided by 4.

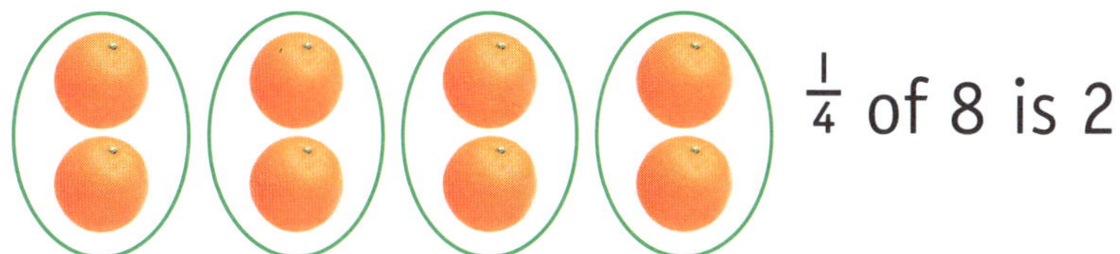

$\frac{1}{4}$ of 8 is 2

1 One half of 8 is 8 divided into 2 equal parts.

$\frac{1}{2}$ of 8 is ________

2 Look at the number 12 and circle fractions of 12.

eg $\frac{1}{2}$ of 12     is 6

a $\frac{1}{4}$ of 12

is ________

b $\frac{1}{3}$ of 12

is ________

c $\frac{1}{6}$ of 12

is ________

d $\frac{1}{12}$ of 12

is ________

Mastery Checklist I can:
- ☐ compare and order fractions
- ☐ colour to show fractions
- ☐ count by fractions
- ☐ work out fractions of a group.

Cakes and Biscuits

Investigation 2

Parents are coming to visit your class and you have to make morning tea. You will need 50 muffins. This recipe makes 20 muffins.

Ingredients:

- 3 cups self-raising flour
- 1 cup of butter
- 1 cup of sugar
- 2 large eggs
- 1 cup of milk
- vanilla essence to taste
- some choc-bits, diced apple or banana

Method:

Place dry ingredients in a bowl.
Mix in wet ingredients. Add choc-bits, apple or banana.

Pour into regular muffin tins and cook for 10–15 minutes at 160 °C.

How will you make 50 muffins using this recipe? Write your answer here.

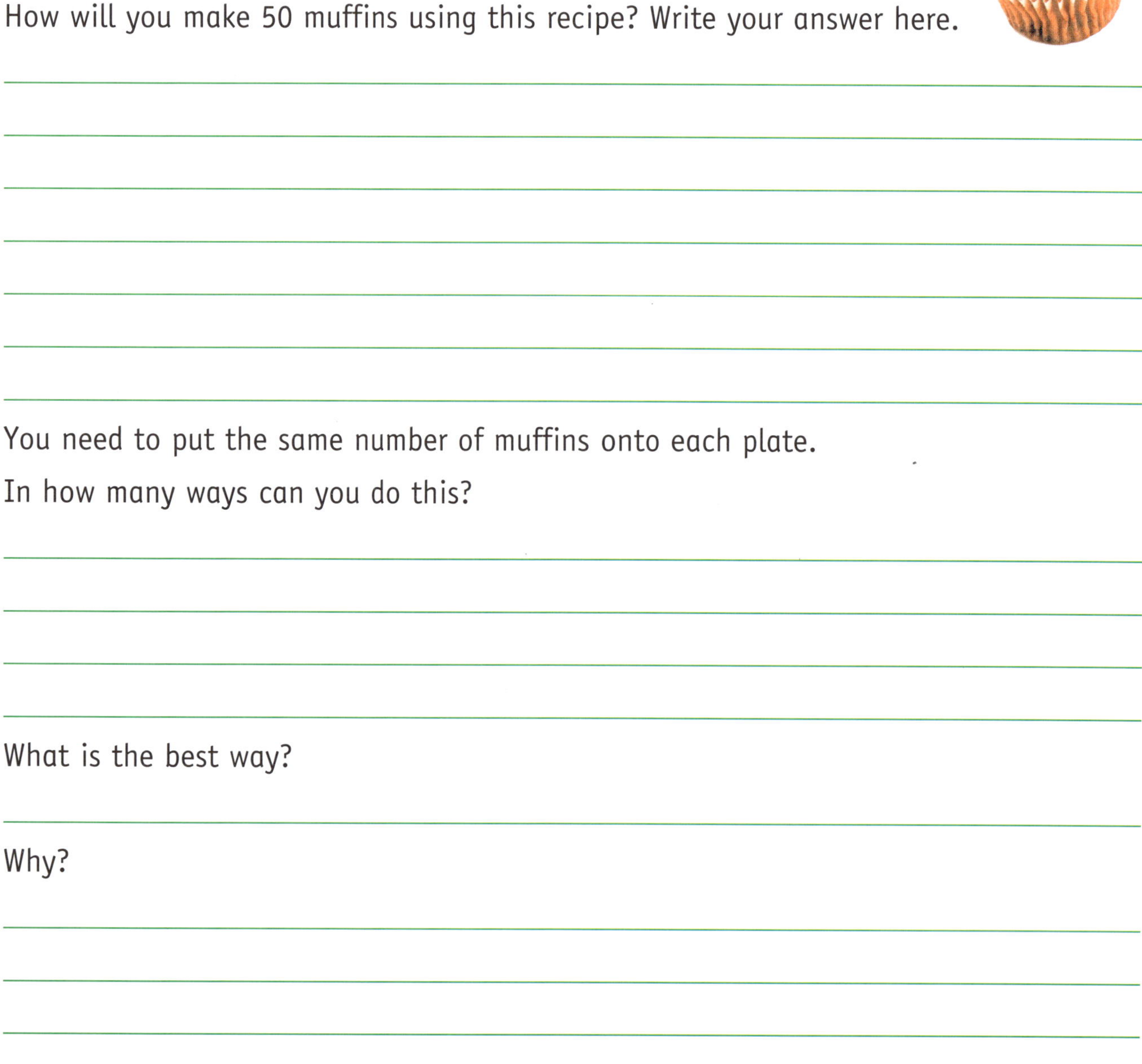

You need to put the same number of muffins onto each plate.

In how many ways can you do this?

What is the best way?

Why?

Cakes and Biscuits

Investigation 2

The Fete is coming and your class has the biscuit stall. Use one of these ingredient lists to work out how much money you can make selling 120 biscuits.

Ingredients – 20 biscuits in a batch

- 1 cup sugar
- 125 g butter, melted
- 1 teaspoon vanilla
- 1 cup plain flour
- 1 cup self-raising flour
- 1 egg, lightly beaten
- sprinkles and decorations

Cost of ingredients $5

Ingredients – 24 biscuits in a batch

- 125 g butter
- $\frac{1}{2}$ cup sugar
- $\frac{1}{2}$ cup brown sugar
- 1 egg
- $\frac{1}{2}$ tsp vanilla essence
- $\frac{1}{4}$ tsp salt
- $1\frac{3}{4}$ cups self-raising flour
- 150 g milk choc chips

Cost of ingredients $5.50

How will you make 120 biscuits?

____

____

____

____

____

____

____

____

____

____

How much will you charge for each biscuit? ____________

Money spent ____________________ Money raised ____________________

To carry out these tasks I need to:

- ☐ use doubling to multiply ingredients
- ☐ calculate how many batches to make
- ☐ calculate how to put biscuits onto trays evenly
- ☐ calculate how much money is spent and raised
- ☐ explain how I solve the problem.

I enjoyed this task! ☆☆☆☆☆

Revision

1 How many minutes have passed when the minute hand moves from 5 to 8?

5 ◯ 8 ◯ 15 ◯ 20 ◯

2 Which object is a pyramid?

 ◯

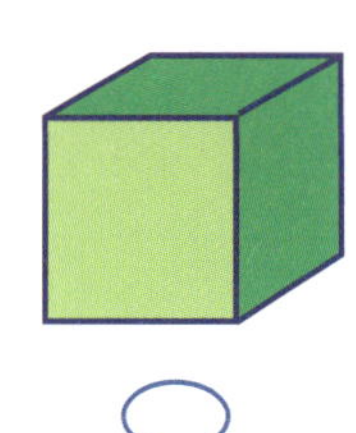 ◯

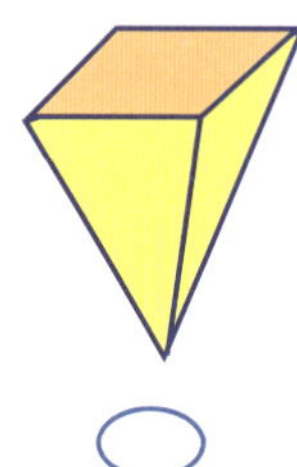 ◯

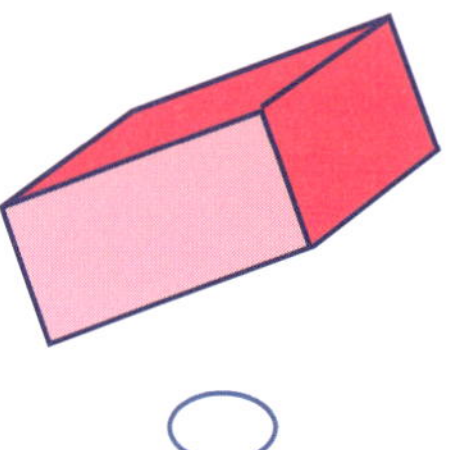 ◯

3 Using only three cards, what is the largest number you can make?

714 ◯ 471 ◯ 741 ◯ 704 ◯

4 Which operation does this number line show?

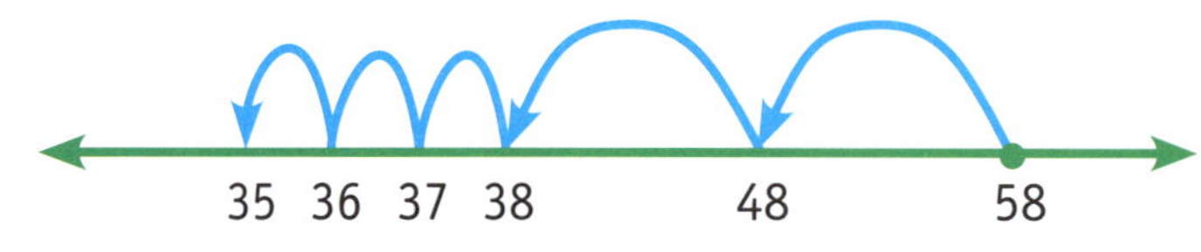

58 + 23 ◯ 35 − 23 ◯ 58 − 23 ◯ 38 − 3 ◯

5 Write the next number in this pattern.

Write your answer in the box.

63 54 45 36 ?

☐

Revision

6 Which label is missing?

Shade one bubble.

0, $\frac{1}{5}$, $\frac{2}{5}$, ☐, $\frac{4}{5}$, $\frac{5}{5}$

$\frac{5}{2}$ ◯ $\frac{3}{5}$ ◯ $\frac{1}{3}$ ◯ $\frac{5}{5}$ ◯

7 What fraction has been shaded?

Write your answer in the box.

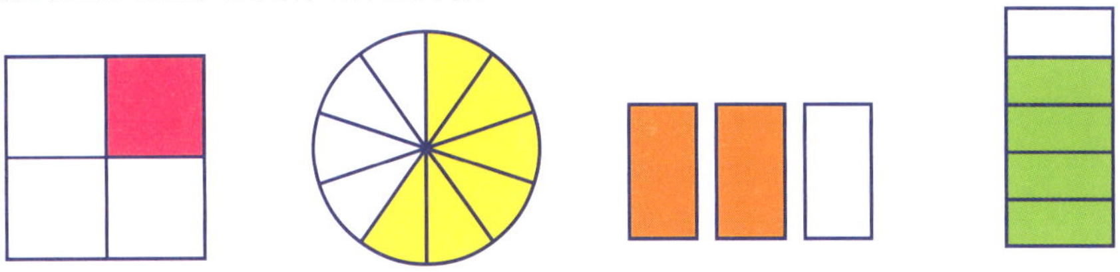

8 18 bunnies are in a row. If 11 hop away how many are left?

11 ◯ 9 ◯ 7 ◯ 8 ◯

Write your answer in the box.

9 Sam started his homework at 4 : 35 pm and finished at 5 : 05 pm.

How long did it take him? ☐ minutes

10 How many working dogs do they have altogether?

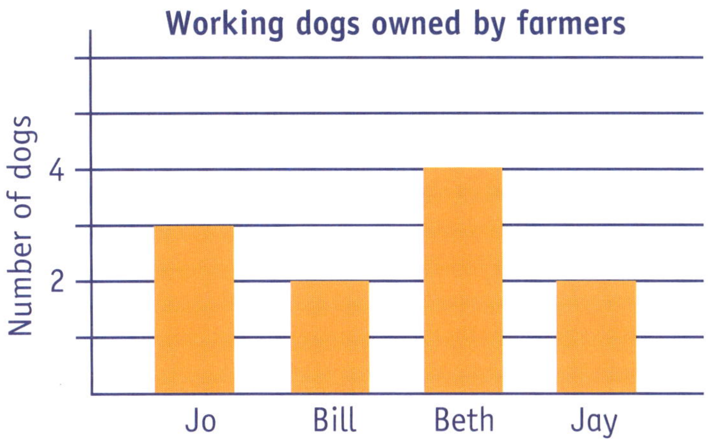

Working dogs owned by farmers

Number of dogs: 2, 4

Jo, Bill, Beth, Jay

Unit 15 Eating in Japan

1 Which items cost less than ¥500?

____

2 Which items cost betwen ¥500 and ¥1000?

____

3 What three items could I buy for a total less than ¥1000?

____

____

4 If I bought the yakitori, the stir fry and a green tea, what change would I get from ¥5000?

____

5 If you had ¥2000, what would you buy? What is the total price of your choice?

____

____

6 Answer true or false.

a You pay more yen than Australian dollars for food in Japan. ____________

b This menu shows that food in Japan is more expensive than in Australia.

____

AC9M3N06 Number MA2-AR-01 Additive relations B • Apply addition and subtraction to familiar contexts, including money and budgeting

Unit 15 Notes and coins

1 Match.

2 Circle the coins to make the amount.

a **$1.10**	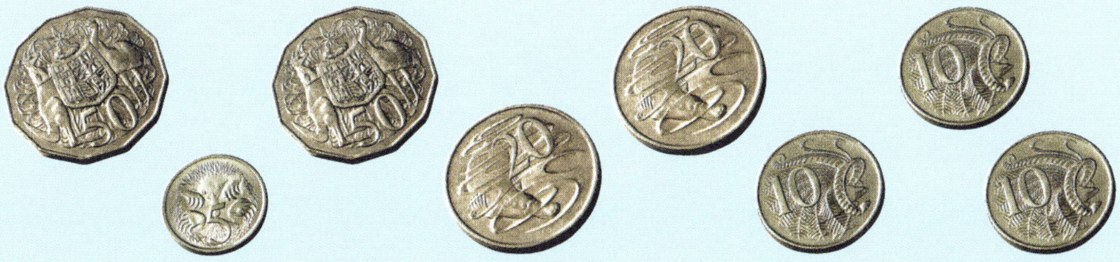
b **$3.45**	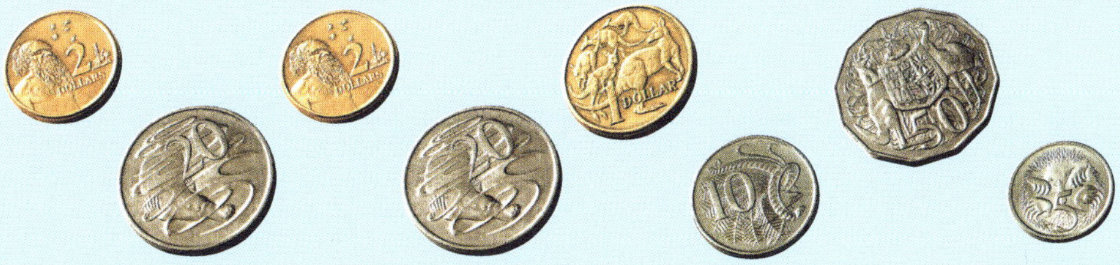
c **$5.80**	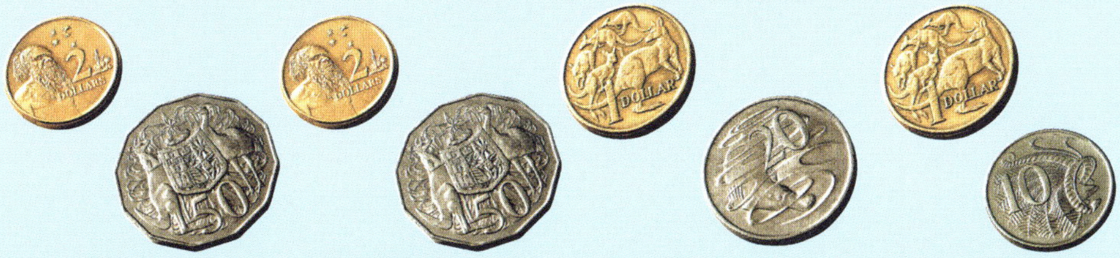
d **$0.95**	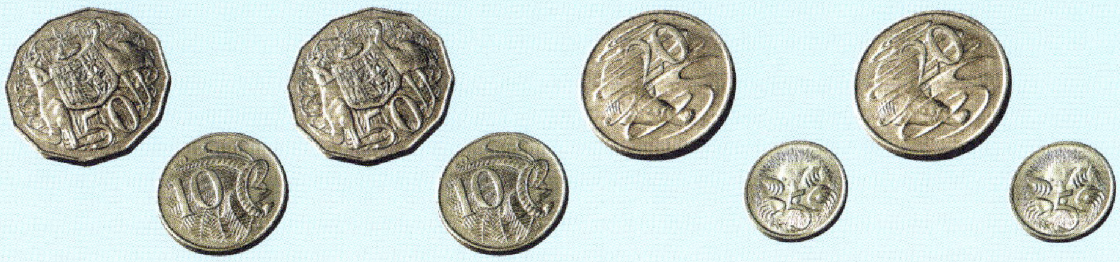

Unit 15 Add and subtract money

Change

Study this menu.

veggie burger
$8.50

milk shake
$4.25

snacks in a bag
$3.80

juice
$3.40

1 What coins would you use to pay for:

a the veggie burger? ______________________

b the milk shake? ______________________

c the snacks? ______________________

d the juice? ______________________

2 a My brother wants one of everything on the menu.
Will a $20 note cover the cost? __________

b What is the total cost? __________

3 What change will I receive from $10 if I buy:

a a veggie burger? __________ b both drinks? __________

4 Complete.

a

+	$5	$36	$19	$1.50	$2.80
$7					

b

+	50c	25c	$2	$18	$1.45
35c					

5 Write two different ways to make each amount with coins.

Amount	Coin combination 1	Coin combination 2
a $1.85		
b $2.40		
c $5.95		

Mastery Checklist I can:
- ☐ add costs and work out change
- ☐ recognise Australian notes and coins
- ☐ choose coins to equal an amount
- ☐ find different combinations of coins to equal an amount.

Unit 16 Number patterns

FRENCH HORN +4

TRUMPET −3

TROMBONE −6

RECORDER −2

CLARINET +5

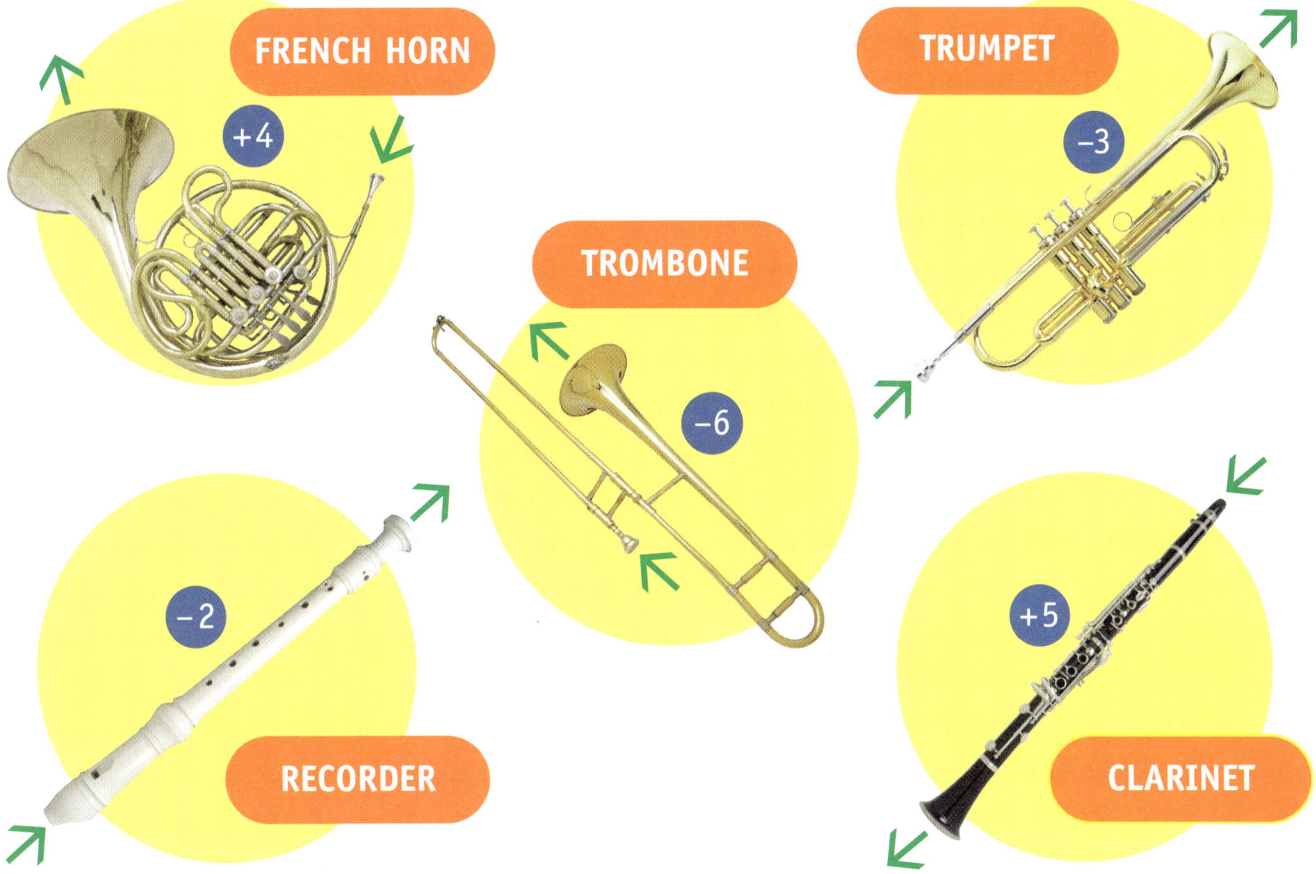

These are magical instruments.

When a number is blown in one end, it changes four times and all four numbers come out the other end. Each instrument has its own rule for making number patterns.

1 What numbers come out of the French horn if 7 is put in?

_______ _______ _______ _______

2 What numbers come out of the trombone if 34 is put in?

_______ _______ _______ _______

3 What happens to a 14 in a:

a trumpet? _______ _______ _______ _______

b clarinet? _______ _______ _______ _______

c recorder? _______ _______ _______ _______

4 What must be put in the clarinet for 40 to come out at the end of 4 changes?

____

Unit 16 Pattern rules

1 Look at page 82. Complete these:

a for the trumpet. Start with 18. ______ ______ ______ ______

Rule = ______ Start with 25. ______ ______ ______ ______

b for the clarinet. Start with 18. ______ ______ ______ ______

Rule = ______ Start with 23. ______ ______ ______ ______

c for the recorder. Start with 18. ______ ______ ______ ______

Rule = ______ Start with 15. ______ ______ ______ ______

d for the French horn. Start with 16. ______ ______ ______ ______

Rule = ______ Start with 11. ______ ______ ______ ______

e for the trombone. Start with 24. ______ ______ ______ ______

Rule = ______ Start with 29. ______ ______ ______ ______

2 This is your kazoo. Decide how it changes numbers and how many changes it makes before it runs out of puff.

KAZOO

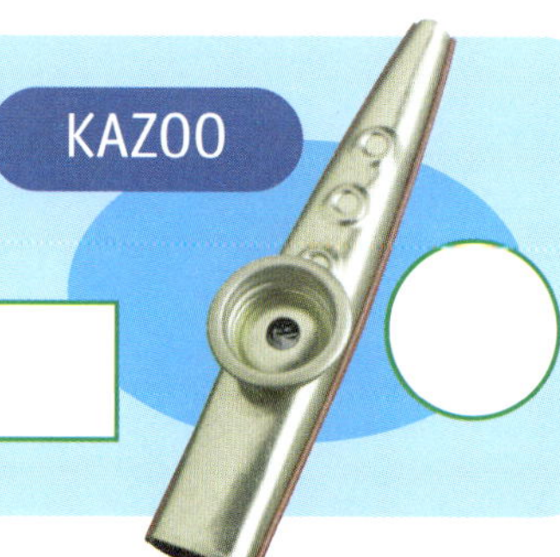

3 Use your kazoo.

a Start with 84. ______ ______ ______ ______

b Start with 110. ______ ______ ______ ______

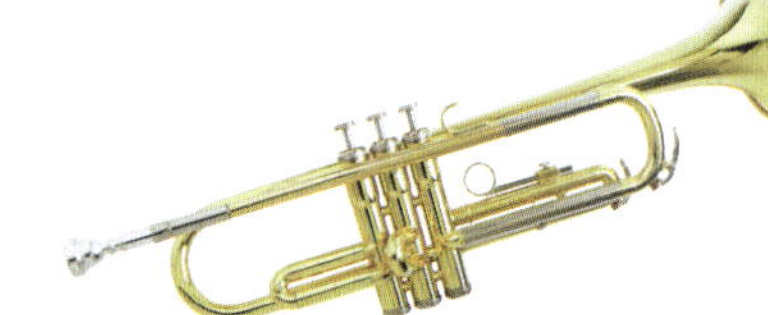

4 Invent a musical instrument and make it add and subtract numbers.

a Instrument name

______

b Changes it makes

______

c Use your instrument.

Start at 92.

______

Draw it here.

Unit 16 Number patterns

1 Write the next three rows.

a

4 + 9 = 13
14 + 9 = 23
24 + 9 = 33

______
______
______

b

8 + 7 = 15
18 + 7 = 25
28 + 7 = 35

______
______
______

c

9 + 7 = 16
19 + 7 = 26
29 + 7 = 36

______
______
______

d

46 - 12 = 34
56 - 12 = 44
66 - 12 = 54

______
______
______

e

89 - 5 = 84
89 - 15 = 74
89 - 25 = 64

______
______
______

f

6 + 6 + 6 = 18
7 + 7 + 7 = 21
8 + 8 + 8 = 24

______
______
______

A **multiple** is the answer you get when you multiply. 5 × 1 = **5**, 5 × 2 = **10**, 5 × 3 = **15**.
So 5, 10 and 15 are multiples of 5.

2 Start at 3. Use a straight line to join it to the next multiple of 3. Continue until you have reached 15.

What shape have you made?

______ Colour this shape.

3, 11, 4, 12, 5, 13, 6, 14, 7, 15, 8, 1, 9, 2, 10

3 Follow the patterns.

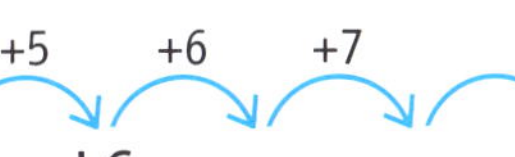

+1 +2 +3 +4 +5 +6 +7

a 1, 2, 4, 7, ____, 16, ____, ____, ____

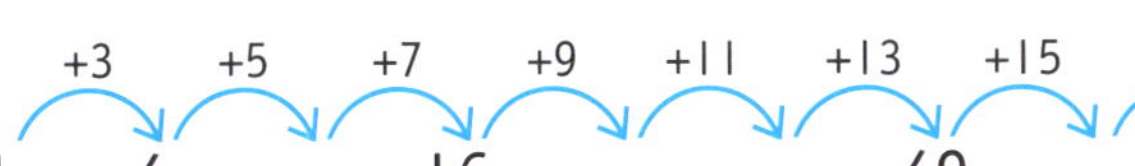

+3 +5 +7 +9 +11 +13 +15

b 1, 4, ____, 16, ____, ____, 49, ____, ____

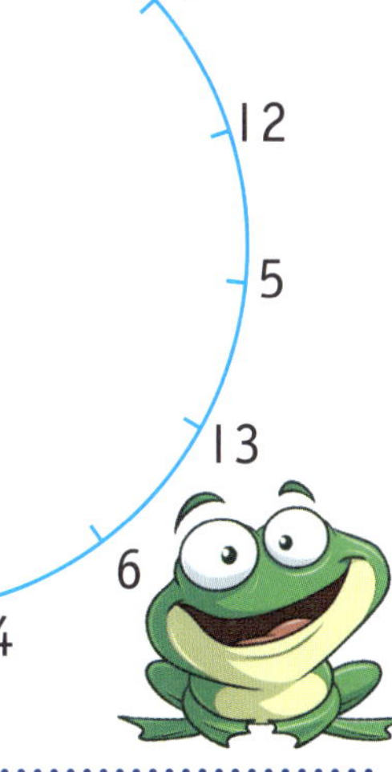

Mastery Checklist I can:
- ☐ follow a rule to make a number pattern
- ☐ start with different numbers to make a number pattern
- ☐ make my own number pattern
- ☐ continue number patterns with addition and subtraction.

Problem solving

Patterns using multiples

Look for the patterns in tables.

1 Complete this multiplication square neatly in pencil.

×	1	2	3	4	5	6	7	8	9	10	11	12
1												
2		4										
3									27			
4												
5					25							
6												
7								56				
8												
9				36								
10										100		
11							77					
12												

2 Colour the multiples of 3.

3 Describe the pattern you coloured.

4 Use different colours, make some different patterns. Try colouring different patterns, using the multiples of 4 and 5.

5 What patterns did you find?

I can solve problems by:

☐ identifying multiples ☐ looking for and identifying patterns.

AC9M3N07 Number **AC9M3A03** Algebra **MAO-WM-01** Working mathematically • communicating thinking and reasoning coherently and clearly
MA2-MR-01 • Multiplicative relations A • Generate and describe patterns • Multiplicative relations B • Use known number facts and strategies

Unit 17 Sides and angles

1 Trace and name these shapes.

2D Shapes
3 sides – triangle
4 sides – quadrilateral
5 sides – pentagon
6 sides – hexagon
7 sides – heptagon
8 sides – octagon

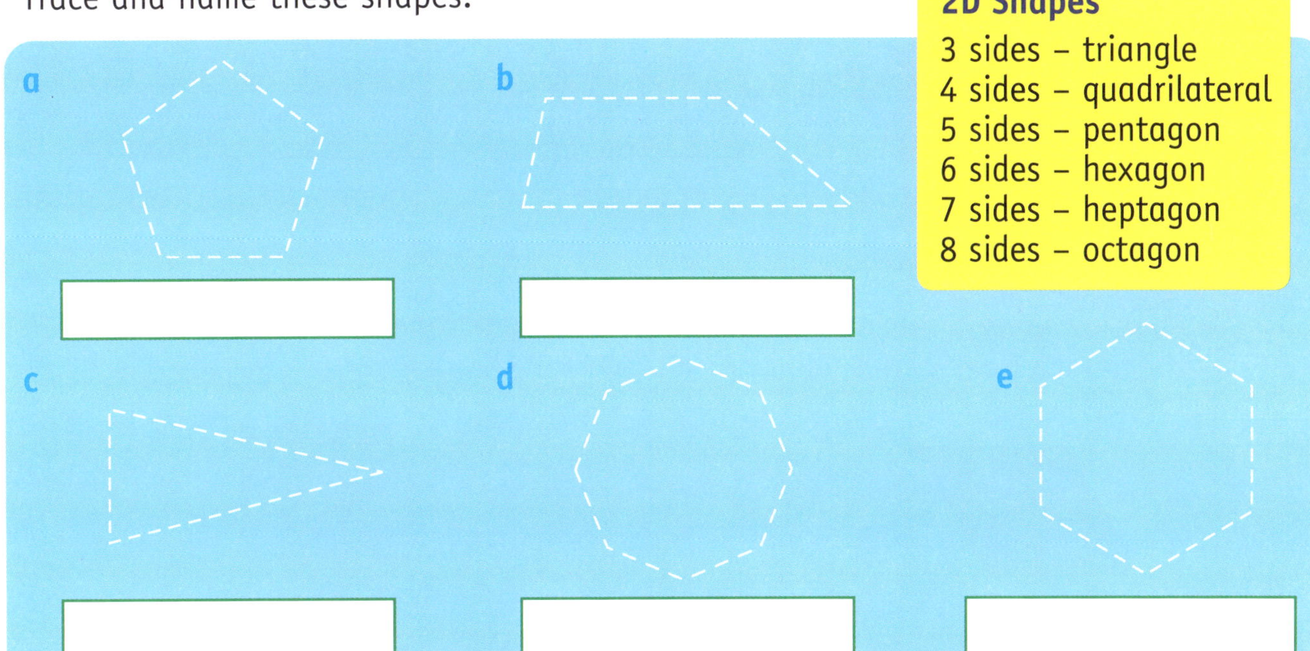

2

	Draw the shape	Name	Number of sides	Number of angles
a		triangle		
b		pentagon		
c		quadrilateral		
d		octagon		
e		hexagon		

Challenge! How many:

circles? ☐ squares? ☐

rectangles? ☐ triangles? ☐

Unit 17 Creating 2D shapes

2D shapes

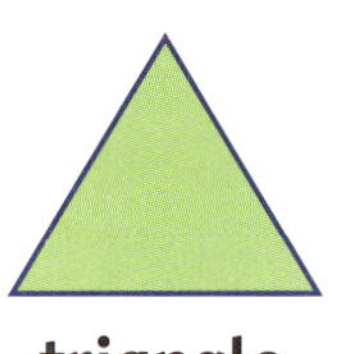
triangle

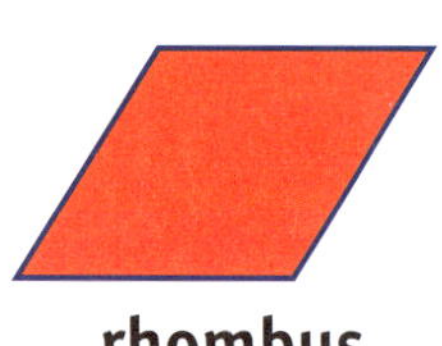
rhombus

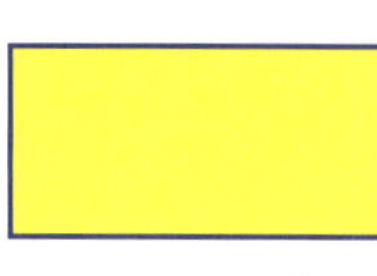
rectangle

square

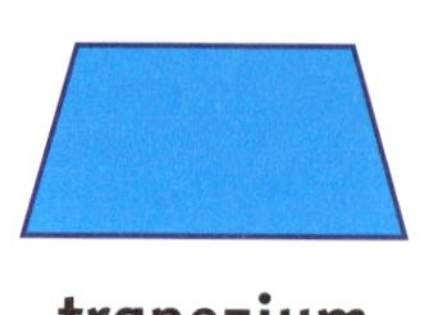
trapezium

You can combine a rhombus and a triangle to form a trapezium.

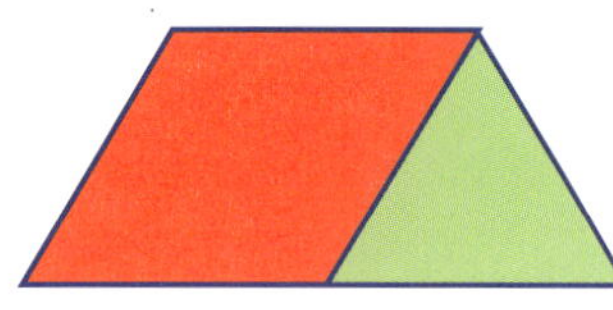

A rectangle and two triangles combine to form a hexagon.

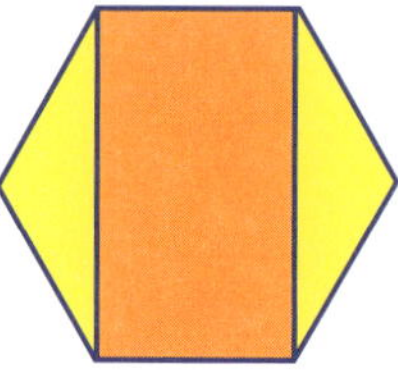

Use combinations of shapes to draw new 2D shapes. See how many different combinations you can find.

Unit 17 Sketching 3D objects

A 3D object has 3 dimensions: height, length and width (depth).

To draw a **triangular prism**:

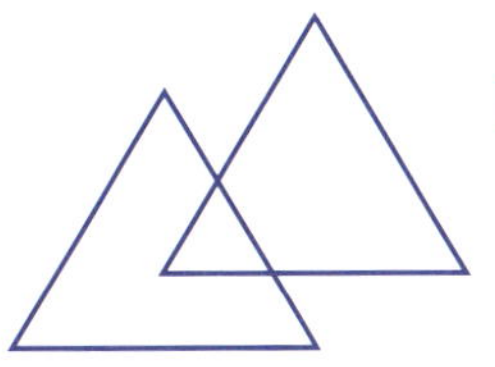

1 Draw two triangles for the bases. Make them the same size, and overlap them.

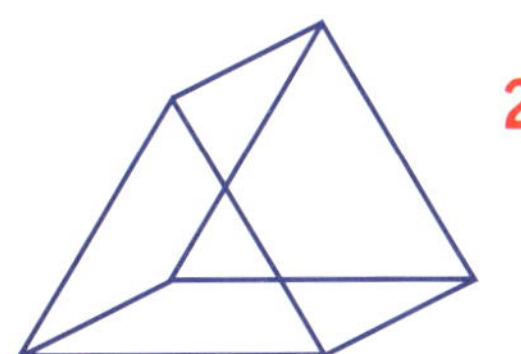

2 Draw straight lines to join the matching corners of the bases.

To draw a **triangular pyramid**:

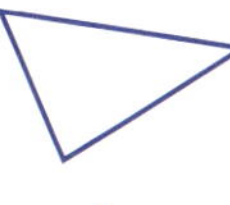

1 Draw the triangle for the base.

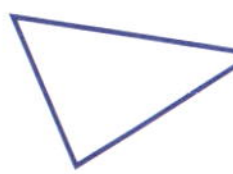

2 Draw a dot for the apex.

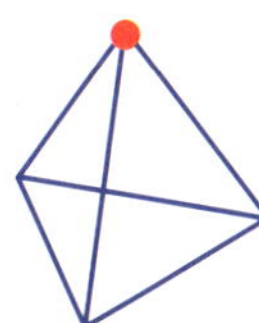

3 Draw a straight line from each corner of the base to the apex.

1 Try drawing these objects.

a cube

b rectangular prism

c square-based pyramid

d pentagon-based pyramid

Unit 17 Nets

A net is a flat (two-dimensional) pattern you can fold to make a 3D object.

This net folds up to make a **rectangular prism**.

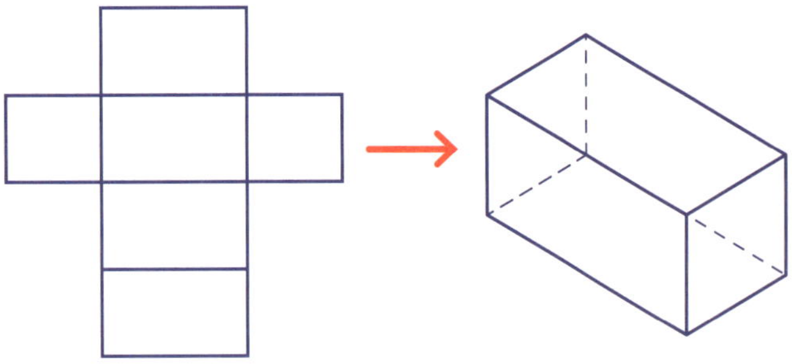

This net folds up to make a **square-based pyramid**.

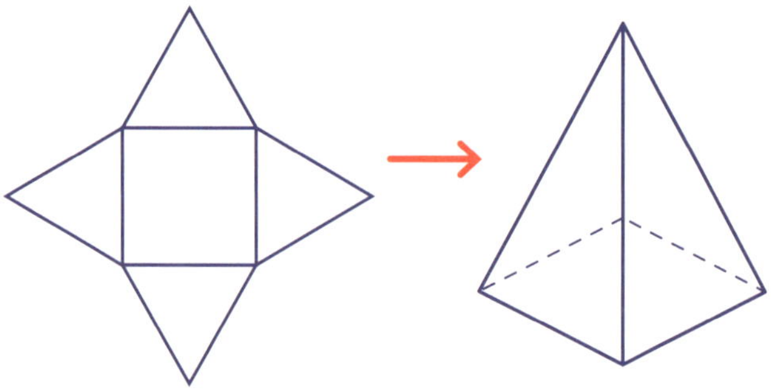

Match the nets with the correct label.

1

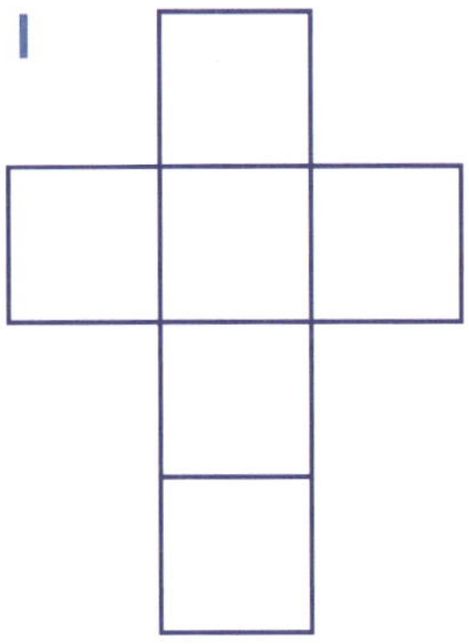

2

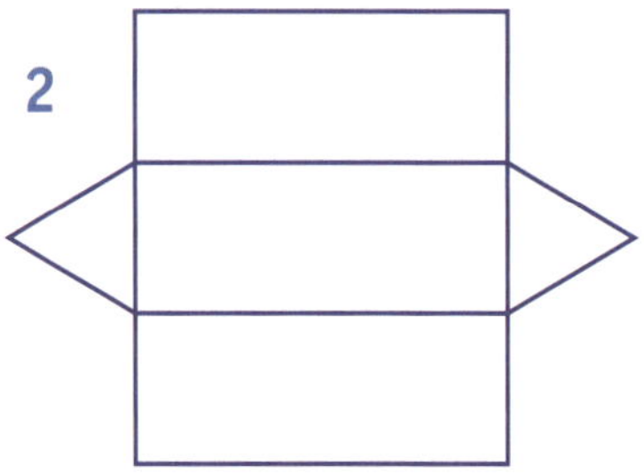

3

cube

rectangular-based pyramid

cylinder

hexagonal prism

triangular prism

cone

triangular pyramid

4

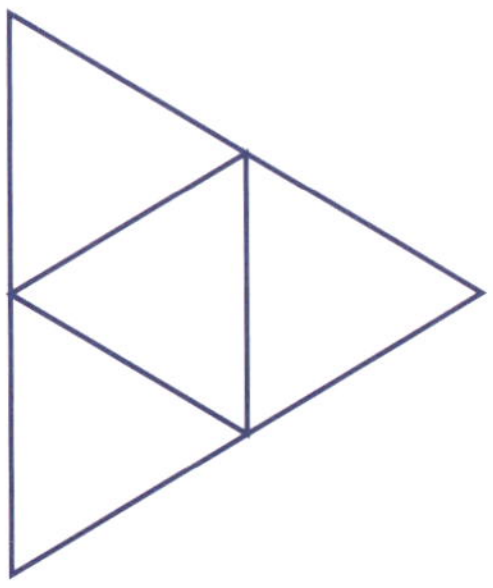

5

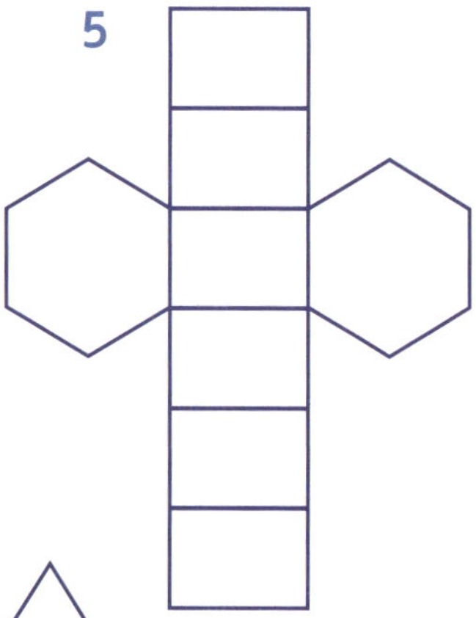

6

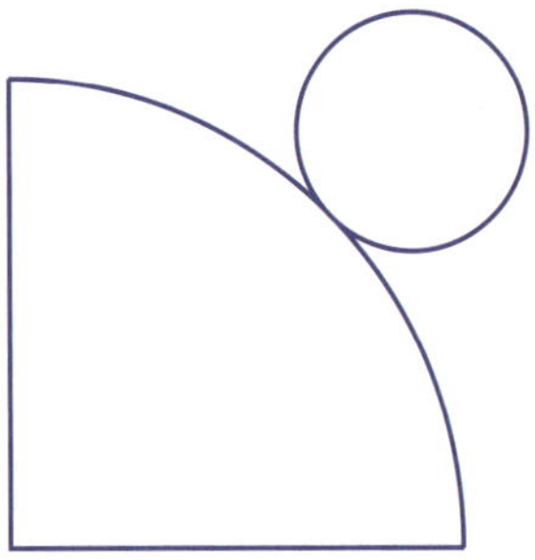

7

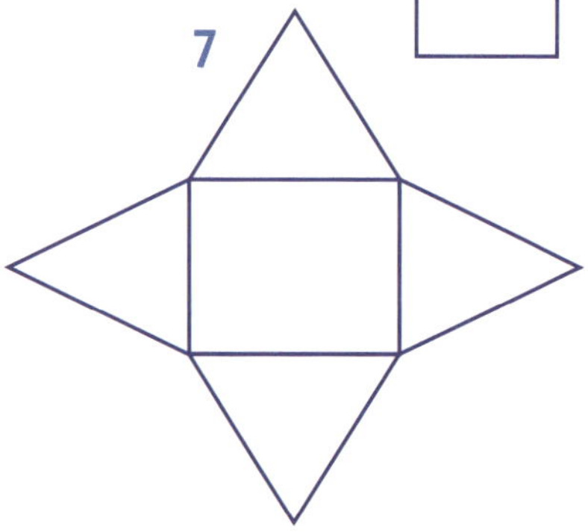

Mastery Checklist I can:

- ☐ identify sides and angles on 2D shapes
- ☐ combine 2D shapes to make new shapes
- ☐ draw prisms and pyramids
- ☐ match nets to 3D objects.

Unit 18 Capacity

1 Which container holds the most? _____

2 Which container holds the least? _____

3 Name two containers that hold about the same amount? _______________

4 Name two containers which hold more than any of these. _______________

____

5 Name two containers which hold less than any of these. _______________

____

6 About how many cups (E) would be needed to fill:

a B? __________ b D? __________ c A? __________ d F? __________

7 Write the containers in order from holds least to holds most.

____

measure capacity

8 Get an empty plastic soft drink bottle and a plastic cup.

a How many cups does the bottle hold? __________

b Does everyone in the class get the same answer? __________

c Why or why not? ____

____

____

Unit 18 The litre

1 Ali used a plastic cup to fill coloured containers with water.

L stands for litre.
5 **L** is 5 litres.

Container	Number of cups needed
Blue	
Green	
Yellow	
Red	
Orange	
Pink	

a How many cups does the green container hold? ________

b Which container holds the most? ________

c Which container holds the least? ________

d How many cups does the orange one hold? ________

e Which two hold about the same?

____

2 Lucy used a different cup. She needed 8 cups to fill the green container.

a Is her cup bigger or smaller than Ali's cup? ________

b About how many of her cups will fill the yellow container? ________

c Is a plastic cup a good measure? ________

Give a reason. ________________

3 a How much milk was in the carton? [ ]

b How much does the jug hold? [ ]

4 Fill an empty 1 litre container with water. Pour it into some empty cups. How many cups does it fill? [ ]

5 Use water and your 1 litre container to find things that hold:

less than 1 litre	about 1 litre	more than 1 litre

Unit 18 Millilitres

These containers measure millilitres.

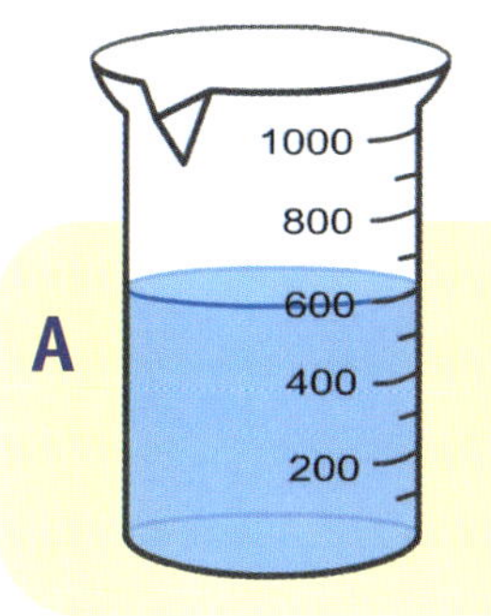

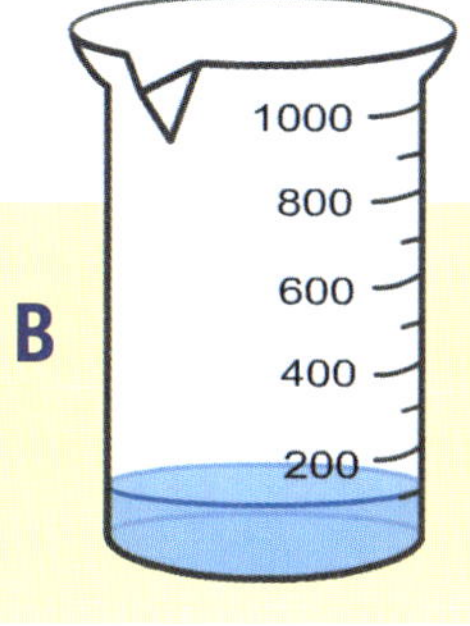

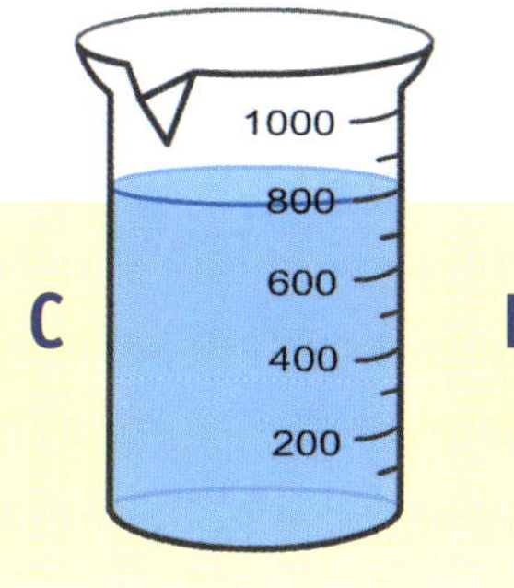

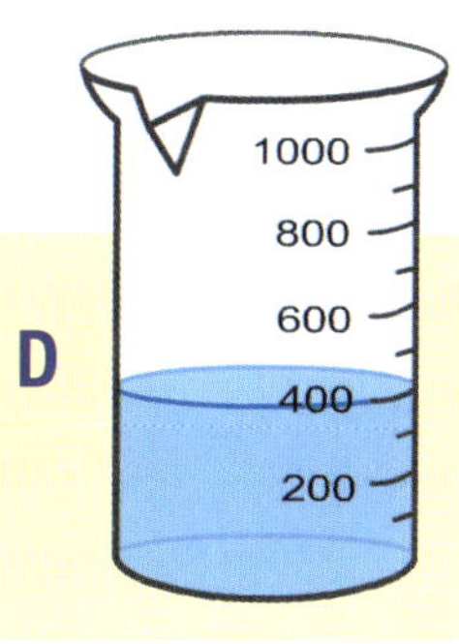

mL is millilitre.
1000 mL = 1 L
500 mL = $\frac{1}{2}$ L

1 How much water is in:

a **A**? ________ b **B**? ________ c **C**? ________ d **D**? ________

2 How much more is in: a **A** than **B**? ________ b **C** than **D**? ________

3 How much must be added to:

a **B** to make 1 L? ________ b **C** to make 1 L? ________

4 Which container is closest to: a 1 L?____ b $\frac{1}{2}$ L?____

5 Name 4 things which could be measured in millilitres.

6 a What is the capacity of **A**? ☐

b What is the capacity of **B**? ☐

c Which container holds more? ☐

d How much more does it hold? ☐

7 True (T) or false (F)?

a A dose of medicine is 5 L. ____

b A car can hold 40 L of petrol. ____

c A glass holds about 250 mL. ____

d The capacity of a cup is 200 L. ____

e My dog drank 1 mL of water today. ____

f The tall vase can hold 1 L of water. ____

Challenge!

estimate capacity, measure to check

On a large plastic bottle place an elastic band to show where you think $\frac{1}{2}$ L is. Check. Try with different containers.

Mastery Checklist

I can:

- ☐ compare the capacities of different containers
- ☐ use a cup to measure capacity
- ☐ compare capacities to 1 litre
- ☐ relate millilitres to litres
- ☐ choose between millilitres and litres.

Unit 19 Presenting data

1 Some friends drew a picture graph of the fish they caught.

a How many people went fishing? ______

b How many fish did Julio catch? ______

c Who caught the most fish? ______

d Who caught twice as many fish as Arthur? ______

e How many fish were caught altogether? ______

f Who said this? "I caught more fish than Julio, but fewer than Mary." ______

2 Mary decided to show the information as a column graph. She drew this.

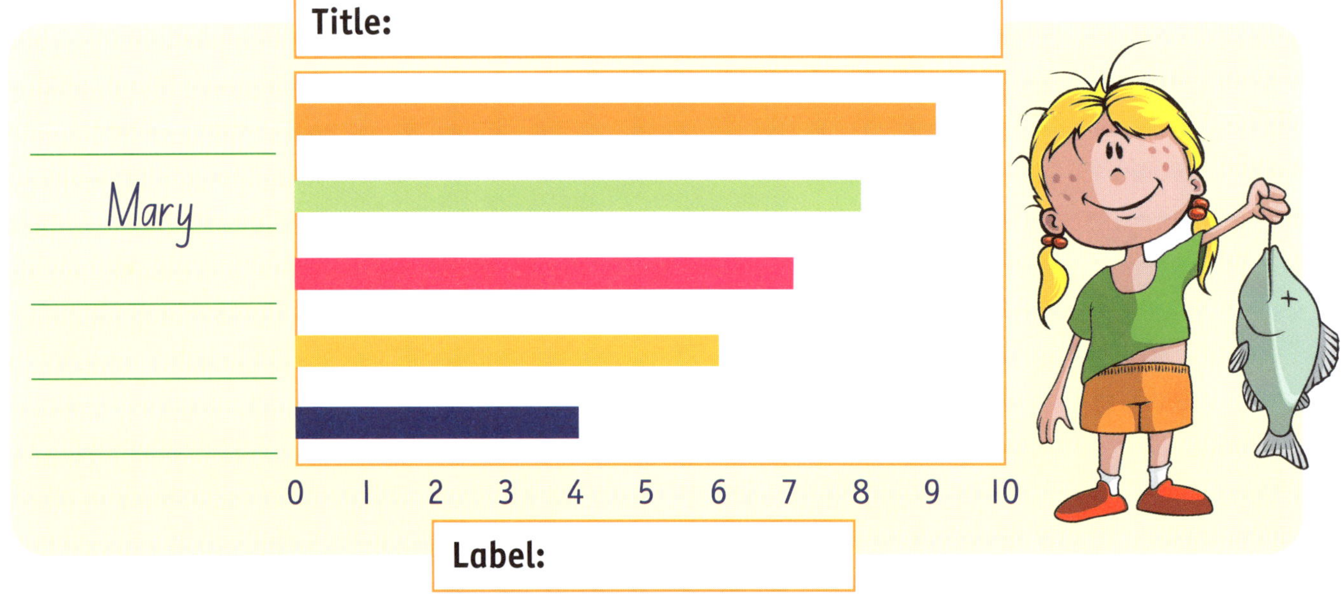

a Complete the column graph by writing the name of each person.

b Write a title on the graph.

c Write the missing label.

3 Conn said he would write a table for the information.

a Complete the table for Conn.

b In which order did he write the names of the people who went fishing? ______

Name	Number of fish caught
Arthur	
Julio	
Conn	7
Mary	
Tessie	

Unit 19 Drawing a column graph

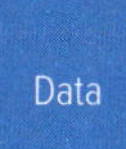

1 Eight children have heavy schoolbags.
Their teacher weighs each bag using books.

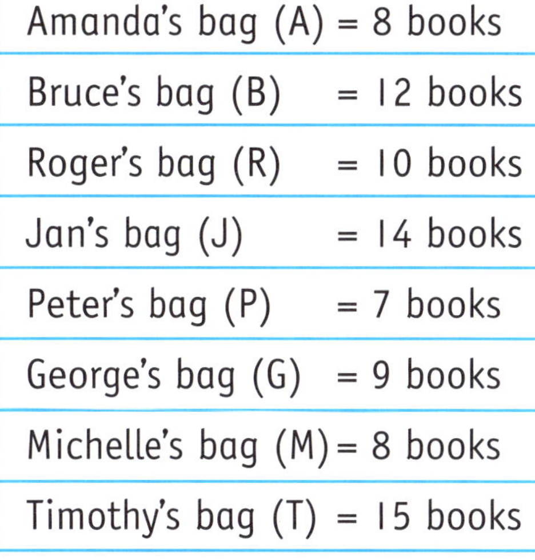

Amanda's bag (A)	= 8 books
Bruce's bag (B)	= 12 books
Roger's bag (R)	= 10 books
Jan's bag (J)	= 14 books
Peter's bag (P)	= 7 books
George's bag (G)	= 9 books
Michelle's bag (M)	= 8 books
Timothy's bag (T)	= 15 books

a How heavy is Roger's bag? __________ books

b Who has the heaviest bag? ______________

c Who has the lightest bag? ______________

d Which two bags have the same mass?

_______________ and _______________

e Write the three students with the heaviest bags from lightest to heaviest.

_______________ , _______________ , _______________

f Whose bag is heavier than George's, but lighter than Bruce's? ______________

g What is the mass, in books, of Peter's bag and Roger's bag together? ______________

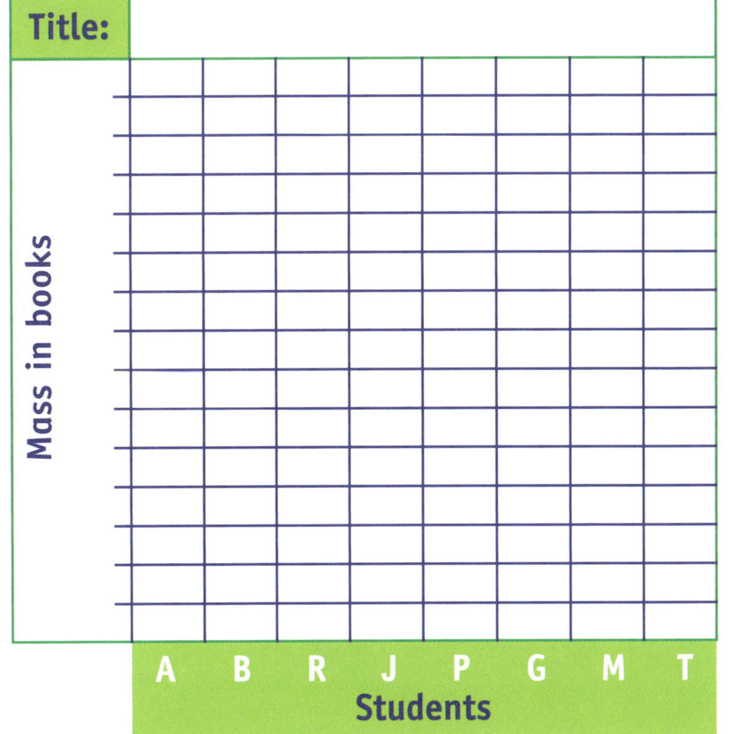

2 a Make a column graph by colouring the spaces.

b Write in the vertical scale.

c Write a title for your graph.

3 True or False?

a Jan's bag is twice as heavy as Peter's bag. ___________

b Roger's bag is lighter than George's bag. ___________

c Timothy's bag has the same mass as Michelle's bag and Peter's bag together. ___________

d Three students have bags lighter than Roger's bag. ___________

Mastery Checklist

I can:
- ☐ answer questions about a picture graph
- ☐ complete a column graph and a table
- ☐ answer questions about a column graph
- ☐ draw a column graph.

Draw a diagram

Find another way to present this information.

Revision Term 2

1 Order from smallest to largest. p 56

9390 9309 9399 9319 9380 9331

_____ _____ _____ _____ _____ _____

2 What is the value of the underlined number? p 58

a 57<u>8</u>2 __________

b <u>9</u>603 __________

3 Use the numerals 6, 7, 8, 9 to write a number with: p 58

a 6 in the hundreds place. __________

b 9 in the ones place. __________

c 7 in the thousands place. __________

4 p 60

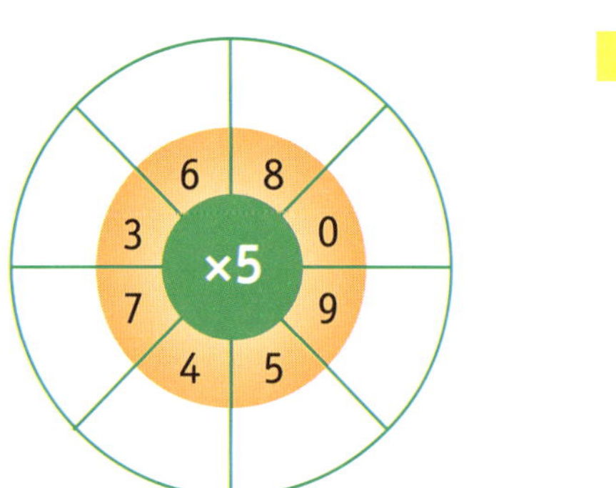

5 Write three more facts. p 63

20 − 13 = 7

____ − ____ = ____

____ + ____ = ____

____ + ____ = ____

6 Count on to complete: p 65

	49	53	50	56	54
−47					

7 Use the number lines. p 66

a

$$\begin{array}{r} 42 \\ -\ 27 \\ \hline \end{array}$$

____

b p 66

$$\begin{array}{r} 81 \\ -\ 56 \\ \hline \end{array}$$

____

8 p 68

a

$$\begin{array}{r} 67 \\ -\ 14 \\ \hline \end{array}$$

b

$$\begin{array}{r} 88 \\ -\ 35 \\ \hline \end{array}$$

c

$$\begin{array}{r} 95 \\ -\ 20 \\ \hline \end{array}$$

9 My frog jumped 58 cm. p 69

Jill's frog jumped 37 cm.

What was the difference? ______

10 Write the next two fractions. p 71

a $\frac{1}{5}$, $\frac{2}{5}$, $\frac{3}{5}$, ______, ______

b $\frac{3}{8}$, $\frac{4}{8}$, $\frac{5}{8}$, ______, ______

11 Order these fractions from smallest to largest. p 71

a $\frac{2}{6}$, $\frac{5}{6}$, $\frac{1}{6}$, $\frac{4}{6}$, $\frac{3}{6}$

_____ _____ _____ _____ _____

b $\frac{7}{8}$, $\frac{2}{8}$, $\frac{1}{8}$, $\frac{5}{8}$, $\frac{8}{8}$

_____ _____ _____ _____ _____

c $\frac{2}{4}$, $\frac{3}{4}$, $\frac{4}{4}$, $\frac{1}{4}$

_____ _____ _____ _____

d $\frac{2}{3}$, $\frac{3}{3}$, $\frac{1}{3}$

_____ _____ _____

12 Circle the diagram for $\frac{1}{4}$. p 71

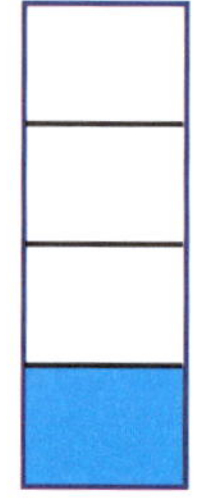

Revision Term 2

13 a Circle $\frac{1}{3}$ of this group. p 73

b Circle $\frac{1}{6}$ of this group.

p 79

14 Write the coins to make the amounts.

a 85c ______________________

b $2.40 ______________________

c $7.15 ______________________

15 Complete. p 80

a

+	$6	$1	$21	$2.20	$1.10	40c
$6						

b

−	$1	$3.70	$1.90	80c	$5	$7
70c						

16 Find the pattern. Write the next three rows. p 83

48 − 13 = 35

58 − 13 = 45

68 − 13 = 55

____

____

____

17 Write something that holds: p 90

a about 1 litre. ______________

b more than 1 litre. ______________

c less than 1 litre. ______________

18 L or mL? p 91

a water in a cup ________

b petrol in a car ________

19 p 93

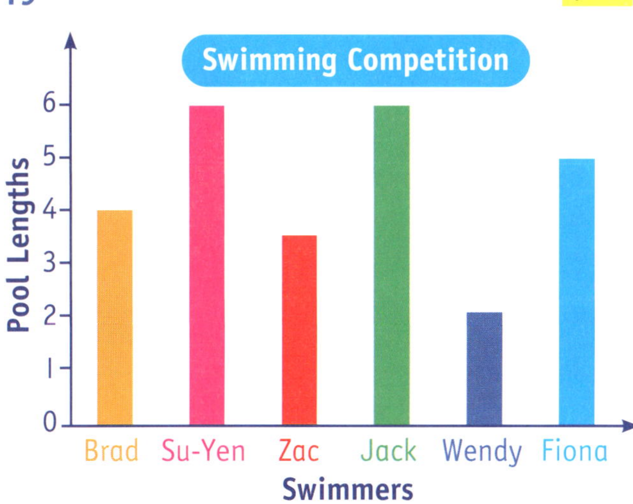

a Who swam the shortest distance?

____

b Which two swimmers swam the same distance?

____

c How many lengths did Zac swim? ________

d How many lengths were swum altogether? ________

e How many people swam in the competition? ________

f What is this graph for?

____

____

____

Unit 20 Addition of money

Riley has $5

Ali has $3.50

Ng has $4.50

Ada has $7

1 Which two toys can each child buy?

a Ada ______________________

b Riley ______________________

c Ali ______________________

d Ng ______________________

2 How much change will they get?

a Ada ____________ b Riley ____________

c Ali ____________ d Ng ____________

3 How many different toys could Ada buy? ________

 AC9M3N02 Number **AC9M3M06** Measurement **MA2-AR-01** Additive relations B • Apply addition and subtraction to familiar contexts, including money and budgeting

1 How many in each group? Find the total.

a

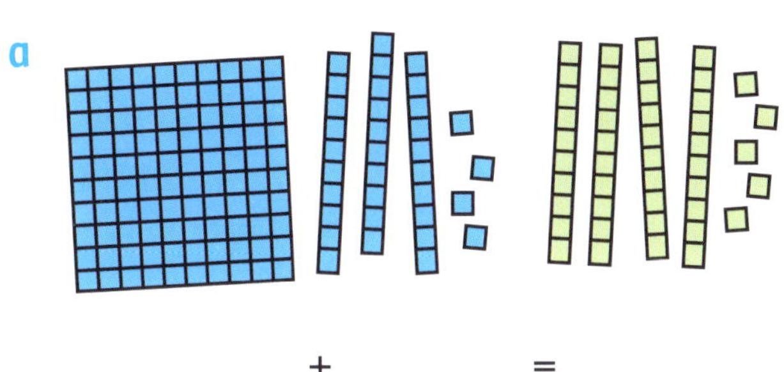

_____ + _____ = _____

b

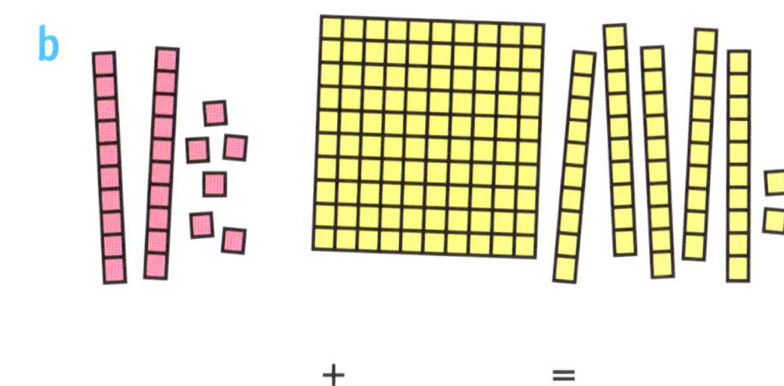

_____ + _____ = _____

c

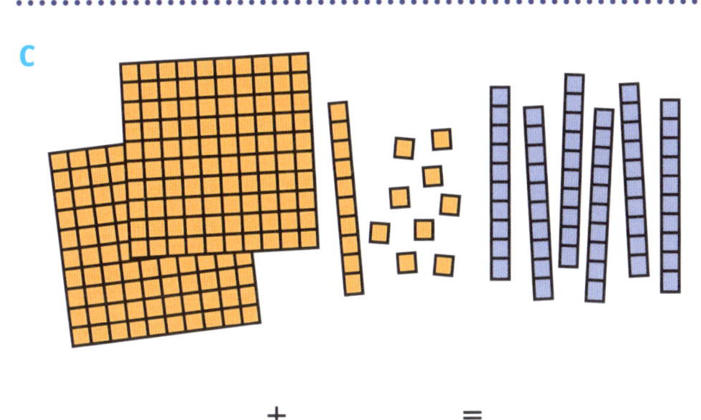

_____ + _____ = _____

d

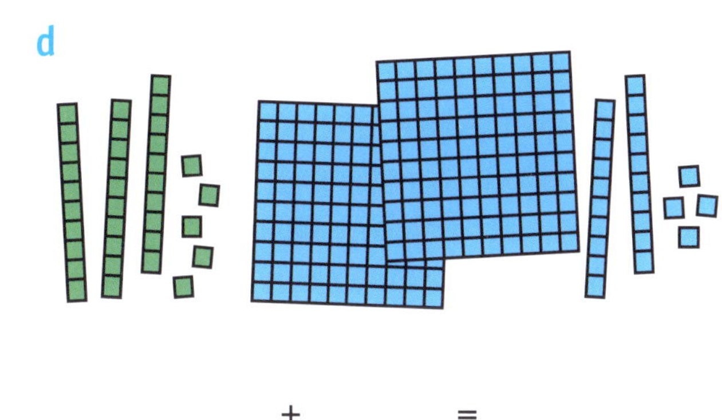

_____ + _____ = _____

2

a $\begin{array}{r} 173 \\ +\ 16 \\ \hline \\ \hline \end{array}$

b $\begin{array}{r} 231 \\ +\ 45 \\ \hline \\ \hline \end{array}$

c $\begin{array}{r} 127 \\ +\ 150 \\ \hline \\ \hline \end{array}$

d $\begin{array}{r} 284 \\ +\ 115 \\ \hline \\ \hline \end{array}$

e $\begin{array}{r} 353 \\ +\ 125 \\ \hline \\ \hline \end{array}$

f $\begin{array}{r} 126 \\ +\ 472 \\ \hline \\ \hline \end{array}$

3

a $\begin{array}{r} 3\ 0 \\ +\ 2\ \square \\ \hline \square\ 9 \\ \hline \end{array}$

b $\begin{array}{r} 2\ \square \\ +\ 6\ 3 \\ \hline \square\ 7 \\ \hline \end{array}$

c $\begin{array}{r} \square\ \square \\ +\ 2\ 4 \\ \hline 9\ 9 \\ \hline \end{array}$

d $\begin{array}{r} 1\ 2 \\ +\ \square\ 2 \\ \hline 8\ \square \\ \hline \end{array}$

e $\begin{array}{r} \square\ 5 \\ +\ 2\ \square \\ \hline 6\ 8 \\ \hline \end{array}$

4 Match each to its answer.

a 172 + 27

c 35 + 243

e 41 + 146

278 199 289

296 379 187

b 283 + 13

d 333 + 46

f 49 + 240

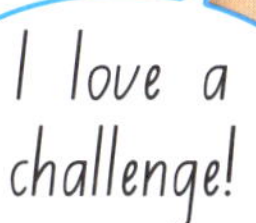

Challenge! Can you buy all the toys on page 99 with $20? Use a calculator.

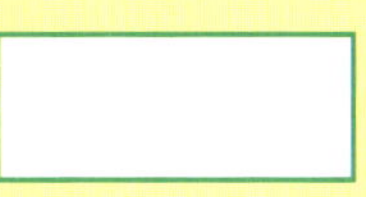

Unit 20 Bar model for addition

Problem	Bar model	Equation
1 Nullah counted crabs at the beach. He counted 75 crabs on Monday. After he counted some more on Tuesday, he had counted 139 crabs altogether. How many crabs did Nullah count on Tuesday?	75 | ? 139 ? = 64	75 + 64 = 139
2 Kylie saw 34 lizards on her hike, before lunch. Then after lunch she saw 27 more. How many lizards did she see altogether?	34 | 27 ? ? = ____	____ + ____ = ____
3 Nellie counted 22 kangaroo paintings, Kirra counted 36 echidna paintings and Maali counted 38 bird paintings. How many paintings did they see altogether?	22 | 36 | 38 ? ? = ____	____ + ____ + ____ = ____
4 Kai picked 39 berries on Saturday. He picked more berries on Sunday but forgot to count them. He had 129 berries altogether. How many berries did he pick on Sunday?	? = ____	____ + ____ = ____
5 Joey carved 14 coolamons in summer and 28 more in winter. How many coolamons did he carve altogether?	? = ____	____ + ____ = ____

AC9M3N06 Number **MA2-AR-01** Additive relations A • Recognise and explain the connection between addition and subtraction

Unit 20 3-digit numbers and money

1 Write a number sentence and the answer.

+			
	230 + 24 = 254		

2

a Which two toys are the same price? ______________ ______________

b Which toy costs the most? ______________

c Which toy is the cheapest? ______________

d Which two toys together cost $8.50? ______________ ______________

e How much would it cost to buy the car and the yo-yo? ______________

f Can I buy the donkey and the softball with $7.50? ______________

g Which toys cost less than $5? ______________

h If you had $10, what would you buy? ______________

i If you had $20, what would you buy? ______________

Unit 20 Mental addition

1 a 65 + 29 = 65 + 30 − 1 = ______ b 38 + 43 = 38 + 40 + 3 = ______

c 43 + 39 = ______________ = ______ d 59 + 38 = ______________ = ______

e 38 + 61 = ______________ = ______ f 47 + 22 = ______________ = ______

g 77 + 13 = ______________ = ______ h 23 + 49 = ______________ = ______

2 a

+ 19

28 42 74 17 65 56 80 33

b

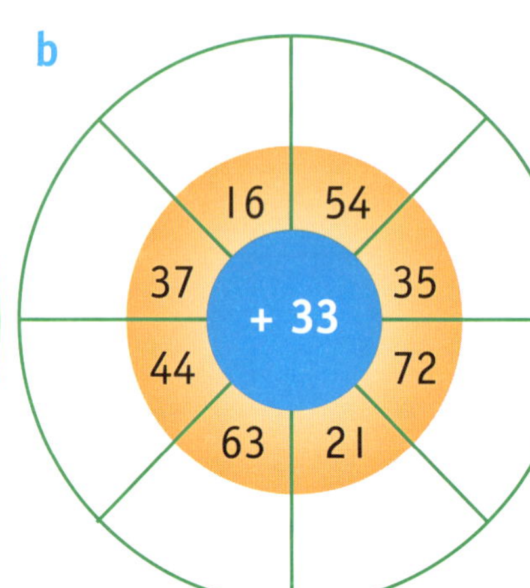

c

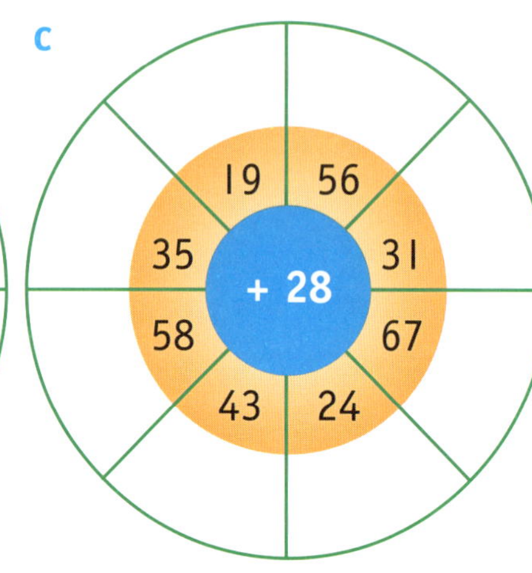

3 Estimate first.

	Estimate	Answer
a 17 + 15		
b 39 + 24		
c 35 + 63		

	Estimate	Answer
d 28 + 13		
e 51 + 37		
f 46 + 29		

4 Jon paid 25c for an apple, 30c for an orange and 45c for a banana.

a How much did he spend? ______________

b How much change from $2? ______________

Work backwards

Look at question 2 on page 99. At the fair Mindy spent exactly $16 on 3 items. Which items did she buy?

Mastery Checklist

I can:

- ☐ add costs and work out change
- ☐ use base 10 blocks to add 3-digit numbers
- ☐ use algorithms to add 3-digit numbers
- ☐ use a bar model to add
- ☐ regroup numbers to add mentally
- ☐ estimate answers to addition.

Unit 21 Multiplication

A

B

C

D

E

F

G

H

1

A	3 + 3 + 3 =	3 × 3 =
B	5 + 5 + 5 + 5 =	
C		
D		
E		
F		
G		
H		

2 Put A and G together and write an addition and a multiplication number sentence.

Unit 21 Multiplication

1 Use different colours to match.

a	2 + 2 + 2 + 2	6 bundles of 6	4 × 2	25
b	5 + 5 + 5 + 5 + 5	4 lots of 2	6 × 6	8
c	6 + 6 + 6 + 6 + 6 + 6	three nines	5 × 5	10
d	9 + 9 + 9	5 groups of 5	7 × 4	36
e	4 + 4 + 4 + 4 + 4 + 4 + 4	1 lot of 10	3 × 9	27
f	10	7 groups of 4	1 × 10	28

2

a	8 + 8 + 8 = ☐ ice-creams	3 × 8 = ☐
b	9 + 9 + 9 + 9 + 9 + 9 + 9 = ☐ hearts	☐ × 9 = ☐
c	5 + 5 + 5 + 5 = ☐ pencils	4 × ☐ = ☐
d	7 = ☐ cakes	☐ × ☐ = ☐
e	☐ + ☐ + ☐ = ☐ apples	☐ × ☐ = ☐
f	☐ + ☐ = ☐ balloons	☐ × ☐ = ☐

Unit 21 Number facts 9×

9 tables 

1	2	3	4	5	6	7	8	9	10	11	12	13
												14
27	26	25	24	23	22	21	20	19	18	17	16	15
28												
29	30	31	32	33	34	35	36	37	38	39	40	41
												42
55	54	53	52	51	50	49	48	47	46	45	44	43
56												
57	58	59	60	61	62	63	64	65	66	67	68	69
												70
83	82	81	80	79	78	77	76	75	74	73	72	71
84												
85	86	87	88	89	90							

Kanga jumps along the path 9 spaces each time.

1 Colour the numbers he will land on.

2 How far did he go in:

a 0 jumps? ______ b 1 jump? ______ c 2 jumps? ______ d 3 jumps? ______

e 4 jumps? ______ f 5 jumps? ______ g 6 jumps? ______ h 7 jumps? ______

i 8 jumps? ______ j 9 jumps? ______ k 10 jumps? ______

3 Look at the coloured numbers.

a What happens to the tens digit each time? ______

b What happens to the ones digit each time? ______

c Add the two digits together each time. What happens? ______

Challenge! With multiples of 9, the digits always add to 9.
eg 8 × 9 = **72**, and 7 + 2 = 9. 12 × 9 = 10**8**, and 1 + 8 = 9
Use this to circle the numbers below that are multiples of 9:

117 252 353 450 518 754 1881 9009

Unit 21 Number facts 5×

1 How many hands? ________

2 How many fingers?

a 2 hands ________ b 12 hands ________

c 7 hands ________ d 0 hands ________

e 6 hands ________ f 3 hands ________

g 4 hands ________ h 10 hands ________

i 9 hands ________ j 8 hands ________

k 11 hands ________ l 5 hands ________

3 Count in 5s.

4 Complete from memory.

×	4	1	5	9	3	7	12	10	6	0	11	8	2
5													

 AC9M3N06 Number AC9M3A03 Algebra MA2-MR-01 Multiplicative relations A • Generate and describe patterns • Multiplicative relations B • Use known number facts and strategies • Use number properties to find related multiplication facts

Unit 21 Number facts practice

3, 4, 5, 10 tables

1 Write the 9 multiplication fact for each badge.

a 

10 x 9 =

b 

c 

d 

e 

f 

g 

h 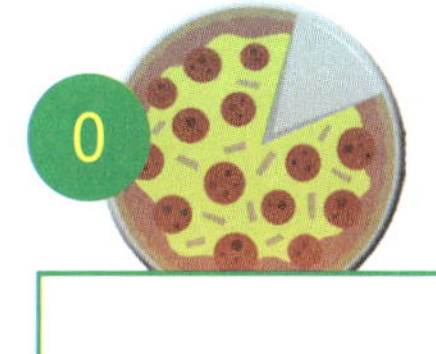

i 

j 

k 

l 

2

×	2	8	5	10	0	7	3	1	6	9	4
4											
10											
6											
3											
9											

3 a 

Mum drew a star with six points.

How many points on 9 stars?

b 

Aunt Jo drew a star with five points.

How many points on 9 stars?

c 

Uncle Bill drew a star with eight points.

How many points on 9 stars?

d 

How many more points are there on Uncle Bill's stars than on Aunt Jo's stars?

Unit 21 Vertical multiplication

1 Write a number sentence for this picture.

☐ × ☐ = ☐

2 Write a number sentence and the answer.

a 10 cars. 4 people in each car. How many people? ☐ × ☐ = ☐

b 5 tricycles. 3 wheels on each tricycle. How many wheels? ☐ × ☐ = ☐

c 3 cases each holding 8 pencils. How many pencils? ☐ × ☐ = ☐

d 5 rows with 10 boys in each row. How many boys? ☐ × ☐ = ☐

e 8 nests with 5 eggs in each nest. How many eggs? ☐ × ☐ = ☐

f 10 pies on each tray. There are 6 trays. How many pies? ☐ × ☐ = ☐

3 Write the answers and match.

$$\begin{array}{r} 6 \\ \times\ 3 \\ \hline \end{array} \quad \begin{array}{r} 8 \\ \times\ 2 \\ \hline \end{array} \quad \begin{array}{r} 7 \\ \times\ 5 \\ \hline \end{array} \quad \begin{array}{r} 10 \\ \times\ 9 \\ \hline \end{array} \quad \begin{array}{r} 4 \\ \times\ 1 \\ \hline \end{array} \quad \begin{array}{r} 8 \\ \times\ 6 \\ \hline \end{array}$$

7 × 5 = ☐ 6 × 3 = ☐ 8 × 2 = ☐ 8 × 6 = ☐ 10 × 9 = ☐ 4 × 1 = ☐

Draw a diagram

Draw pictures to show:

2 rows of 6	5 groups of 3 stars	4 lots of 7 apples
2 × 6 = ☐	5 × ☐ = ☐	☐ × ☐ = ☐

Mastery Checklist I can:

- ☐ use equal groups to multiply
- ☐ connect repeated addition with multiplication
- ☐ remember the 3×, 4×, 5×, 6×, 9× and 10× tables
- ☐ solve multiplication stories
- ☐ use multiplication algorithms.

Problem solving

Vegetable garden

Victor is planning gardens of lettuces, tomatoes and radishes. He wants to plant them in rows of equal numbers of plants. He has 30 lettuce, 32 tomato and 36 radish plants. How can he plant them in these garden beds?

Key: ● = lettuce ▲ = tomato ◆ = radish

I can solve problems by:

☐ dividing numbers ☐ writing algorithms.

Unit 22 Sharing

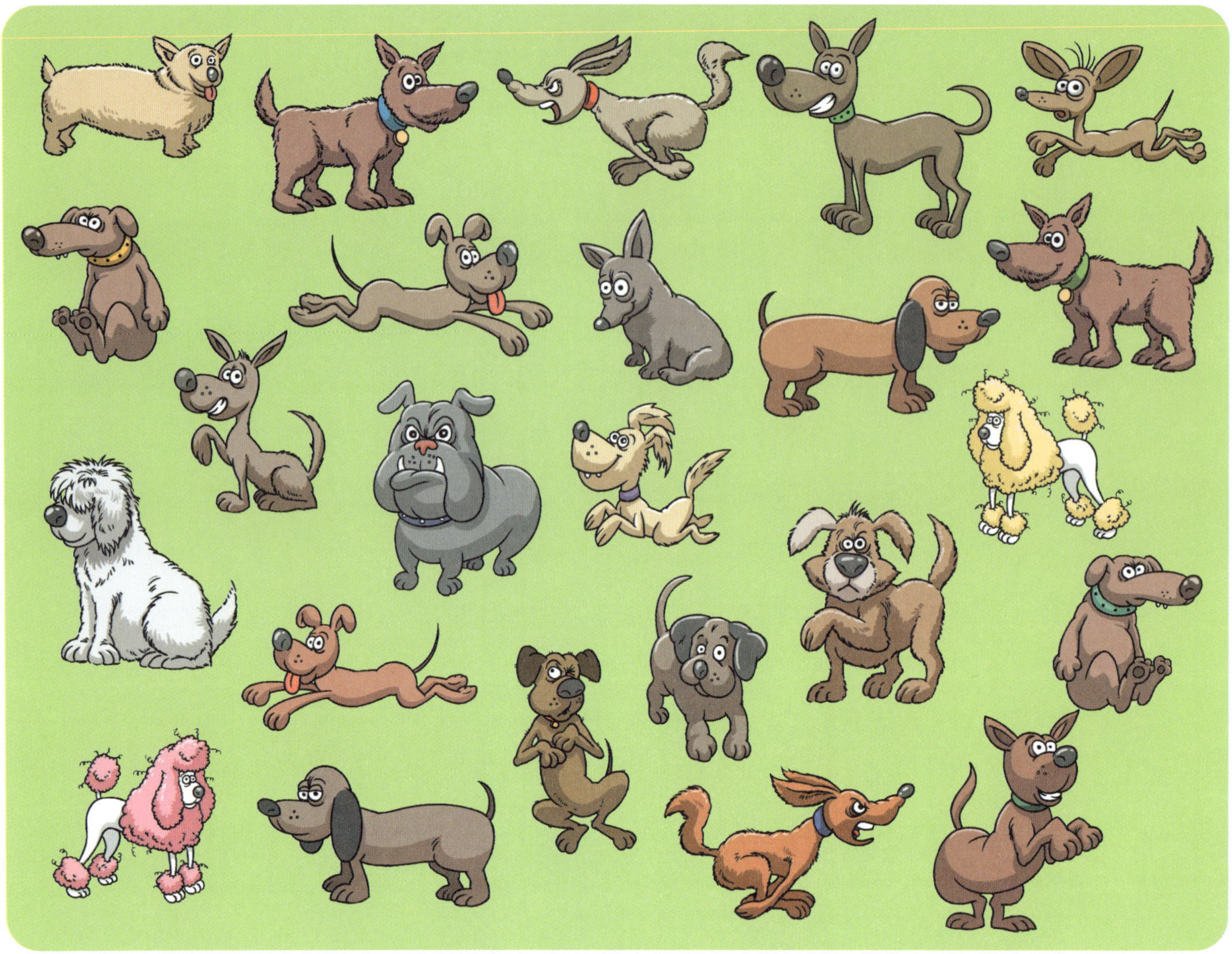

1 These dogs all need good homes. How many dogs are there? _______

2 How many dogs would each person get if they were fairly shared by:

a 4 people? _______ b 3 people? _______

c 2 people? _______ d 24 people? _______

e 6 people? _______ f 8 people? _______

g 1 person? _______ h 12 people? _______

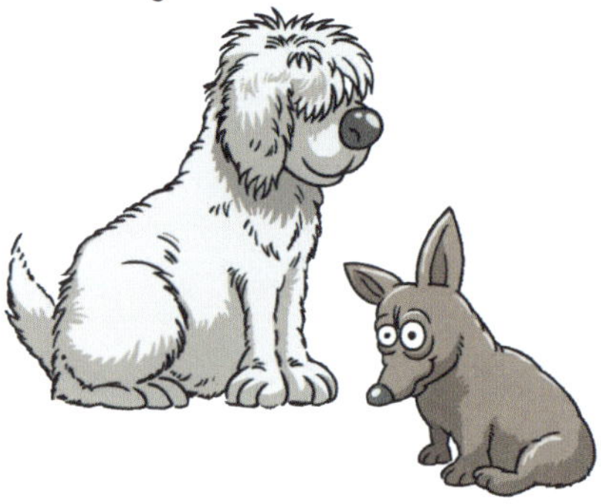

3 Tom took half the dogs. How many did he take? _______

4 Ella took one quarter of the dogs. How many did she take? _______

5 If five people wanted the dogs, would they each get a fair share? _______

Why? ____

____

6 Are there other ways to share which are not fair? _______

Unit 22 Fair shares

Fair shares means an equal number in each share.

1 a Are these shares fair? ______

b Why? ______________________

____

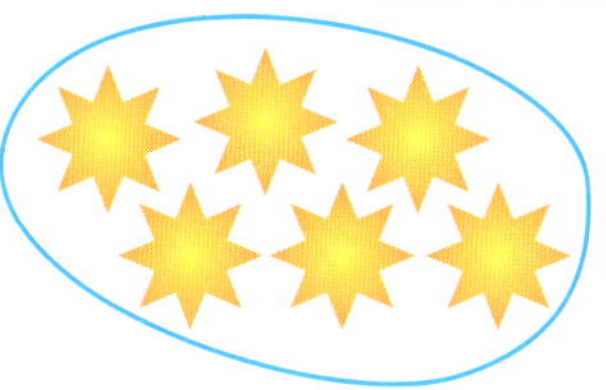

2 a Make 5 fair shares.

One share ______

b Make 4 fair shares.

One share ______

c Make 10 fair shares.

One share ______

3 Circle to make fair shares. How many in each share?

a

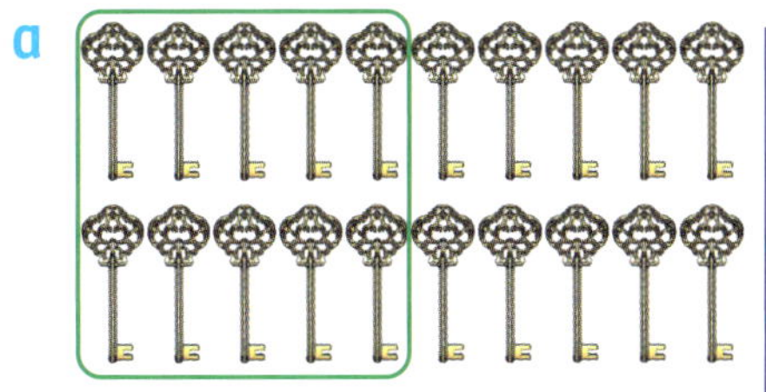

2 shares ______

b

3 shares ______

c

4 shares ______

d

5 shares ______

e

10 shares ______

f

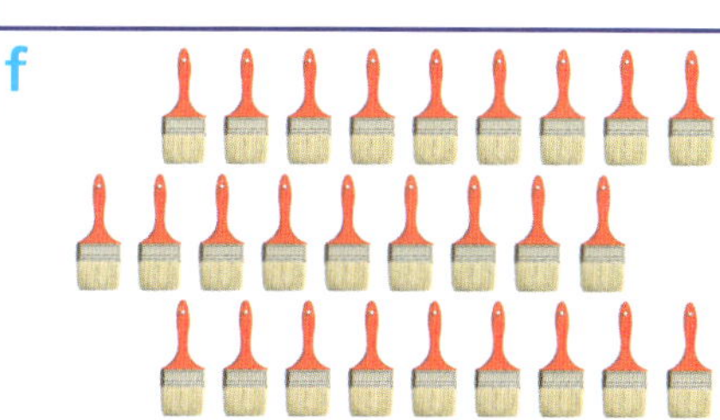

9 shares ______

g

8 shares ______

h

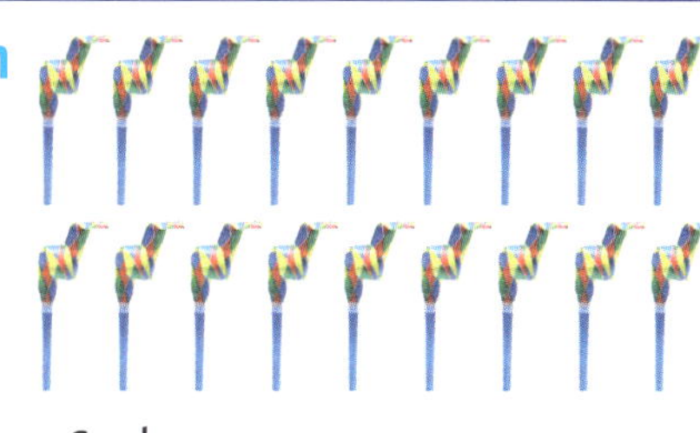

6 shares ______

i

4 shares ______

4 a Share 20 lollies into 5 packets. How many lollies in each packet? ______

b Share 15 apples onto 5 plates. How many apples on each plate? ______

c Place 10 children into 2 equal groups. How many children in each group? ______

d Place 36 crayons equally into 9 boxes. How many crayons in each box? ______

e Share 28 coins among 4 girls. How many coins does each girl get? ______

Unit 22 Equal groups

1 a Circle groups of 5 pots.

How many pots? ______

How many groups? ______

b Circle groups of 5 hats.

How many hats? ______

How many groups? ______

c Circle groups of 3 eggs.

How many eggs? ______

How many groups? ______

2 a Circle groups of 3 hearts.

How many groups? ______

How many hearts? ______

b Circle groups of 4 hearts.

How many groups? ______

How many hearts? ______

c Circle groups of 2 hearts.

How many groups? ______

How many hearts? ______

3 There are 24 rockets.

a Circle 3 equal groups.

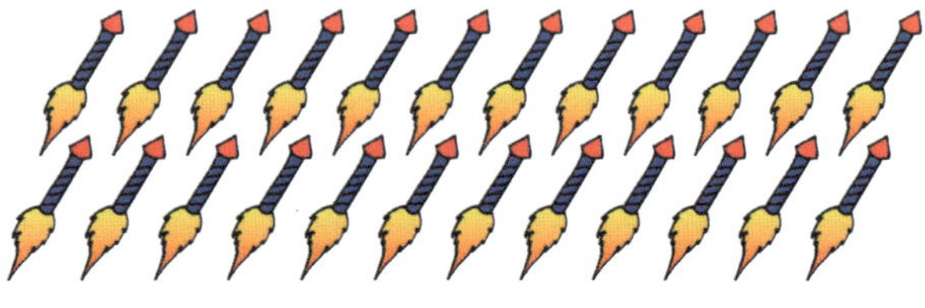

How many in each group? ______

b Circle 6 equal groups.

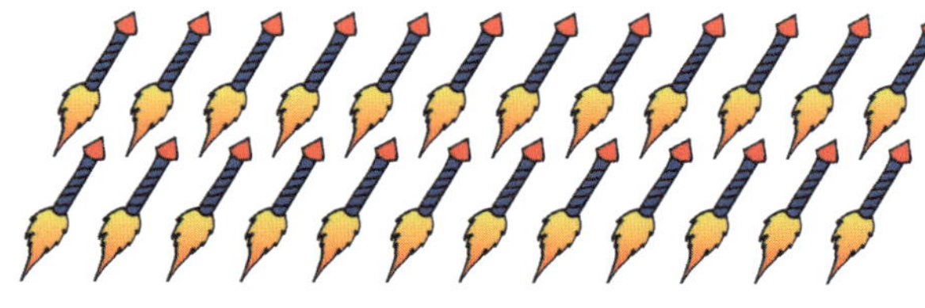

How many in each group? ______

c Circle 2 equal groups.

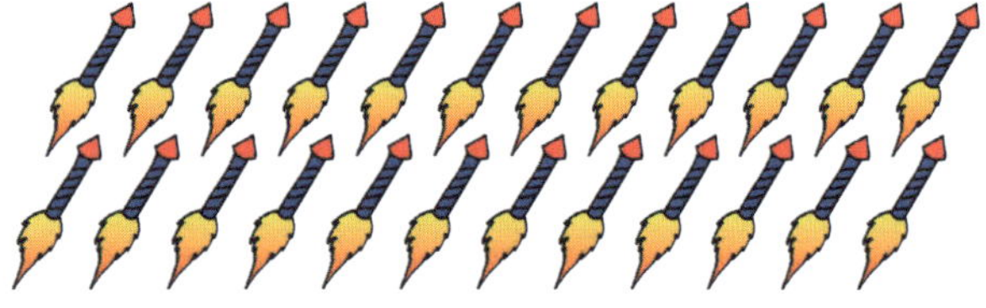

How many in each group? ______

d Circle 8 equal groups.

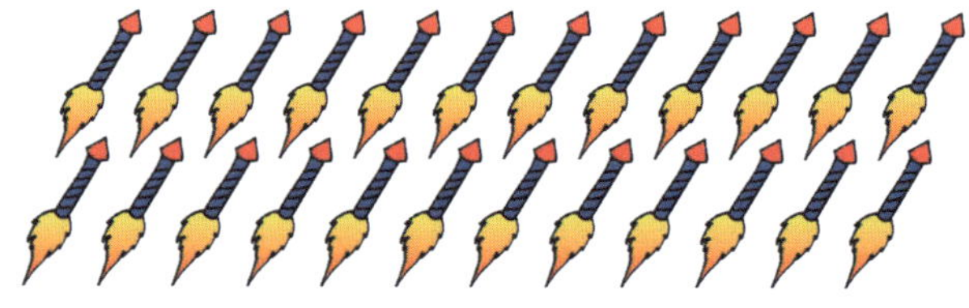

How many in each group? ______

Mastery Checklist I can:
- ☐ work out fair shares
- ☐ work out fractions of a group
- ☐ make equal groups.

Problem solving

Grandpa's treat

Grandpa has 36 fifty-cent coins. He says that he could share them evenly among his grandchildren even if he had 2, 3, 4, 5, 6, 7, 8 or 9 grandchildren. Is he right? Show your working.

Yes, he can share between 2 grandchildren. **36 ÷ 2 = 18   2 × 18 = 36**

I can solve problems by:

☐ dividing and related multiplication ☐ writing algorithms.

Unit 23 Equivalent fractions

$\frac{1}{2}$	$\frac{1}{2}$	halves

$\frac{1}{3}$	$\frac{1}{3}$	$\frac{1}{3}$	thirds

$\frac{1}{4}$	$\frac{1}{4}$	$\frac{1}{4}$	$\frac{1}{4}$	quarters

$\frac{1}{5}$	$\frac{1}{5}$	$\frac{1}{5}$	$\frac{1}{5}$	$\frac{1}{5}$	fifths

$\frac{1}{8}$	$\frac{1}{8}$	$\frac{1}{8}$	$\frac{1}{8}$	$\frac{1}{8}$	$\frac{1}{8}$	$\frac{1}{8}$	$\frac{1}{8}$	eighths

$\frac{1}{10}$	$\frac{1}{10}$	$\frac{1}{10}$	$\frac{1}{10}$	$\frac{1}{10}$	$\frac{1}{10}$	$\frac{1}{10}$	$\frac{1}{10}$	$\frac{1}{10}$	$\frac{1}{10}$	tenths

1 How many in 1 whole?

a halves ____ b fifths ____ c thirds ____ d tenths ____ e quarters ____

2 How many:

a quarters make $\frac{1}{2}$? ____ b tenths make $\frac{1}{2}$? ____ c eighths make $\frac{1}{2}$? ____

d eighths make $\frac{1}{4}$? ____ e fifths make $\frac{3}{10}$? ____ f tenths make $\frac{5}{5}$? ____

3 Circle the larger fraction.

a $\frac{1}{5}$ $\frac{1}{10}$ b $\frac{1}{8}$ $\frac{1}{2}$ c $\frac{1}{4}$ $\frac{1}{5}$ d $\frac{1}{3}$ $\frac{2}{5}$ e $\frac{3}{5}$ $\frac{1}{2}$

4 True (T) or false (F)? The larger the denominator the smaller the fraction. ____

How do you know? ________________

5 Write three fractions that are smaller than $\frac{1}{2}$. ____ ____ ____

What do you notice about their denominators? ________________

 AC9M3N02 Number **MA2-PF-01** Partitioned fractions A • Model and represent unit fractions, and their multiples, to a complete whole on a number line • Partitioned fractions B • Represent fractional quantities equal to and greater than one

Unit 23 Fraction names

Working with fractions

1 Match.

$\frac{2}{10}$ $\frac{7}{8}$ $\frac{4}{5}$ $\frac{3}{4}$

7 out of 8 equal parts

2 out of 10 equal parts

3 out of 4 equal parts

4 out of 5 equal parts

four-fifths

seven-eighths

two-tenths

three-quarters

2 = numerator
5 = denominator
This means 2 equal parts out of 5.

---

2 Write the fraction coloured.

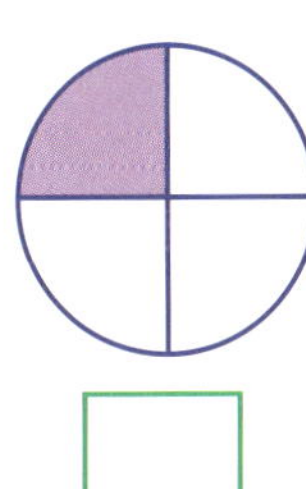

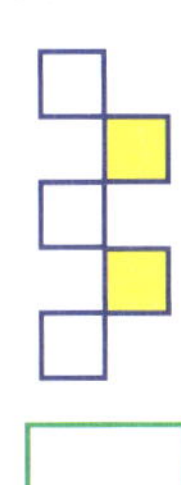

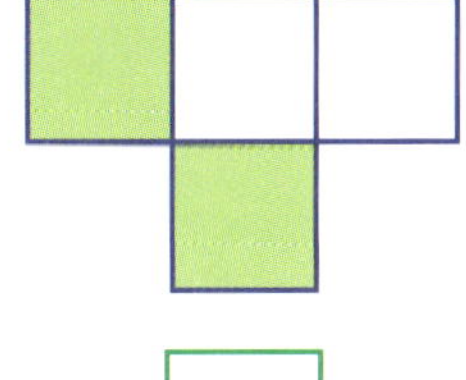

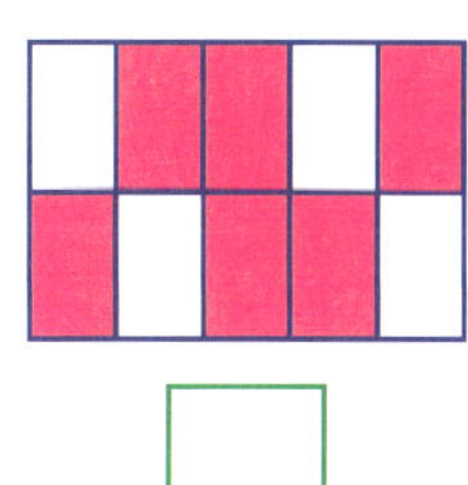

---

3 Colour to match the fraction.

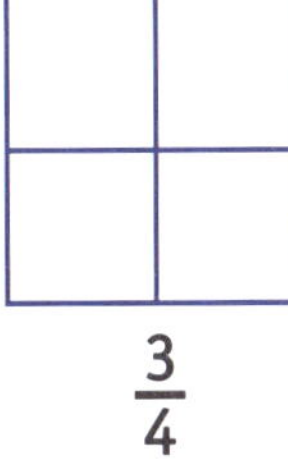

$\frac{3}{4}$

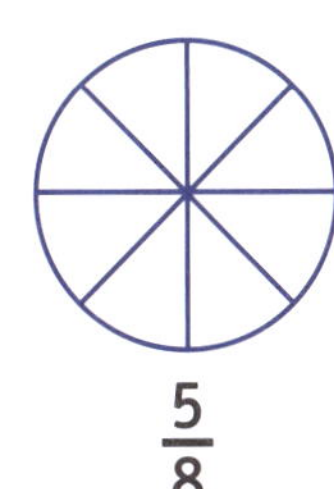

$\frac{5}{8}$

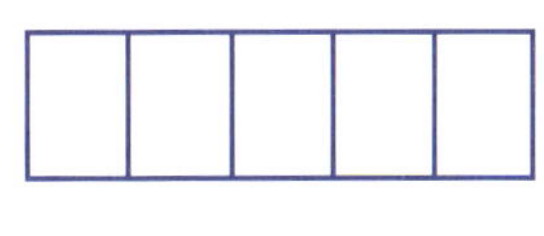

$\frac{2}{5}$

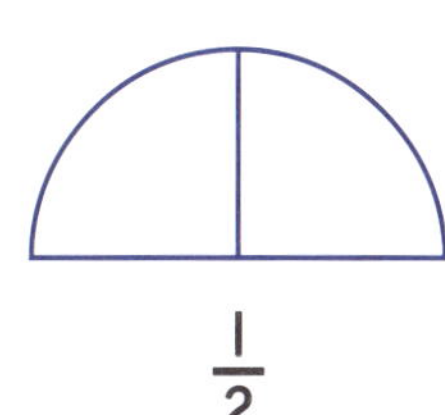

$\frac{1}{2}$

---

4 Look at page 112. Write another name for:

a one-quarter ______________

b one-half ______________

c one-fifth ______________

d five-tenths ______________

---

5 Draw a diagram to show:

$\frac{4}{5}$

$\frac{3}{8}$

Unit 23 Parts of a group

1 What is one-half of:

a 10 pears? _____

b 14 tomatoes? _____

c 16 onions? _____

2 What is one-quarter of:

a 8 mangoes? _____

b 12 peas? _____

c 16 mushrooms? _____

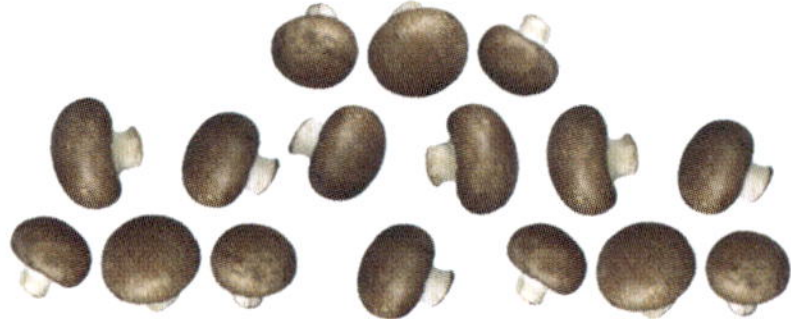

3 What is one-fifth of:

a 5 chillies? _____

b 10 oranges? _____

c 15 pumpkins? _____

4 Draw.

a $\frac{1}{5}$ of 10 bananas

b $\frac{1}{8}$ of 24 cherries

c $\frac{3}{4}$ of 8 apples

5 **a** $\frac{1}{2}$ of a bunch of grapes = 10. 1 whole bunch of grapes = _______

b $\frac{1}{2}$ of a dozen eggs = 6. 1 whole dozen eggs = _______

c $\frac{1}{4}$ of a bag of sweets = 3. 1 whole bag of sweets = _______

d $\frac{1}{5}$ of a box of plums = 6. 1 whole box of plums = _______

e $\frac{1}{10}$ of a packet of biscuits = 5. 1 whole packet of biscuits = _______

Mastery Checklist I can:

- ☐ work out how many fractions in one whole
- ☐ work out equivalent fractions
- ☐ recognise fraction names
- ☐ colour to show a fraction
- ☐ work out fractions of a group.

AC9M3N02 Number **MA2-PF-01** Partitioned fractions A • Model and represent unit fractions, and their multiples, to a complete whole on a number line • Partitioned fractions B • Represent fractional quantities equal to and greater than one

Problem solving

Fractions at the party

1 There are 20 party hats to give out.

$\frac{1}{2}$ of them are red. $\frac{1}{4}$ of them are blue.

$\frac{1}{5}$ of them are green. The rest are pink.

Colour the hats correctly. Circle and label the groups with their fractions.

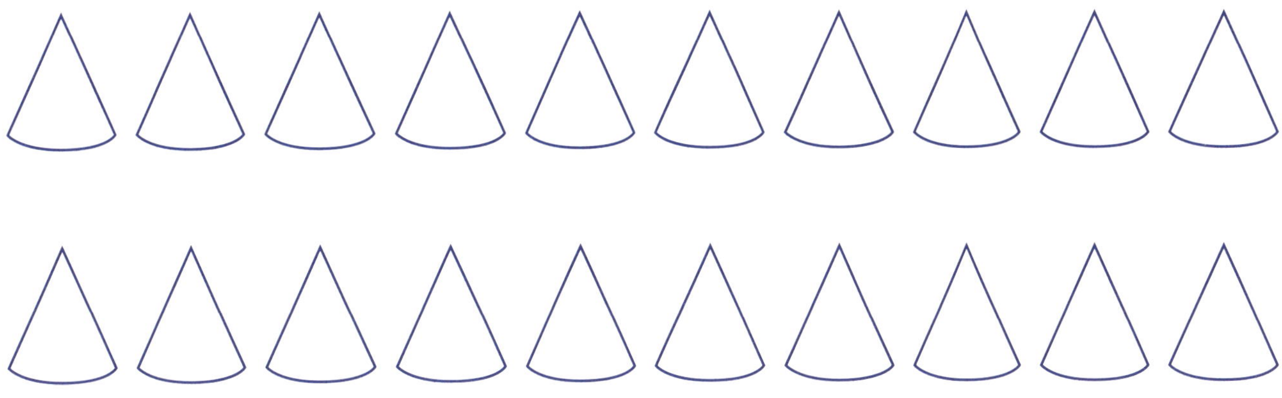

2 Answer true or false.

a $\frac{1}{2}$ of 20 hats is more than $\frac{1}{5}$ of 20 hats. ____________

b $\frac{1}{5}$ of 20 hats is more than $\frac{1}{4}$ of 20 hats. ____________

c $\frac{1}{4}$ of 20 hats is half as much as $\frac{1}{2}$ of 20 hats. ____________

d $\frac{1}{2}$ is the same as $\frac{1}{5}$ of the hats and $\frac{1}{4}$ of the hats together. ____________

How do you know? ____

e $\frac{1}{2}$ of the hats plus $\frac{1}{4}$ of the hats is all the hats. ____________

How do you know? ____

3 Write two of your own statements about the fractions of the hats.

____

____

____

____

____

I can solve problems by:

☐ understanding fractions of an amount ☐ using diagrams.

Holidays!

Investigation 3

survey the class

It's time for a holiday!
You need to plan everything.

Decide where you will go — camping, the snow, a city or the beach.

1 Survey your class to find the best place.

Tally

1 Camping ____________________

2 Snow ____________________

3 City ____________________

4 Beach ____________________

2 Display your results here.

3 Choose what holiday you want to go on.

____

4 Choose the month you will be away. Fill in the calendar.
Colour the 7 days you plan to be on holiday.

Month ____________________

Sun	Mon	Tues	Wed	Thurs	Fri	Sat

Leaving home: ____________________ Arriving back: ____________________

AC9M3ST03 Statistics MA2-DATA-01 • MA2-DATA-02 Data A • Interpret and compare data • Data B • Select and trial methods for data collection

5 What will you do on your holiday? Plan the days.

6 You can only take 3 shirts and 2 pairs of jeans or 2 skirts. Draw your clothes and the different outfits. How many different outfits can you wear? ______

To carry out these tasks I need to:

- ☐ ask survey questions
- ☐ make a tally
- ☐ make a horizontal column graph
- ☐ read a calendar and record days on it
- ☐ explain choice of time
- ☐ calculate time and cost for activities
- ☐ draw diagrams to show choices of clothing.

I enjoyed this task!

☆☆☆☆☆

Revision

1

Write your answer in the box.

Su-Yin bought two toys and spent $7.30. Which two toys did she buy?

Shade one bubble.

2 What is the total value of these notes and coins?

$73.50 ◯ $68.50 ◯ $23.50 ◯ $73.00 ◯

3 Josef bought a drink for $1.50 and a sandwich for $2.20.
How much change did he get from $5?

$1.30 ◯ $3.70 ◯ $2.30 ◯ $0.70 ◯

$2.20

$1.50

4 4 out of 10 squares are coloured pink. What is another name for $\frac{4}{10}$?

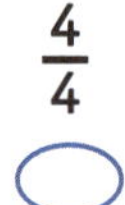
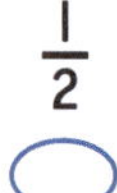

$\frac{4}{4}$ ◯ $\frac{2}{4}$ ◯ $\frac{1}{2}$ ◯ $\frac{2}{5}$ ◯

Write your answer in the box.

5 Complete.

a

37	63
?	

? = ________

b

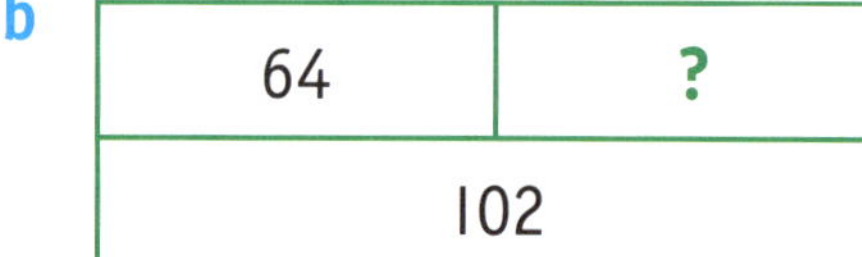

64	?
102	

? = ________

Revision

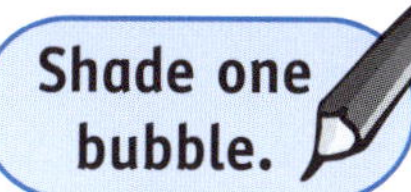

6 Joh started his bushwalk at  . He walked for two hours.

Which clock shows his finishing time?

7 Ahmed had to make 6 fair shares from these cupcakes.

How many in each share? 3 4 5 6

8 This graph shows how many glasses of water these children drank on Monday.

How many glasses did Murphy and Ari drink altogether?

10 5 8 9

Ben	5 glasses
Murphy	4 glasses
Harriet	3 glasses
Ari	6 glasses
Lily	2 glasses

9 Which child made correct estimations of the capacity of these containers?

	Tamsie	Jacque	Hiram	Lottie
Tea cup	Less than $\frac{1}{2}$ L	About 1 L	About $\frac{1}{2}$ L	About $\frac{1}{2}$ L
Juice carton	About 2 L	About 2 L	About 1 L	Less than $\frac{1}{2}$ L
Yoghurt carton	About $\frac{1}{2}$ L	About $\frac{1}{2}$ L	Less than $\frac{1}{2}$ L	About 1 L
Milk jug	About 1 L	Less than $\frac{1}{2}$ L	About 2 L	About 2 L

10 How many angles in this shape?

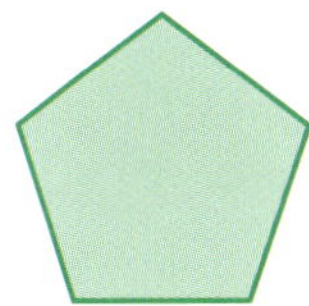

10 7 5 3

11 Which shape is a pyramid?

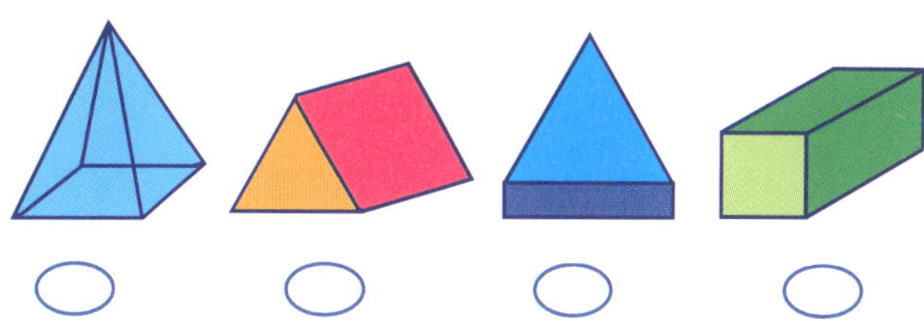

Unit 24 Describing patterns

1 Write the missing term, then write a reason for your answer.

a $\frac{1}{2}$, $\frac{1}{4}$, $\frac{1}{8}$, ______

Reason ______________________________

b $1.80, $1.70, ______ , $1.50, $1.40, $1.30

Reason ______________________________

c 2, 7, 12, ______ , ______ , 27

Reason ______________________________

d 25, 40, ______ , 70, ______ , ______

Reason ______________________________

e 36, 45, 54, 63, ______ , 81

Reason ______________________________

f 10, 120, 230, ______ , ______ , 560

Reason ______________________________

2

9 × 6	5 × 3
3 × 4	double 27
8 + 7	4 × 4
36 − 4	1 dozen
9 + 3 + 4	9 × 5
100 − 55	8 × 4

3 Use a calculator.

a Press AC b Press 5 c Press + + d Press =

e What does your calculator show? ______ f Press = again.

g Keep pressing = and write the answers. ______ ______ ______ ______

h What is the pattern? ______________________________

Unit 24 Patterns of nines

1 a $0 \times 9 =$ _____, 9×0 = _____   b $1 \times 9 =$ _____, 9×1 = _____

c $2 \times 9 =$ _____, ________ = _____   d $3 \times 9 =$ _____, ________ = _____

e $4 \times 9 =$ _____, ________ = _____   f $5 \times 9 =$ _____, ________ = _____

g $6 \times 9 =$ _____, ________ = _____   h $7 \times 9 =$ _____, ________ = _____

i $8 \times 9 =$ _____, ________ = _____   j $9 \times 9 =$ _____, ________ = _____

k $10 \times 9 =$ _____, ________ = _____   l $11 \times 9 =$ _____, ________ = _____

2 Write the pattern for adding 9 in this table.

Order of term	1	2								
Term	7	16	25							

3 Complete the patterns.

a 3 12 ☐ 30 39 ☐ ☐ 66 75 ☐ ☐ ☐

b 90 ☐ ☐ 63 ☐ 45 ☐ ☐ 18 ☐ ☐

4 a Colour the 9s pattern red. Continue to 100.

1	2	3	4	5	6	7	8	9	10
11	12	13	14	15	16	17	18	19	20
21	22	23	24	25	26	27	28	29	30
31	32	33	34	35	36	37	38	39	40
41	42	43	44	45	46	47	48	49	50
51	52	53	54	55	56	57	58	59	60
61	62	63	64	65	66	67	68	69	70
71	72	73	74	75	76	77	78	79	80
81	82	83	84	85	86	87	88	89	90
91	92	93	94	95	96	97	98	99	100

b Colour the 3s pattern green. Continue to 100.

1	2	3	4	5	6	7	8	9	10
11	12	13	14	15	16	17	18	19	20
21	22	23	24	25	26	27	28	29	30
31	32	33	34	35	36	37	38	39	40
41	42	43	44	45	46	47	48	49	50
51	52	53	54	55	56	57	58	59	60
61	62	63	64	65	66	67	68	69	70
71	72	73	74	75	76	77	78	79	80
81	82	83	84	85	86	87	88	89	90
91	92	93	94	95	96	97	98	99	100

c Colour the 6s pattern yellow. Continue to 100.

1	2	3	4	5	6	7	8	9	10
11	12	13	14	15	16	17	18	19	20
21	22	23	24	25	26	27	28	29	30
31	32	33	34	35	36	37	38	39	40
41	42	43	44	45	46	47	48	49	50
51	52	53	54	55	56	57	58	59	60
61	62	63	64	65	66	67	68	69	70
71	72	73	74	75	76	77	78	79	80
81	82	83	84	85	86	87	88	89	90
91	92	93	94	95	96	97	98	99	100

d Which numbers are coloured on all three grids? ________________

e How is the 6 pattern different? ________________

Challenge! Complete these patterns.

215, 224, 233 ☐ ☐ ☐ ☐ ☐

528, 519, 510 ☐ ☐ ☐ ☐ ☐

Unit 24 Table patterns

1 Complete the pattern and write the rule.

a 4 13 22 31 ____ ____ ____ ____ Rule ____________

b 52 46 40 34 ____ ____ ____ ____ Rule ____________

c 11 15 19 23 ____ ____ ____ ____ Rule ____________

d 85 76 67 58 ____ ____ ____ ____ Rule ____________

e 9 18 9 18 ____ ____ ____ ____ Rule ____________

2 Write the pattern for 7s in this table.

Order of term	1	2	3								
Term	7	14									

3 Complete these addition and subtraction patterns.

a $18 + 9 =$ ______

______ $- 9 = 18$

b $36 + 9 =$ ______

______ $- 9 = 36$

c $36 - 9 =$ ______

______ $+ 9 = 36$

d ______ $- 6 = 54$

$54 + 6 =$ ______

e $72 - 8 =$ ______

______ $+ 8 = 72$

f $81 - 7 =$ ______

______ $+ 7 =$ ______

4 a Write your own pattern using addition or subtraction.

____ ____ ____ ____ ____ ____ ____ ____

b Write the rule. ____________

5 Colour each path across the river.

Mastery Checklist I can:
- ☐ find patterns in numbers
- ☐ write the missing term in a pattern
- ☐ use a calculator to make number patterns
- ☐ follow a rule to make a number pattern
- ☐ complete addition and subtraction patterns.

AC9M3N07 Number

Unit 25 Position

1 Draw the cake they choose.

Mandy	Mitch	Milly	Min	Mark
top row, on the left	bottom row, 2nd from the right	middle row, on the right	bottom row, on the left	top row, in the middle

2 Write the position of:

a the cupcake with the cherry on top. ______________________

b the meringue snowman. ______________________

c the cream frog. ______________________

d the apricot cheesecake. ______________________

e the strawberry slice. ______________________

3 Write the names and positions of the three cakes you like best.

a ______________________

b ______________________

c ______________________

Unit 25 Rows and columns

Position 

1 Which letter is:

a third column, top row? _____

b last column, bottom row? _____

c fifth column, second row? _____

d second last column, third row from the bottom? _____

e third column from the right, fourth row from the top? _____

f These letters spell a word. What is the word? __________

U	P	G	A	D	C
D	S	K	V	E	B
F	B	Y	O	A	N
G	R	O	T	E	F
H	I	L	N	M	R

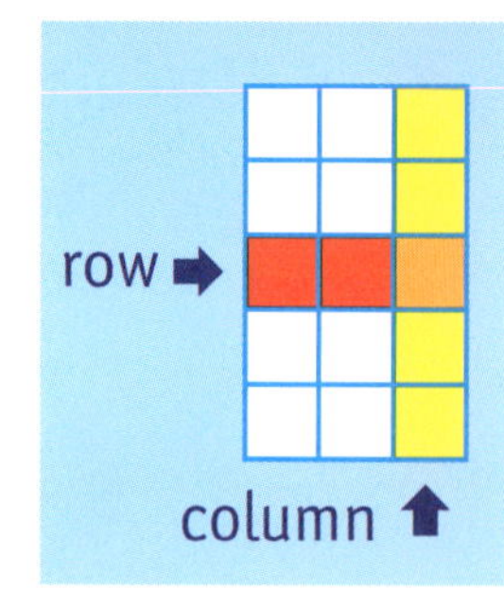

2 Here is the map of 3B's classroom.

Tim	Simon	Kirsty	Zoe	Samad		
Lionel	Bob	Adam		Chloe	Gill	Lenny
	Chris	Brian	Amy	Samir	Lilly	Gopal
Lucy	Sam	Jim	Judith	Joe	Ajit	Leah
				Miss Brown		

a How many children are in Miss Brown's class? _______

b Who is sitting next to Brian? __________

c Who is sitting in front of the teacher? __________ __________

d Who is sitting behind Lionel? __________

e How many children are in Chloe's row? _______

f Rodger wants to sit in the third row. Who will he sit next to? __________

g Joe was talking. He was sent to sit behind Kirsty. Mark his new seat on the map.

h Draw in red how Joe would get to his new seat.

i Lucy wanted to borrow a pencil. She walked across the front of the room and down the aisle between Ajit and Leah. She asked the person in the third row on her left.

Who did she ask? __________

j Write directions for the path Adam would take to sit next to Samad.

____

Unit 25 Street map

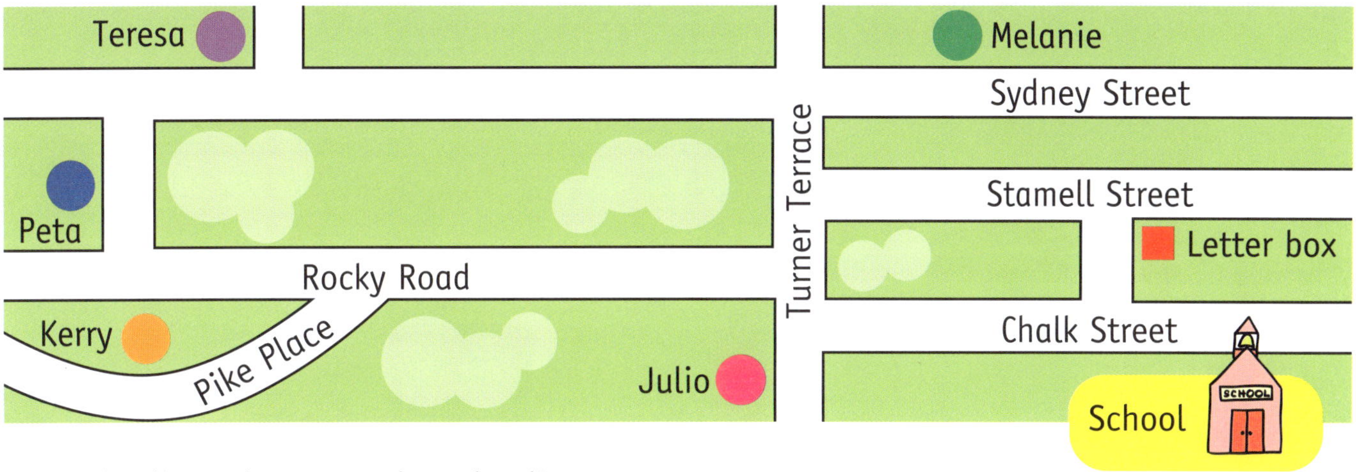

Position

Teresa
Melanie
Sydney Street
Peta
Turner Terrace
Stamell Street
Letter box
Rocky Road
Kerry
Pike Place
Julio
Chalk Street
School

1 a Who lives closest to the school? ______________________

b On which street does Melanie live? ______________________

c Who lives at the corner of two streets? ______________________

d Peta went to visit her friend. She walked out her front gate, turned left, then turned right. She walked past Turner Terrace, and entered a house on her left.

Who did she visit? ____________

e Draw the path she followed in red.

f Who lives furthest from Julio? ____________

2 Teresa's mum asked her to post a letter on her way to school. In green, draw her path to school.

3 Write directions to tell how Kerry walks home from school.

____

____

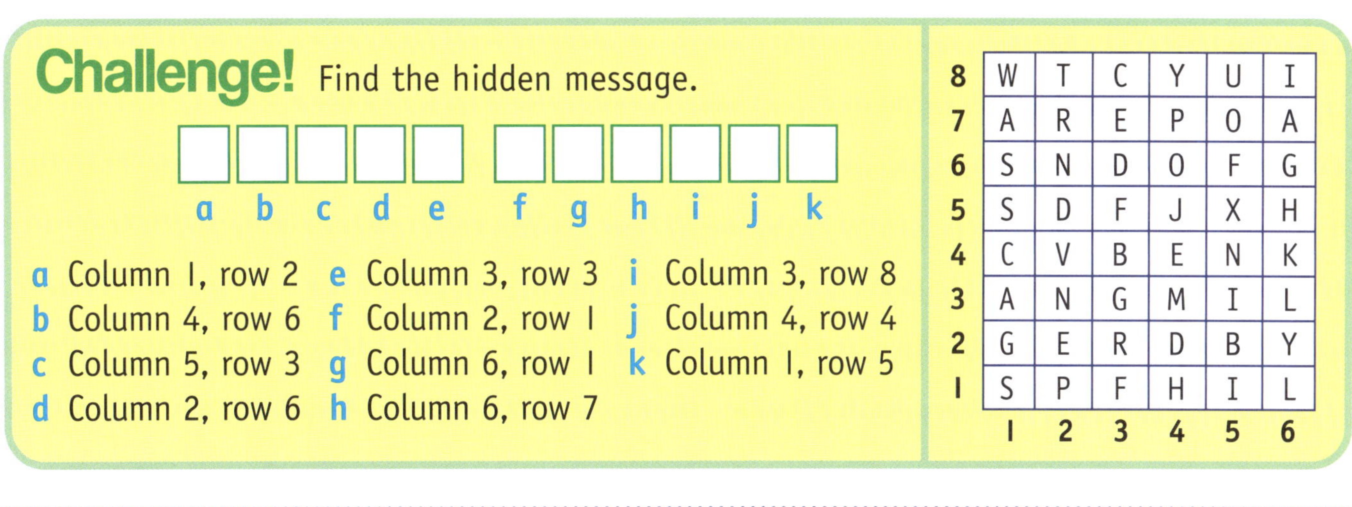

Challenge! Find the hidden message.

a	b	c	d	e		f	g	h	i	j	k

a Column 1, row 2
b Column 4, row 6
c Column 5, row 3
d Column 2, row 6
e Column 3, row 3
f Column 2, row 1
g Column 6, row 1
h Column 6, row 7
i Column 3, row 8
j Column 4, row 4
k Column 1, row 5

8	W	T	C	Y	U	I
7	A	R	E	P	O	A
6	S	N	D	O	F	G
5	S	D	F	J	X	H
4	C	V	B	E	N	K
3	A	N	G	M	I	L
2	G	E	R	D	B	Y
1	S	P	F	H	I	L
	1	2	3	4	5	6

Mastery Checklist I can:
☐ describe the position of an object in a group
☐ use columns and rows to identify a position
☐ understand directions on a street map.

Problem solving

Make a picture map

You and your friends are going on a mission to find lost gold.

7							
6	N ↑						
5							
4							
3							
2							
1		HOME					
	A	B	C	D	E	F	G

1 Put these things on the map: mountains in the middle, a river to cross, swamps and a forest.

2 Write some directions for how you are going to get there. Use coordinates to describe your movements. Remember to put the letter first, eg B4.

____

____

____

____

I can solve problems by:

☐ understanding position ☐ drawing paths.

Unit 26 Mass

measure and compare mass

Find three small boxes. Label them **A**, **B** and **C**. Fill each box with sand.

1 a Feel the weight of each box.

b Write the boxes in order from lightest to heaviest.

lightest ______ ______ ______ heaviest

2 Use balance scales to order the boxes.

lightest ______ ______ ______ heaviest

3 a Empty the boxes and fill them with something different, eg marbles or blocks.

b Order the boxes from lightest to heaviest.

lightest ______ ______ ______ heaviest

4 Is the order the same each time? ________

5 How could you weigh this book using sand or marbles?

____

6 Do you know a better method to weigh this book?

____

Unit 26 Weighing in kilograms

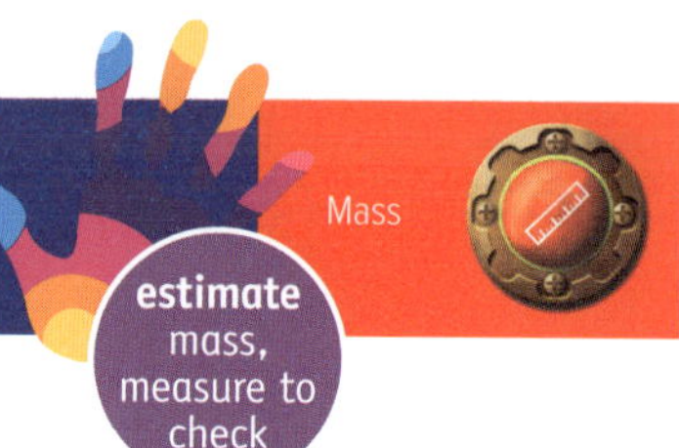

1 Hold a one kilogram weight. Feel how heavy it is.

Estimate whether these items are heavier or lighter than 1 kg. Use balance scales to check.

Objects are weighed in kilograms. kg is the short way to write kilograms.

Item	Estimate	Balance scales
a 2 maths books		
b a pencil case		
c a book box		
d a full lunch box		
e 1 brick		
f a bottle of water		

2 a

The pumpkin weighs ______ than 1 kg.

b

The apple weighs ______ than 1 kg.

3 Write five items that are weighed in kilograms, eg sugar.

______ ______ ______ ______ ______

4 What is the mass for each object?

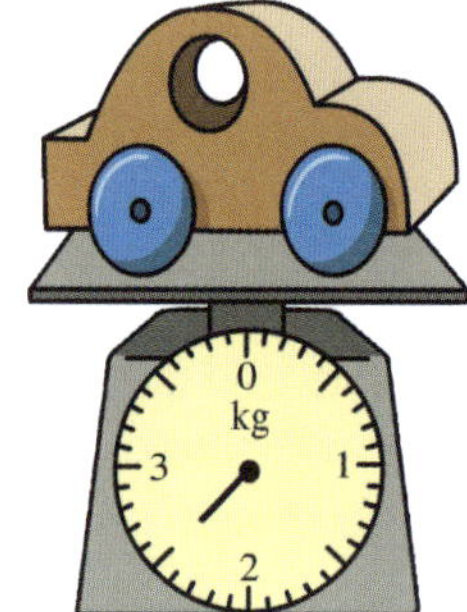

a ______ kg b ______ kg c ______ kg d ______ kg

e Order the objects from lightest to heaviest.

______ ______ ______ ______

Mastery Checklist I can:
- ☐ compare the masses of real-life objects
- ☐ compare masses to 1 kilogram
- ☐ read scales in kilograms
- ☐ use balance scales.

Problem solving

Heavy duty

1 You can carry 7 kg and your little sister can carry 5 kg.

How many ways can you carry all these bags between you?

Solutions: ______________________________

____

____

____

2 How can you find the heaviest of three similar objects with only a balance scale and no weights?

Solution: ______________________________

____

____

____

3 How can you weigh your dog when he won't stand still on the scales?

Hint: *Use these.*

____

____

____

____

I can solve problems by:

☐ understanding mass ☐ measuring and comparing masses.

Unit 27 Symmetry

Patterns 

Line of symmetry
both halves match exactly when folded on the line of symmetry eg

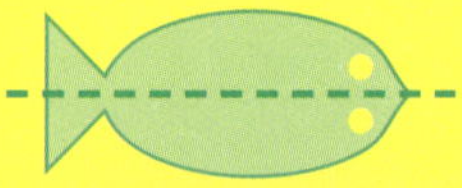

A

B

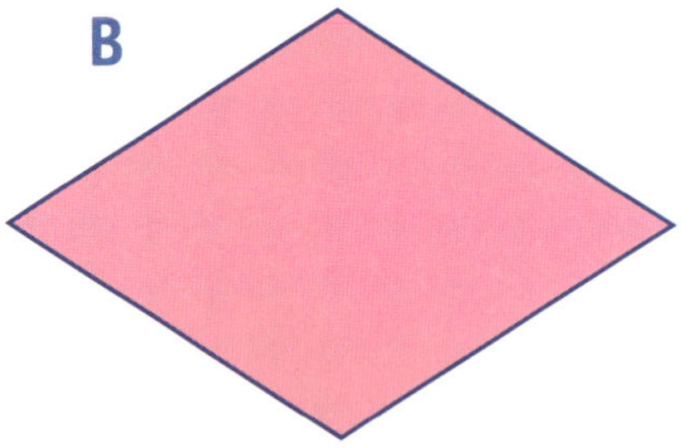

C

D

E

F

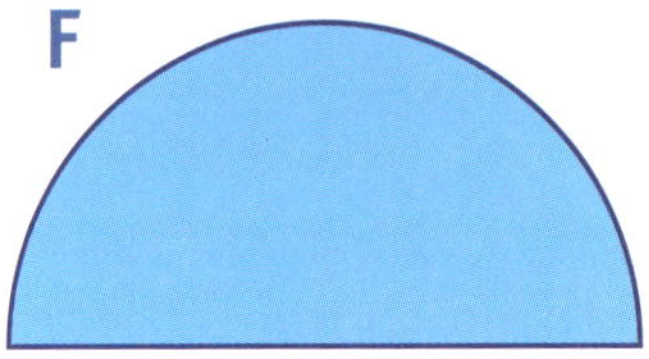

G

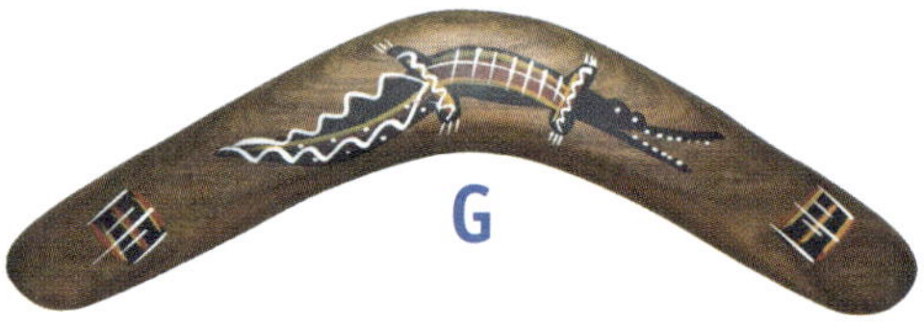

H

I

J

1 Inspect the shapes. If possible, draw in 1 line of symmetry.

2 Which shapes have more than 1 line of symmetry? ______

3 a Which shapes do not have a line of symmetry? ______

b Why? ______

4 Draw two more letters and two more shapes that have a line of symmetry.

a Letters	b Shapes

Unit 27 Symmetrical shapes

1 Place a mirror on each dotted line. Write the name of the object. Draw the missing part.

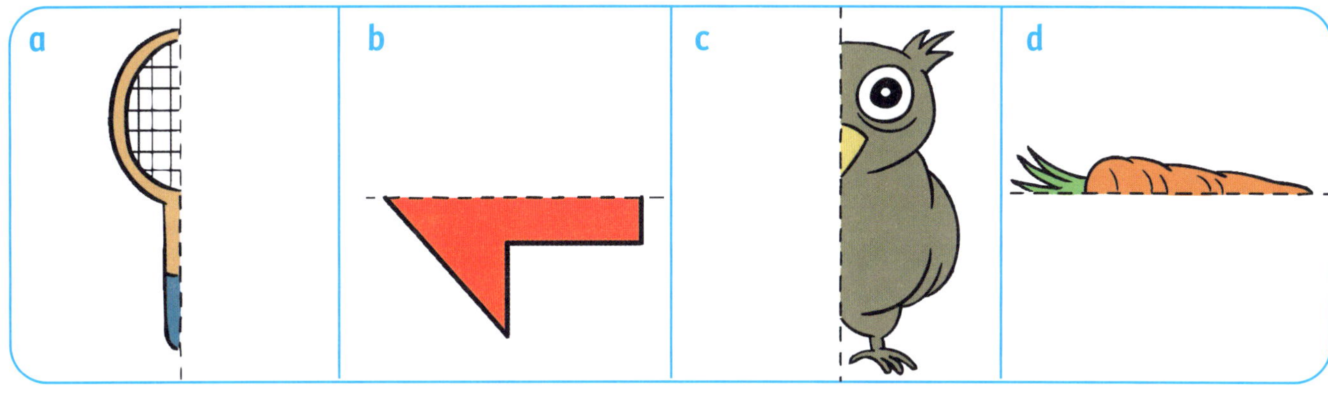

2 a Look at these shapes. Colour those that are symmetrical.

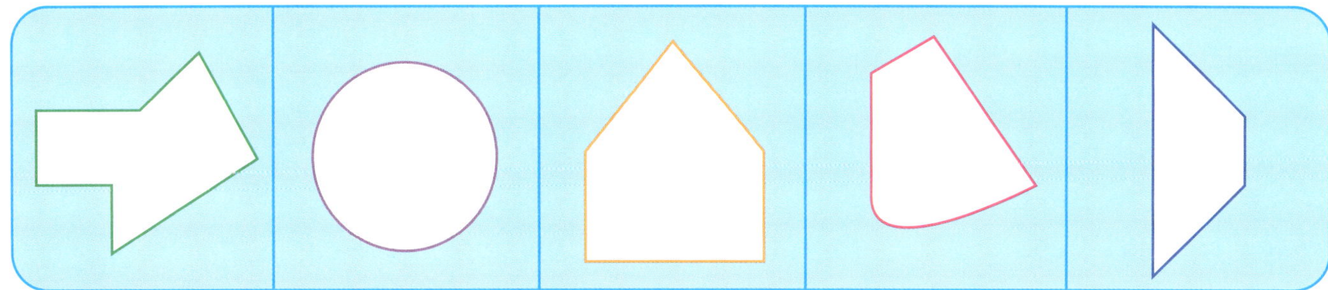

b Draw a line of symmetry on those you coloured.

3 Complete each of these drawings to make a symmetrical design.

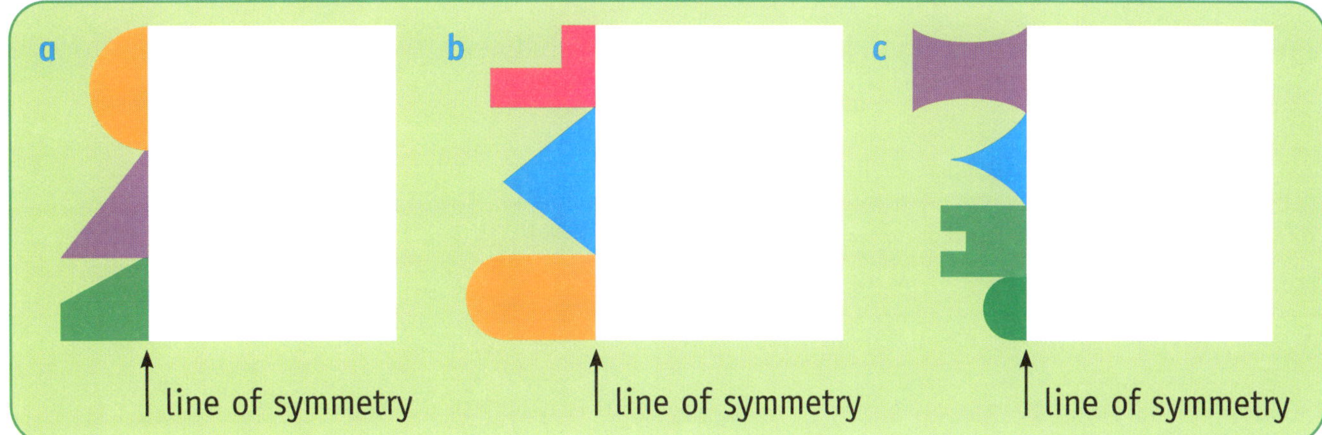

Challenge!

What are the answers?

line of symmetry

Mastery Checklist

I can:

- ☐ identify lines of symmetry
- ☐ draw symmetrical letters and shapes
- ☐ complete symmetrical designs.

Unit 28 Passing time

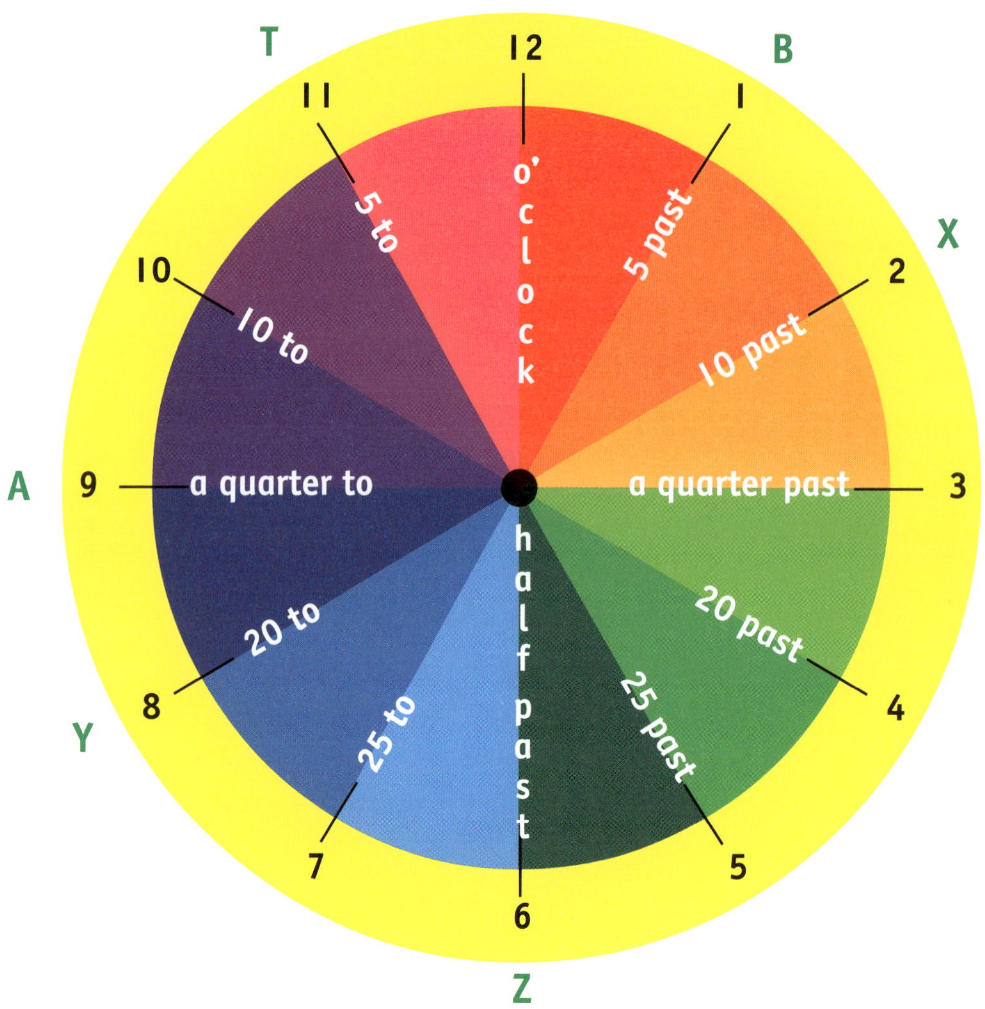

1 Study the analogue clock and count the minutes between the letters, counting clockwise.

a A and B ______________ b X and Y ______________ c T and Z ______________

2 Write the analogue time 5 minutes after:

a 10 past 5 ______________ b 20 past 4 ______________

c 5 past 3 ______________ d a quarter past 7 ______________

3 Write the analogue time 10 minutes before:

a 20 past 2 ______________ b a quarter past 6 ______________

c 10 past 8 ______________ d half past 9 ______________

4 Write the analogue time 15 minutes after:

a 25 past 4 ______________ b twenty to 11 ______________

c half past 7 ______________ d ten to 5 ______________

5 Write the analogue time 5 minutes before:

a twenty to 3 ______________ b ten to 12 ______________

Unit 28 am and pm

am is ante meridiem – before midday

pm is post meridiem – before midnight

1 Write am or pm.

a go to bed ________ b eat breakfast ________

c wake up ________ d finish school ________

e get dressed ________ f morning recess ________

g do homework ________ h eat afternoon tea ________

2 Write the above activities in the order you do them.

a ________ b ________

c ________ d ________

e ________ f ________

g ________ h ________

3 Name two things which take you:

a about one hour to do. ________

b about 10 minutes to do. ________

c about 2 minutes to do. ________

d only a few seconds to do. ________

4 Number these from shortest time (1) to longest time (6).

Watch one TV show.	
Clean my shoes.	
Feed the dog.	
Clean my teeth.	
Eat my lunch.	
Drink a glass of water.	

5 Circle the shortest time and cross the longest time.

a	1 week	1 month	1 hour	1 day
b	1 day	1 second	1 hour	1 week
c	1 month	1 year	1 fortnight	1 week

Unit 28 Time facts

1 a Draw a circle around the earliest time.

10:31 pm | 3:10 am | 1:30 pm | 10:30 am

b Draw a circle around the latest time.

2:45 am | 6:40 pm | 11:30 pm | 11:50 am

2 Number these times in order from earliest to latest.

5:10 pm ☐ | 12:00 noon ☐  | 7:45 am ☐  | 1:10 am ☐

3 Complete.

¼ past 7	get dressed	7:15
	go to school	:
	start school	:
	have lunch	:
	eat dinner	:

4 Yindi has three chores to do on Saturday:

- vaccuming – 1 hour
- wash the car – 45 minutes
- stack the dishwasher – 25 minutes.

Write the chores where they will fit into Yindi's schedule.

Saturday
8 am: breakfast
9 am: soccer
11 am:
12 noon: lunch
1 pm: shopping
2 pm:
2:40 pm: dance
4 pm:
4:45 pm: Nan visiting

Unit 28 Time and action

1 How many hours have passed:

a between 1 pm and 4 pm? ________

b between 11 am and 1 pm? ________

c between 6 pm and 12 midnight? ______

d between 10 am and 9 pm? ________

2 Write a reasonable activity that takes about this much time.

a 15 minutes ________________________

b 25 minutes ________________________

c 2 hours ________________________

d 1 hour 5 minutes ________________________

3 How many minutes have passed? What might you do in this time?

a between 3:45 pm and 4:15 pm

____

____

b between 5:10 am and 5:24 am

____

____

c between 12 noon and 12:32 pm

____

____

d between 11:26 am and 11:38 am

____

____

4 Show the two times on the clocks and answer the question.

a Cam started to clean the car at 9:10 am. He finished at 9:45 am.

How long did it take him to clean the car?

____

b Joan's appointment was at 3:20 pm but she arrived at 3:50.

How late was she?

____

Challenge!

Mum says, "Meet me here at four o'clock." As time passes, you look at your watch 4 times. How long do you have each time?

2:45  3:05 [ ] 3:25  3:50 [ ]

Mastery Checklist I can:

- ☐ tell time to the nearest 5 minutes
- ☐ work out times before and after
- ☐ use am and pm
- ☐ work out how long activities take
- ☐ show time on a clock.

Unit 29 Reading a table

SSL Table — Central Districts

	Games	Won	Lost	Drawn	Points
Giants	8	6	1	1	26
Bradies	8	6	2	0	24
Dragons	8	5	3	0	20
Furies	8	4	3	1	18
Brongoes	7	4	3	0	16
Tigers	8	4	4	0	16
Meteors	7	2	5	0	8
Wallabies	8	2	6	0	8

Here is the Schools Soccer League results table for this year.

1 What are the points for the:

a Wallabies? ________ b Giants? ________

c Dragons? ________ d Meteors? ________

2 a How many points do the teams score for a win? ________

b How many points do they get for a draw? ________

3 How many rounds have been played by most teams? ________

4 Who has yet to play their eighth game? ________

5 Which two teams had a draw? ________

6 If the Brongoes win their 8th round match, what will the top 4 teams be?

____

7 Could the Furies become the league leaders after playing two more games? ________

How? ________

8 If the Tigers win the next 4 games, will they be leaders? ________

Why? ________

Challenge! Update the table using these results:

Round 8 Brongoes 4 Meteors 2

Round 9 Giants 3 Wallabies 1 Bradies 2 Dragons 1

Meteors 4 Furies 3 Brongoes 2 Tigers 2

Who is top of the table now? ________

Unit 29 Graphs

Data

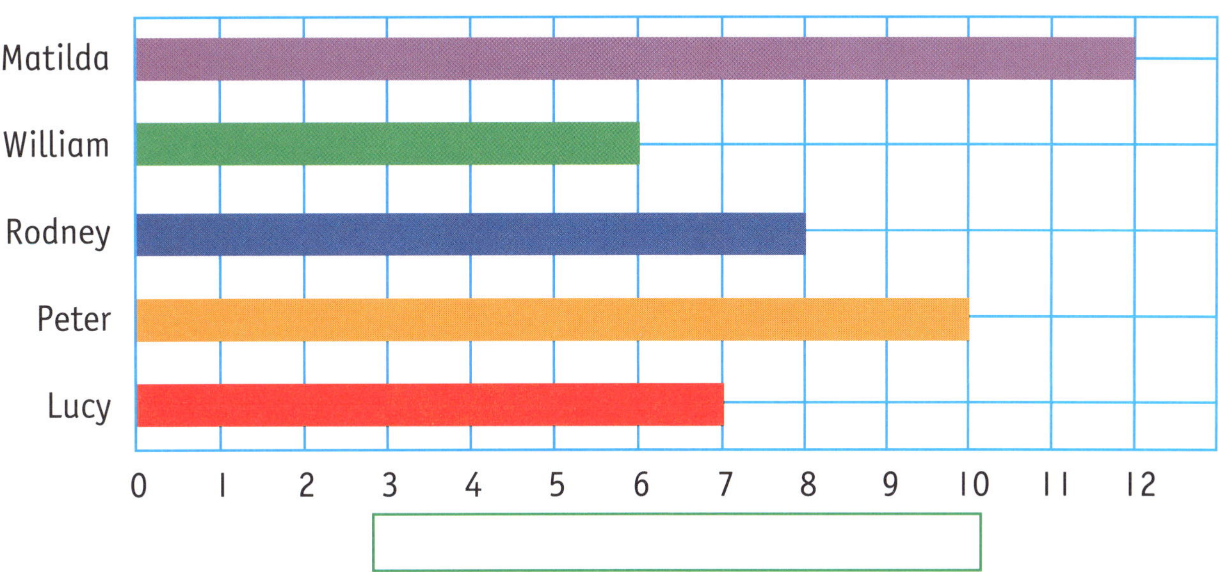

1 a How many students compared homework? ________

b Write the label for the bottom numbers.

c Who did the most homework? ________________

d Who did the least homework? ________________

e Who did 8 hours of homework? ________________

f Name three students who did more homework than Lucy.

________________ ________________ ________________

2 Draw a picture graph to show the same information. Use one clock to show one hour. Label your graph clearly.

Unit 29 Collecting data

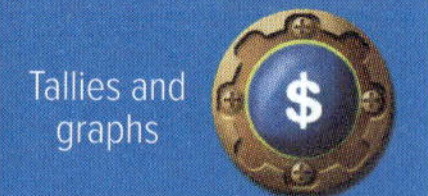

Tally marks are in groups of 5

卌 || = 7

Tallies and graphs

Which do they like most?

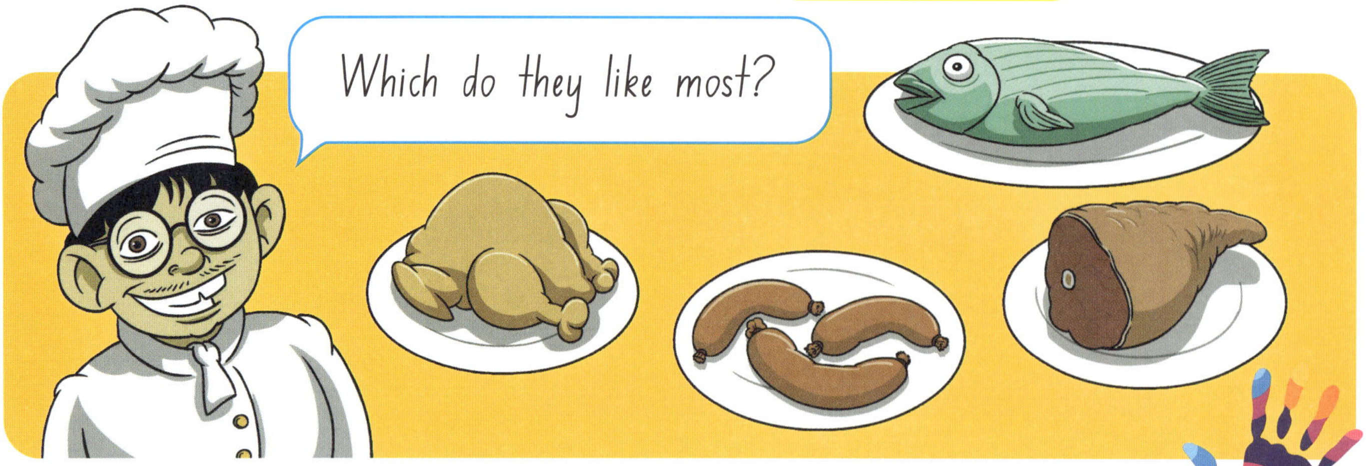

survey the class

1 Ask each child in your class to choose one.

a Use this tick sheet.

b Now use tally marks.

2 Make a column graph to show these choices. Remember all the labels.

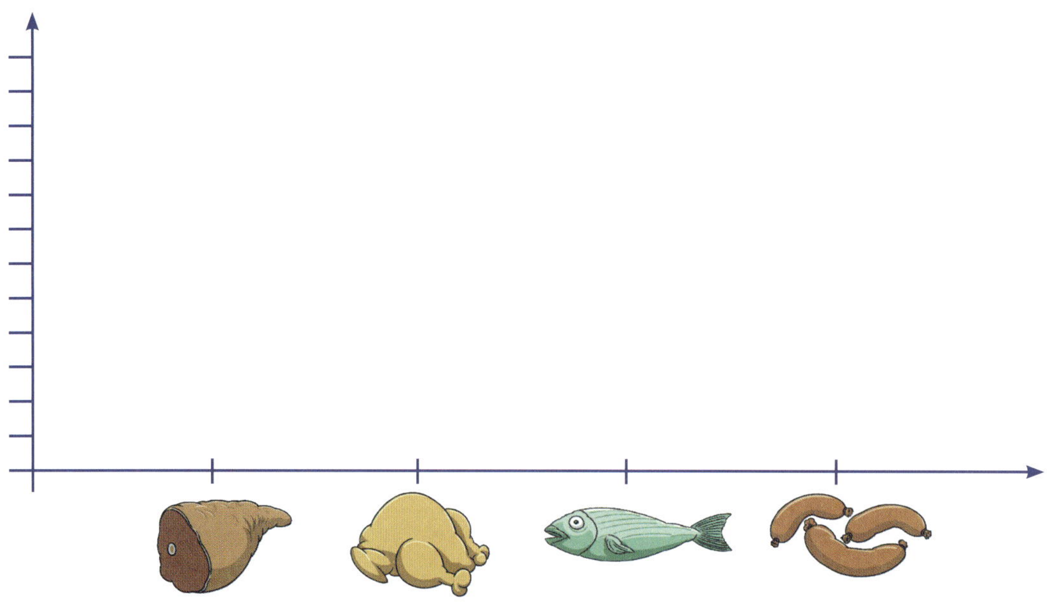

Unit 29 Chance

1 What is the likelihood of each happening? Use one of these words.

certain · likely · unlikely · impossible

a You will eat a boiled egg for breakfast tomorrow. ______

b Your teacher will have purple hair next week. ______

c It will rain next Wednesday. ______

d My mother is older than me. ______

e You will eat food tomorrow. ______

f Next month is September. ______

2 From this bag, which colour:

a is most likely to be drawn out? ______

Why? ______

b is least likely to be drawn out? ______

Why? ______

c will never be drawn out? ______

Why? ______

d Which colours have the same chance? ______

Why? ______

Challenge!

Write down:

- 3 things you think are FAIR and
- 3 things you think are UNFAIR.

FAIR	UNFAIR

Mastery Checklist I can:
- ☐ answer questions about a table
- ☐ answer questions about a column graph
- ☐ make a picture graph
- ☐ collect data and use tally marks
- ☐ make a column graph
- ☐ understand certain, likely, unlikely and impossible.

Revision Term 3

1 Sam had $5. He bought one chocolate for $3.20 and one lollipop for 60c. p 96

a How much did he spend? ______

b How much change did he get? ______

2 p 97

a $174 + 13 =$ ______ b $383 + 15 =$ ______ c $460 + 37 =$ ______

3 Fill in the boxes. p 97

a $2\square + 54 = \square 9$

b $\square 2 + 34 = 7\square$

c $64 + \square\square = 78$

4 p 101

a $9 \times 5 =$ ______ b $9 \times 0 =$ ______

c $3 \times 9 =$ ______ d $9 \times 4 =$ ______

5 Use colours to match. p 102

9 + 9 + 9	six fours
7 × 5	27
6 groups of 4	6 × 3
10 × 0	7 + 7 + 7 + 7 + 7
3+3+3+3+3+3	0

6 Each chapter in a book has 8 pages. How many pages has Liam read if he's read 9 chapters? p 103

______

7 p 106

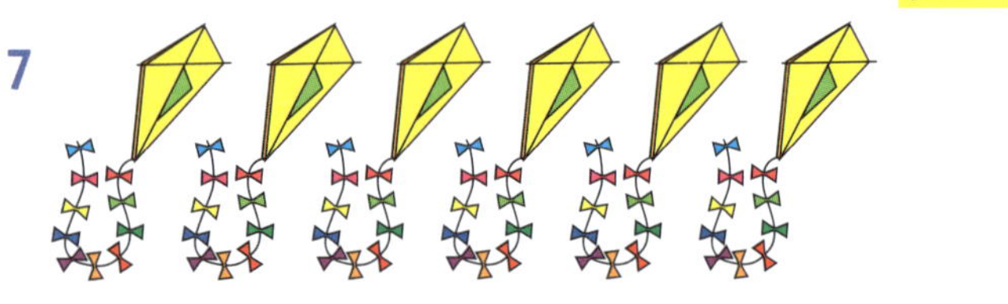

a How many kites? ______

b How many bows on each kite? ______

c How many bows altogether? ______

d ______ × ______ = ______

8 p 106

a 4×1 ______ b 5×3 ______ c 4×9 ______ d 10×6 ______

9 Make fair shares. p 109

7 shares. 1 share = ______

10 a Draw 24 balls. p 110

b How many groups of 4? ______

c How many groups of 3? ______

d How many groups of 12? ______

11 Circle the larger fraction. $\frac{1}{2}$, $\frac{1}{5}$ p 112

12 True or false? p 112

a $\frac{1}{2}$ is the same as $\frac{2}{4}$ ______

b $\frac{1}{2}$ is more than $\frac{2}{5}$ ______

13 Colour the fraction to match. p 113

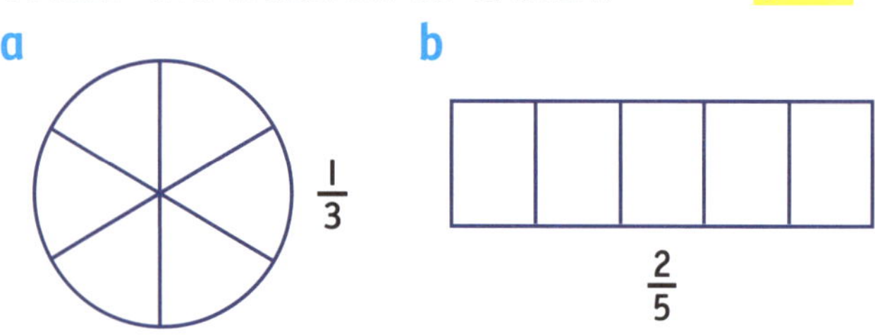

a $\frac{1}{3}$ b $\frac{2}{5}$

14 What is: p 114

a $\frac{1}{4}$ of 12 oranges? ______

b $\frac{1}{3}$ of 15 beans? ______

Revision Term 3

15 Write the missing terms. 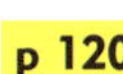 p 120

a $1.80, $1.60, ____, $1.20, ____

b 25, 33, 41, ____, ____, 65

16 Write the pattern for adding 6 in this table. p 121

Order of the term	1	2	3			
Term	6					

17 p 123

What is:

a on the top row in the middle?

____

b in the middle row on the left?

____

Write the position of:

c the jacket. ____

____

d the sunglasses. ____

____

18 Name something that is: 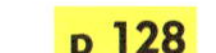 p 128

a heavier than 1 kg.

____

b lighter than 1 kg.

____

19 How much does it weigh?  p 128

a

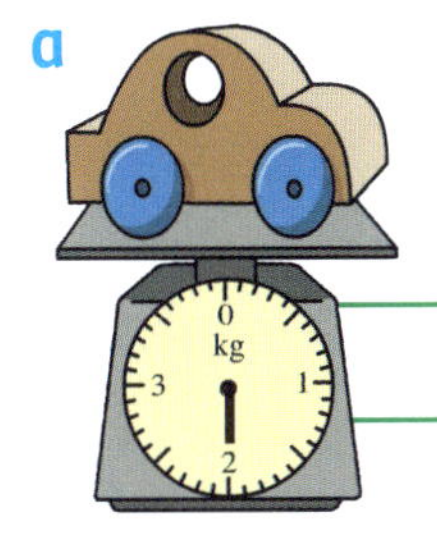

b

20 Draw both times on the clocks. p 135

The writing lesson started at 11:40 am and went for 35 minutes. Write the time it finished in words.

____

21 What is the likelihood of: p 139

a the school holidays being 3 months long? ____

b it raining next week? ____

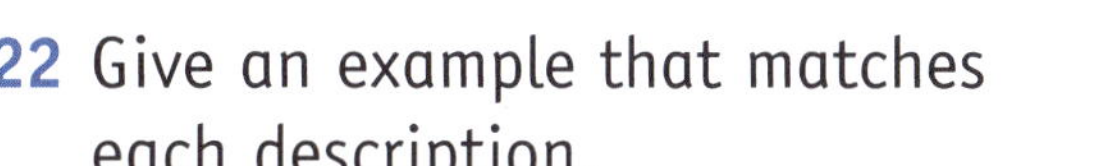

22 Give an example that matches each description. p 139

a certain ____

____

b impossible ____

____

c likely ____

____

d unlikely ____

____

23 Look at the bag of cubes. p 139

a Which colour is least likely to be drawn out? ____

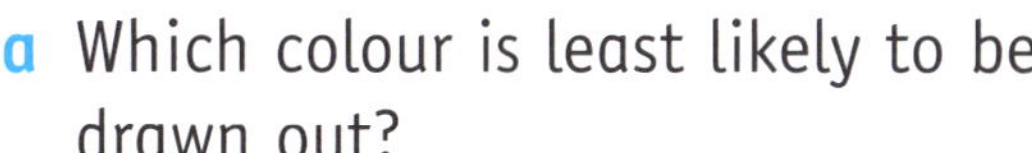

b Which two colours have the same chance? ____ and ____

c Which colour will never be drawn out? Circle it.

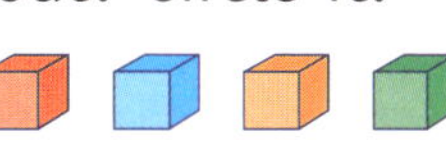

Unit 30 Number facts 7×

Multiplication

JULY						
S	M	T	W	T	F	S
				1	2	3
4	5	6	7	8	9	10
11	12	13	14	15	16	17
18 19	20	21	22	23	24	25
26 27	28	29	30	31		

AUGUST						
S	M	T	W	T	F	S
1	2	3	4	5	6	7
8	9	10	11	12	13	14
15	16	17	18	19	20	21
22	23	24	25	26	27	28
29	30	31				

SEPTEMBER						
S	M	T	W	T	F	S
			1	2	3	4
5	6	7	8	9	10	11
12	13	14	15	16	17	18
19	20	21	22	23	24	25
26	27	28	29	30		

1 How many days in 1 week? ______

2 Use the calendar to help you work out the number of days in:

a 3 weeks. ______ b 6 weeks. ______ c 4 weeks. ______ d 2 weeks. ______

e 10 weeks. ______ f 8 weeks. ______ g 5 weeks. ______ h 7 weeks. ______

i 9 weeks. ______ j 0 weeks. ______ k 11 weeks. ______ l 12 weeks. ______

3 Complete.

4

×	6	10	2	8	4	0	7	3	9	1	5
7											

5 It takes 7 minutes to eat 1 hotdog. How long will it take to eat 8 hotdogs?

______

6 1 toy aeroplane costs $7. How much will 5 toy aeroplanes cost? ______

7 There are 7 flowers on each plant. How many flowers are there on 7 plants?

______

8 Make up your own '7' story.

____

____

____

____

____

Unit 30 Number facts 8×

1 How many legs on:

a 1 spider? ______ b 6 spiders? ______ c 4 spiders? ______ d 9 spiders? ______

e 2 spiders? ______ f 10 spiders? ______ g 3 spiders? ______ h 8 spiders? ______

i 7 spiders? ______ j 5 spiders? ______ k 0 spiders? ______ l 11 spiders? ______

2 Join.

3 Complete these as quickly as you can.

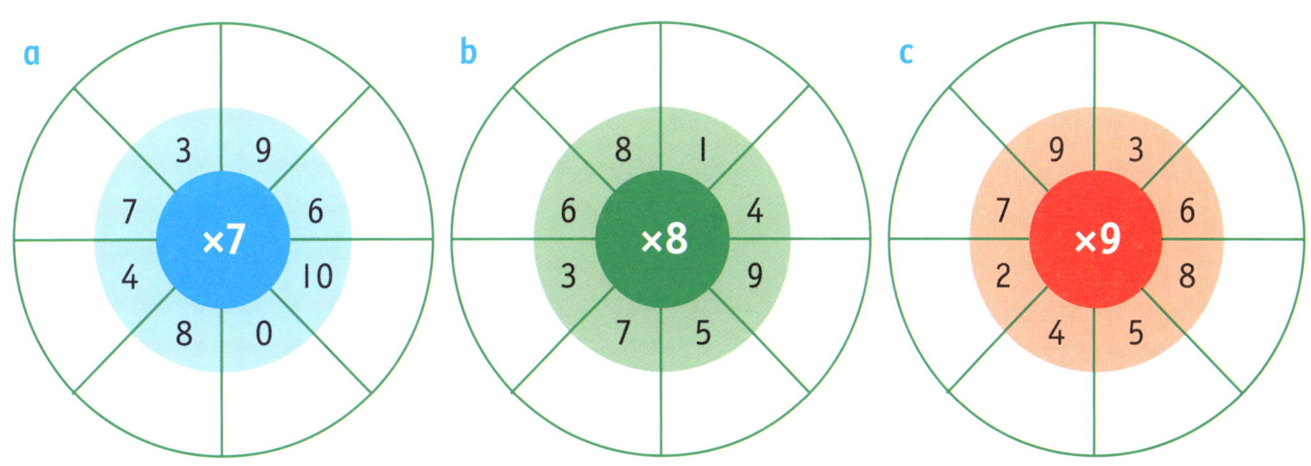

Unit 30 Multiplication facts

A

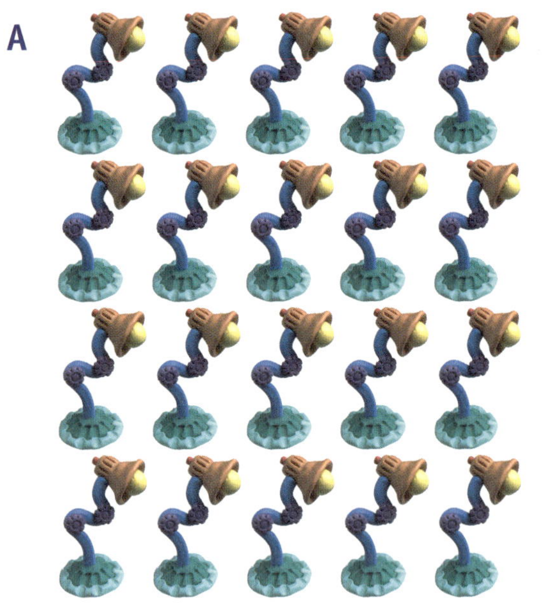

B

C

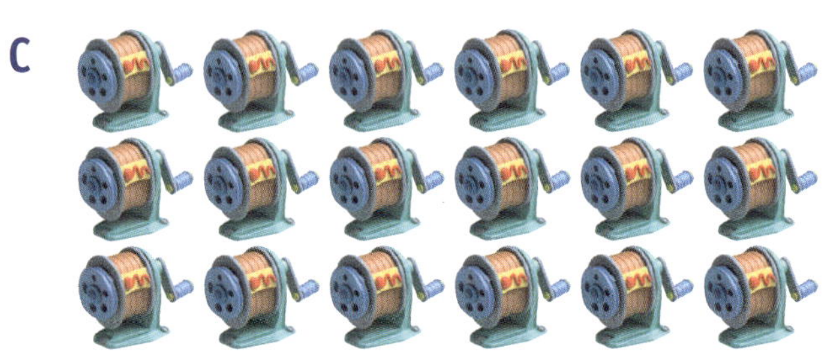

D

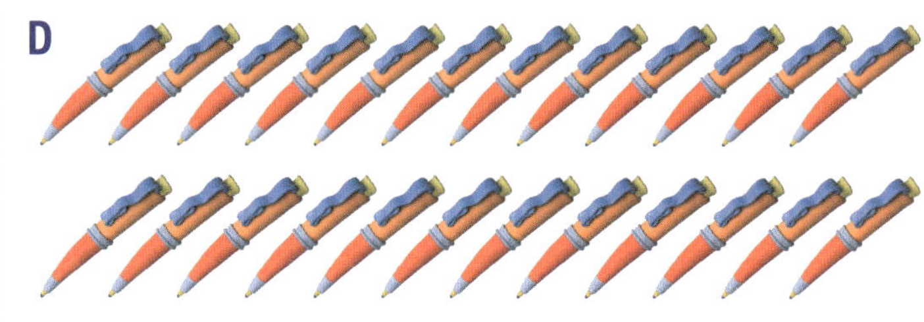

E

F

Write as many multiplication facts as you can for each group.

A	B	C

D	E	F

Unit 30 Products

Product is the answer when numbers are multiplied.

Match the number sentence to its answer.
Then write the letter in the secret message.

1 6 × 7 =
2 9 × 8 =
3 4 × 4 =
4 8 × 6 =
5 3 × 7 =
6 5 × 4 =
7 9 × 6 =
8 7 × 7 =

9 a $\begin{array}{r} 8 \\ \times\ 4 \\ \hline \end{array}$ b $\begin{array}{r} 9 \\ \times\ 3 \\ \hline \end{array}$ c $\begin{array}{r} 10 \\ \times\ 0 \\ \hline \end{array}$ d $\begin{array}{r} 7 \\ \times\ 9 \\ \hline \end{array}$ e $\begin{array}{r} 5 \\ \times\ 7 \\ \hline \end{array}$ f $\begin{array}{r} 8 \\ \times\ 8 \\ \hline \end{array}$

10 Write the product of:

a 6 and 4 ______ b 3 and 6 ______ c 9 and 1 ______ d 2 and 5 ______
e 4 and 3 ______ f 7 and 4 ______ g 6 and 6 ______ h 8 and 7 ______

11 Fill in the missing facts.

eg		4 groups of 6	$\begin{array}{r} 6 \\ \times\ 4 \\ \hline \end{array}$	6 × 4	24
a		3 groups of 8			
b			$\begin{array}{r} 5 \\ \times\ 5 \\ \hline \end{array}$		
c					16

Unit 30 Multiples

3, 4, 5, 10 tables

1	2	3	4	5	6	7	8	9	10
11	12	13	14	15	16	17	18	19	20
21	22	23	24	25	26	27	28	29	30
31	32	33	34	35	36	37	38	39	40
41	42	43	44	45	46	47	48	49	50
51	52	53	54	55	56	57	58	59	60
61	62	63	64	65	66	67	68	69	70
71	72	73	74	75	76	77	78	79	80
81	82	83	84	85	86	87	88	89	90
91	92	93	94	95	96	97	98	99	100

1 a Colour the multiples of 7 yellow.

b Colour the multiples of 8 red.

c Colour the multiples of 9 green.

d Which numbers have been coloured more than once?

____

e Why? _______________

____

____

____

____

2 Colour the multiples of the middle number.

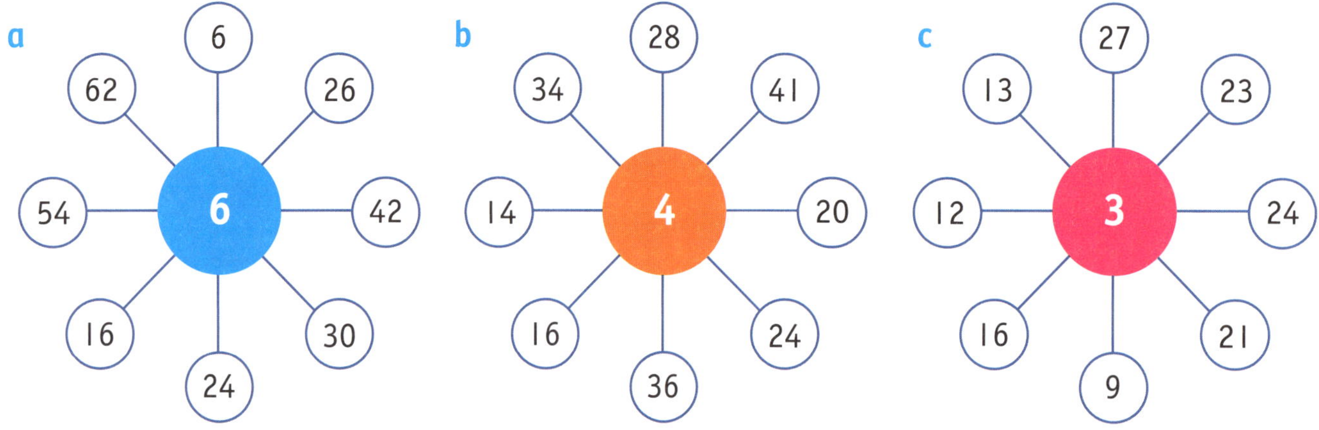

3 What is the value of each pile?

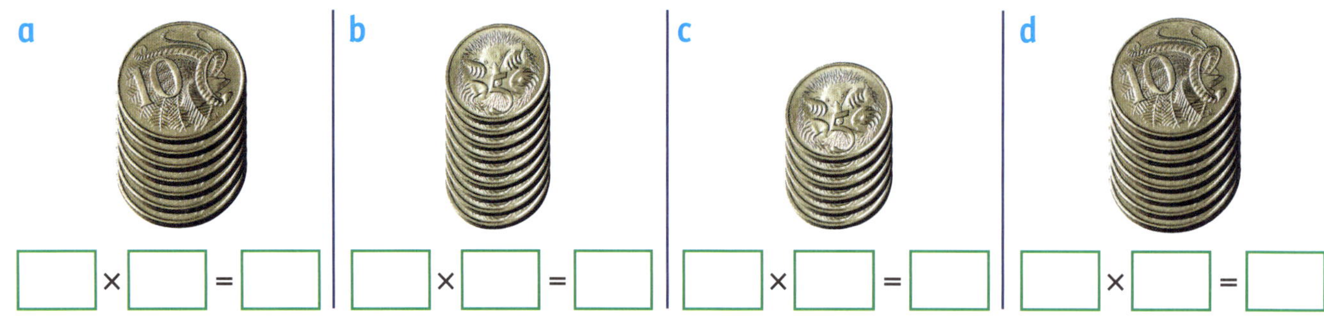

a ☐ × ☐ = ☐

b ☐ × ☐ = ☐

c ☐ × ☐ = ☐

d ☐ × ☐ = ☐

Mastery Checklist I can:
- ☐ remember the 7× and 8× tables
- ☐ write different multiplication facts for a picture array
- ☐ find the product
- ☐ show multiples on a 100 square
- ☐ identify multiples.

Problem solving

Operations

1 Lily has 8 pairs of socks. How many socks altogether?

$8 \times 2 =$ ☐

Answer ☐ socks

2 Jarrah bought 10 apples for 8 cents each. How much did he spend?

☐ × ☐ = ☐

Answer ☐

3 Liam has 5 children. Each child has 4 T-shirts. How many T-shirts altogether?

☐ × ☐ = ☐

Answer ☐ T-shirts

4 Ruby gathers 4 eggs every day. How many eggs in 1 week?

☐ × ☐ = ☐

Answer ☐ eggs

You write the questions.

5 ______________________________

____

____

____

____

☐ × ☐ = ☐ Answer 30 bananas

6 ______________________________

____

____

____

____

☐ × ☐ = ☐ Answer 48 monsters

7 Use a calculator.

Farmer Lei had 14 paddocks. There were 25 cows in each of 4 paddocks and 34 sheep in each of 3 paddocks.

a How many cows? ☐ × ☐ = ☐

b How many sheep? ☐ × ☐ = ☐

c How many animals altogether?

____

I can solve problems by:

☐ using multiplication ☐ writing questions and algorithms.

Unit 31 Division

These are stamps used in the country of Weirdo.

1 Wrod only ever bought 5c stamps. How many could he buy for:

a 40c? ______ b 30c? ______ c 15c? ______ d 5c? ______ e 50c? ______

2 Wred only bought 10c stamps. How many could she buy for:

a 60c? ______ b 90c? ______ c 20c? ______ d 50c? ______ e 70c? ______

3 Weid only bought $2 stamps. How many could he buy for?

a $14? ______ b $8? ______ c $18? ______ d $6? ______ e $12? ______

4 Wido had $13. Could she buy eight $2 stamps? ________

Why? ______________________________

5 How much for: a seven 5c stamps? __________ b five $5 stamps? __________

6 Wodi has 85c. How many 10c stamps can she buy? __________

7 a How much to buy 1 of each stamp? __________

b How much change from $10? __________

Challenge! Make a list

Werd has a package to send. List the ways she can make $3.10 using 5 or less stamps.

Unit 31 The division sign

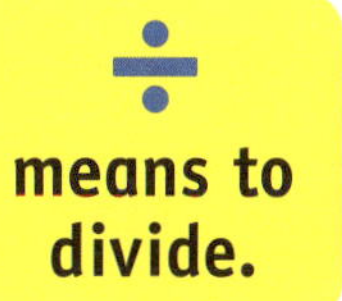

1 Divide 20 cars into 4 equal groups.

20 ÷ 4 = ______

There are ______ cars in each group.

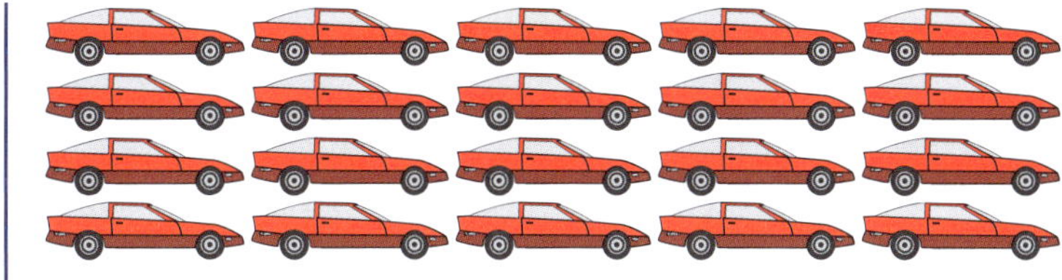

2 Divide 16 leaves into 8 equal groups.

16 ÷ 8 = ______

There are ______ leaves in each group.

3 Divide 24 stars into 6 equal groups.

24 ÷ 6 = ______

There are ______ stars in each group.

4 Divide 18 cats into 3 equal groups.

18 ÷ 3 = ______

There are ______ cats in each group.

5 Divide 32 dice into 4 groups.

32 ÷ 4 = ______

There are ______ dice in each group.

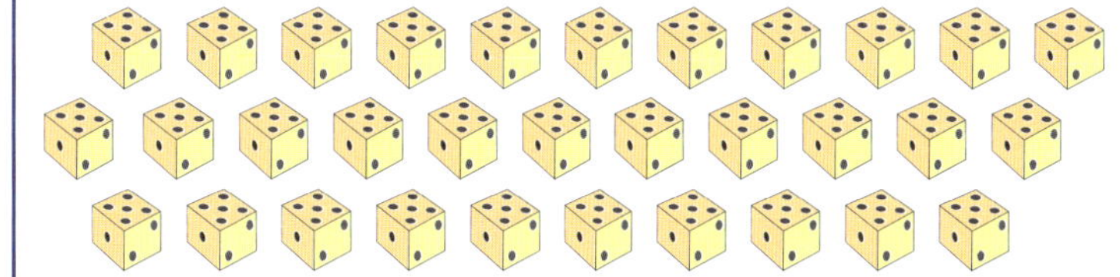

6 Divide 24 foxes into groups of 8.

24 ÷ 8 = ______

There are ______ groups of foxes.

7 Divide 15 girls into groups of 3.

15 ÷ 3 = ______

There are ______ groups of girls.

8 Divide 20 bugs into groups of 5.

20 ÷ 5 = ______

There are ______ groups of bugs.

9 Divide 22 fish into groups of 2.

22 ÷ 2 = ______

There are ______ groups of fish.

Unit 31 Using the division sign

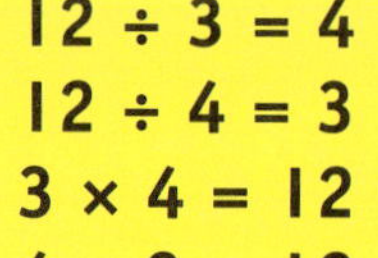

1 Use this group of 24 ice-creams to help you to divide.

a 24 ÷ 8 = ______ b 24 ÷ 6 = ______

c 24 ÷ 3 = ______ d 24 ÷ 24 = ______

e 24 ÷ 4 = ______ f 24 ÷ 1 = ______

2 Use this group of 30 bears to help you to divide.

a 30 ÷ 10 = ______

b 30 ÷ 6 = ______

c 30 ÷ 3 = ______

d 30 ÷ 5 = ______

e 30 ÷ 30 = ______

f 30 ÷ 1 = ______

3 Complete these number sentences.

a 5 × 6 = ______	b 3 × 6 = ______	c 4 × 8 = ______	d 10 × 9 = ______
30 ÷ 5 = ______	18 ÷ 3 = ______	32 ÷ 4 = ______	90 ÷ 10 = ______
30 ÷ 6 = ______	18 ÷ 6 = ______	32 ÷ 8 = ______	90 ÷ 9 = ______

4

a 42 ÷ 7 = ______	b 10 ÷ 5 = ______	c 20 ÷ 10 = ______	d 40 ÷ 10 = ______
e 27 ÷ 9 = ______	f 48 ÷ 8 = ______	g 49 ÷ 7 = ______	h 36 ÷ 6 = ______
i 54 ÷ 9 = ______	j 35 ÷ 5 = ______	k 9 ÷ 9 = ______	l 100 ÷ 10 = ______

5 a 30 balls are packed into boxes of 6. How many boxes are needed?

☐ ÷ ☐ = ☐

b Mrs Lim is making 50 cupcakes. She puts 10 cupcakes on each tray. How many trays are needed?

☐ ÷ ☐ = ☐

c 5 children share 25 biscuits equally. How many biscuits each?

☐ ÷ ☐ = ☐

d Mr Baker has 60 apples. He puts 6 apples in each bag. How many bags?

☐ ÷ ☐ = ☐

Mastery Checklist I can:
- ☐ solve money division problems
- ☐ recognise ÷
- ☐ divide into equal groups to solve problems
- ☐ connect division to multiplication
- ☐ solve division word problems.

Problem solving

Bags to pack

Jerry, Sam and Tye bought 48 grocery items. They wanted to find how many ways they could pack them equally into bags. Jerry found the most ways. Sam thought of 3 ways, 1 less than Tye. Tye thought of 4 less than Jerry. How many ways did Jerry find?

What might be the ways that Jerry thought of, apart from this way?

$2 \times 24 = 48$

$48 \div 2 = 24$

I can solve problems by:

☐ using multiplication and division ☐ writing algorithms.

Unit 32 Writing 4-digit numbers

Number words

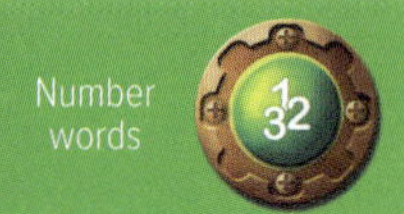

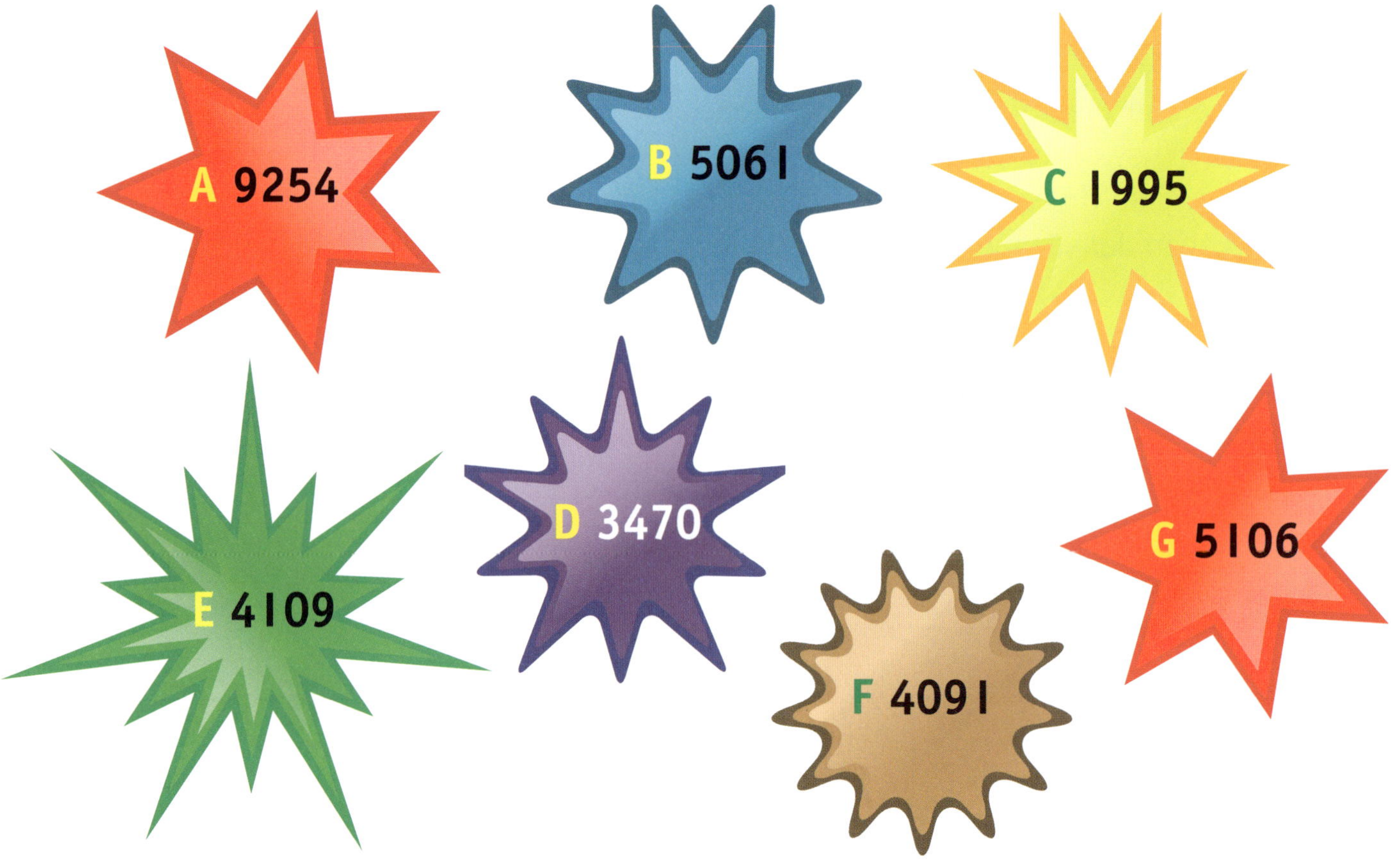
A 9254
B 5061
C 1995
D 3470
E 4109
F 4091
G 5106

1 Write each number in words.

A ______________________________

B ______________________________

C ______________________________

D ______________________________

E ______________________________

F ______________________________

G ______________________________

2 Write the numbers in ascending order.

3 Which number is:

a closest to 4000? ____________ b closest to 6000? ____________

4 Which number comes:

a after 1995? ____________ b before 4091? ____________

c before 5061? ____________ d after 4109? ____________

Unit 32 Rounding thousands

1 Round these numbers to the nearest thousand.

a 7430 ______ b 8199 ______
c 2506 ______ d 6794 ______
e 1245 ______ f 4009 ______
g 8952 ______ h 3673 ______
i 9367 ______ j 5801 ______

To round to the nearest thousand look at the hundreds place.
1704 → 2000
1407 → 1000
Remember
1, 2, 3, 4 go down.
5, 6, 7, 8, 9 go up.

2 Write the number 10 more than:

a	3654	
b	2871	
c	9108	
d	8235	
e	5096	

3 Write the number 10 less than:

a	8463	
b	2028	
c	9612	
d	5579	
e	3105	

4 Write the number 100 more than:

a	7398	
b	1427	
c	5006	
d	2192	
e	945	

5 Write the number 100 less than:

a	5650	
b	1901	
c	9436	
d	3198	
e	8072	

6 6105 5160 5016 5601 6510

Write the number:

a with thousands digit 5 and ones digit 1. ______
b with hundreds digit 1 and ones digit 5. ______
c with hundreds digit 5 and ones digit 0. ______
d with thousands digit 5 and ones digit 6. ______

Work backwards

What number am I?
My thousands digit is 2 more than my tens digit.
My tens digit is 3 less than my hundreds digit.
My hundreds digit is 4 more than my ones digit which is 2. ______

Unit 32 Using numeral expanders

1 Write these numbers.

a 7 Thousands 6 Hundreds 2 Tens 9 Ones ______

b 9 Thousands 4 Hundreds 5 Tens 2 Ones ______

c 4 Thousands 7 Hundreds 0 Tens 3 Ones ______

d 1 Thousands 0 Hundreds 8 Tens 6 Ones ______

e 6 Thousands 3 Hundreds 5 Tens 0 Ones ______

These are expanded numbers.

2 Complete these numeral expanders.

a 5218

☐ Thousands ☐ Hundreds ☐ Tens ☐ Ones

☐ ☐ Hundreds ☐ Tens ☐ Ones

☐ ☐ ☐ Tens ☐ Ones

☐ ☐ ☐ ☐ Ones

b 3964

☐ Thousands ☐ Hundreds ☐ Tens ☐ Ones

☐ ☐ Hundreds ☐ Tens ☐ Ones

☐ ☐ ☐ Tens ☐ Ones

☐ ☐ ☐ ☐ Ones

3 Use the numeral expanders above to express:

a 5218 as ______ thousands, ______ tens, ______ ones

b 5218 as ______ hundreds, ______ tens, ______ ones

c 5218 as ______ tens, ______ ones

4 How many hundreds in:

a 7450? ______ b 6307? ______ c 2094? ______ d 8813? ______

5 How many tens in:

a 1638? ______ b 5920? ______ c 4107? ______ d 9022? ______

6 How many ones in:

a 7004? ______ b 2500? ______ c 1234? ______ d 9990? ______

Mastery Checklist I can:
- ☐ write 4-digit numbers in different ways
- ☐ round numbers
- ☐ add and subtract 10 and 100
- ☐ understand place value to thousands.

Unit 33 Denominators

equivalent – having the same value, equal to

$\frac{1}{1} = 1$

The denominator 1 divides one whole into 1 part.

$\frac{1}{2}$	$\frac{1}{2}$

The denominator 2 divides one whole into two equal parts.

$\frac{1}{4}$	$\frac{1}{4}$	$\frac{1}{4}$	$\frac{1}{4}$

The denominator 4 divides one whole into 4 equal parts.

$\frac{1}{8}$	$\frac{1}{8}$	$\frac{1}{8}$	$\frac{1}{8}$	$\frac{1}{8}$	$\frac{1}{8}$	$\frac{1}{8}$	$\frac{1}{8}$

The denominator 8 divides one whole into 8 equal parts.

1 $\frac{1}{4}$ is one of four parts.

a $\frac{2}{4}$ is ________ of four parts.

b $\frac{3}{4}$ is ________ of four parts.

c $\frac{4}{4}$ is ________ of four parts.

d Are all four parts the same size? ________ Why? ______________________

e Which fraction is the largest? ________

What is another name for this? ______________________

2 a Colour the fractions.

$\frac{1}{8}$ 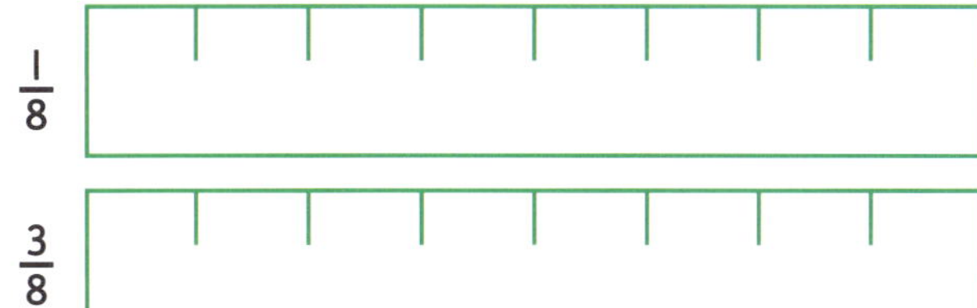

$\frac{2}{8}$ 

$\frac{3}{8}$ 

$\frac{4}{8}$ 

$\frac{5}{8}$ 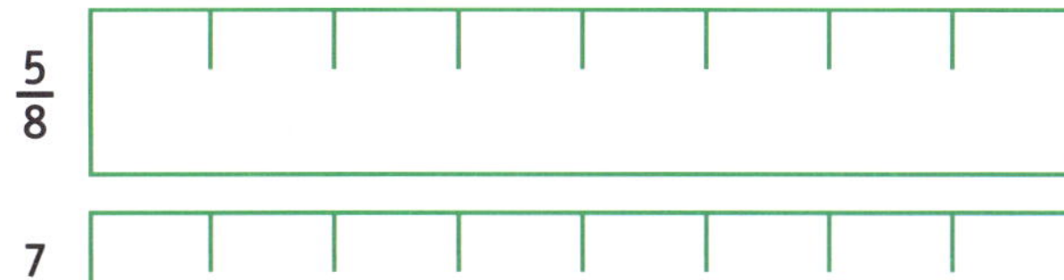

$\frac{6}{8}$ 

$\frac{7}{8}$ 

$\frac{8}{8}$ 

b Find the fraction which is equivalent to $\frac{1}{4}$. ____________ $= \frac{1}{4}$.

c Find the fraction which is equivalent to $\frac{3}{4}$. ____________ $= \frac{3}{4}$.

Unit 33 Writing Decimals

A decimal fraction is a fraction written with a decimal point.

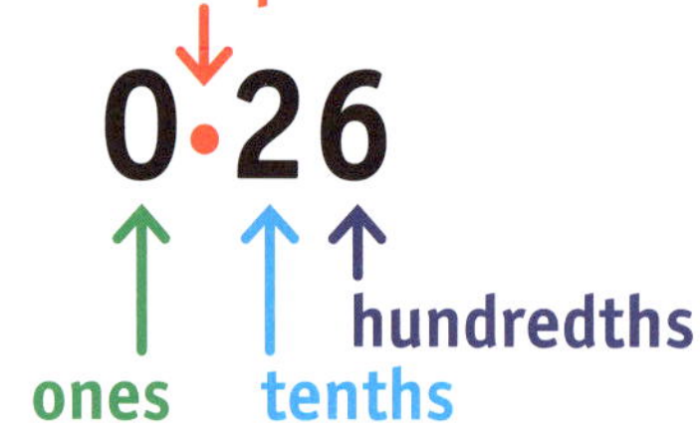

0·26

no whole numbers

2 tenths

6 hundredths

1 Complete the table.

Decimal fraction	Ones	·	Tenths	Hundredths
eg 0·15	0	·	1	5
a 0·63				
b 0·24				
c 0·57				
d 0·89				
e 0·99				

2 Write the missing values.

Fraction	Hundredths	Decimal
eg $\frac{65}{100}$	65 hundredths	0·65
a $\frac{52}{100}$		
b		0·34
c	97 hundredths	
d $\frac{78}{100}$		
e		0·45
f	19 hundredths	
g	7 hundredths	
h		0·10
i $\frac{80}{100}$		
j	24 hundredths	
k		0·15
l	33 hundredths	

Unit 33 Tenths and hundredths

1 Match.

A

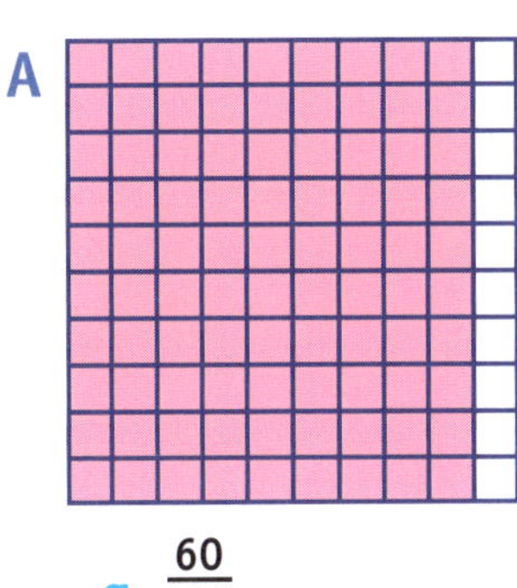

B

C

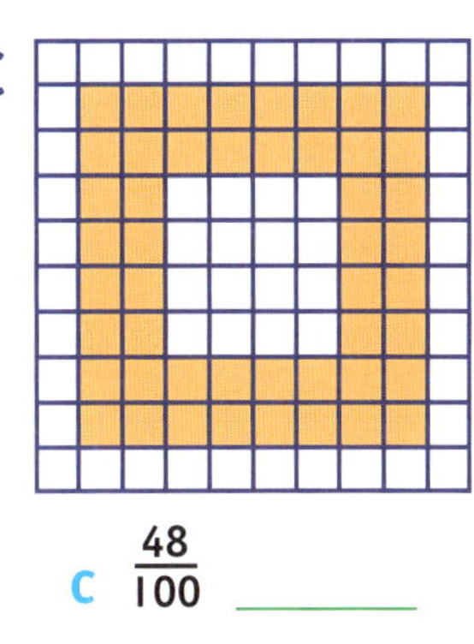

D

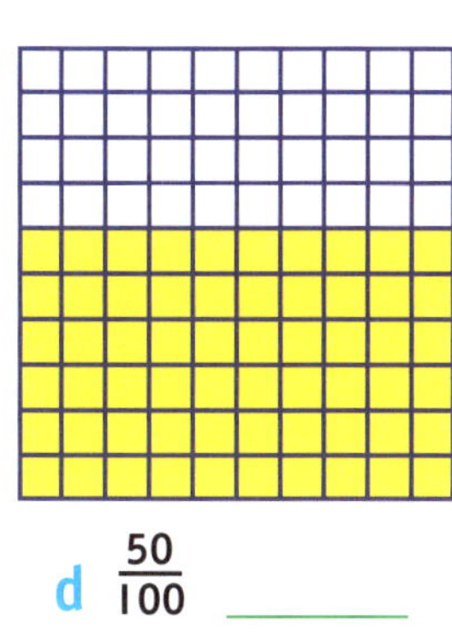

a $\frac{60}{100}$ ______ b $\frac{90}{100}$ ______ c $\frac{48}{100}$ ______ d $\frac{50}{100}$ ______

2 Colour the fraction on each hundred square. Complete the equivalent fractions.

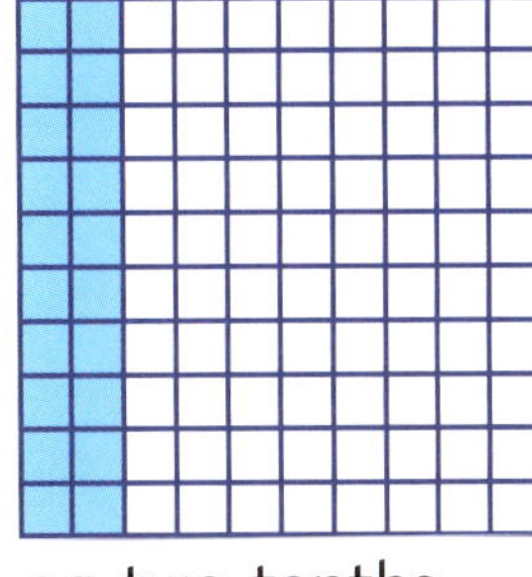

eg two tenths

$= \frac{20}{100} = 0.2$

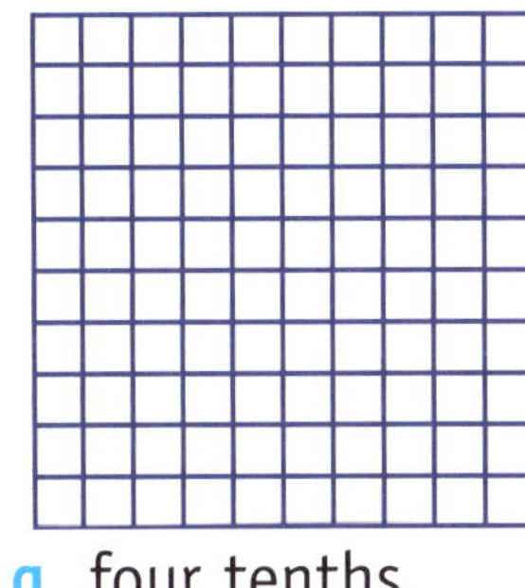

a four tenths

$= \frac{\square}{100} =$ ______

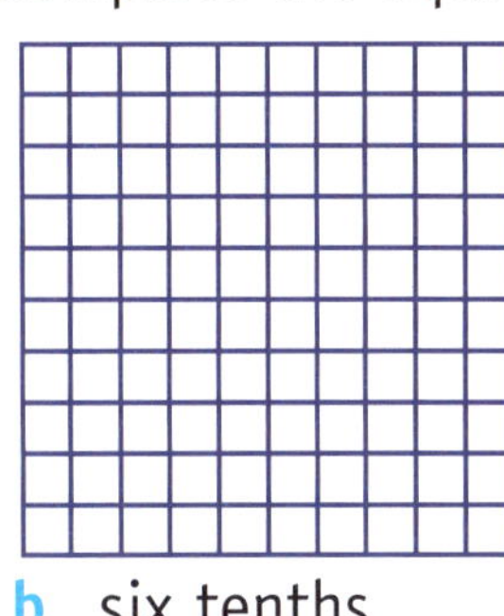

b six tenths

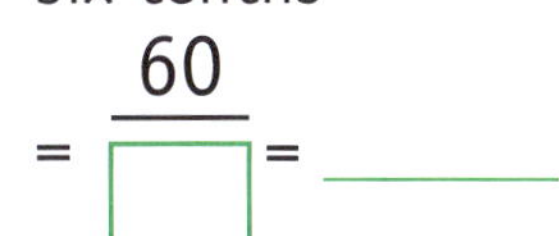

$= \frac{60}{\square} =$ ______

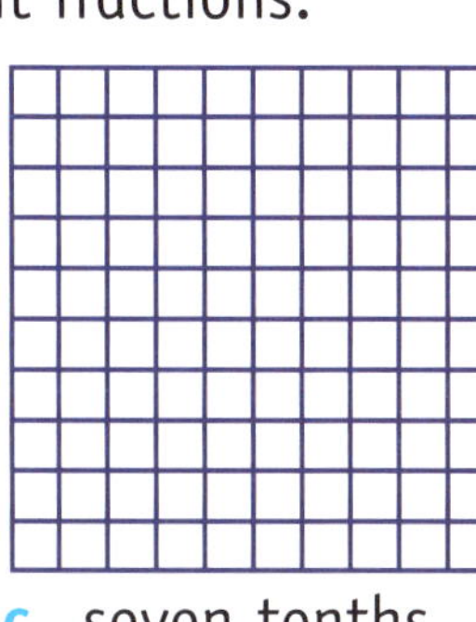

c seven tenths

$= \frac{\square}{100} =$ ______

3 Complete:

a two tenths = ______ hundredths b five tenths = ______ hundredths

c nine tenths = ______ hundredths d eighty hundredths = ______ tenths

4 Show by using two colours that the following statements are true.

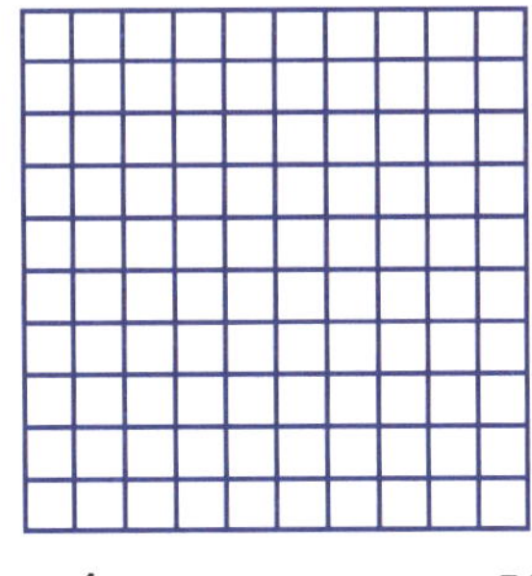

a $\frac{4}{10}$ is less than $\frac{50}{100}$

b $\frac{20}{100}$ equals $\frac{2}{10}$

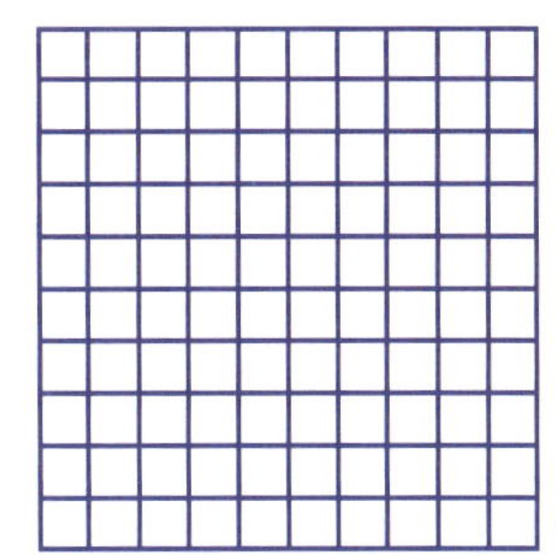

c $\frac{70}{100}$ is more than $\frac{3}{10}$

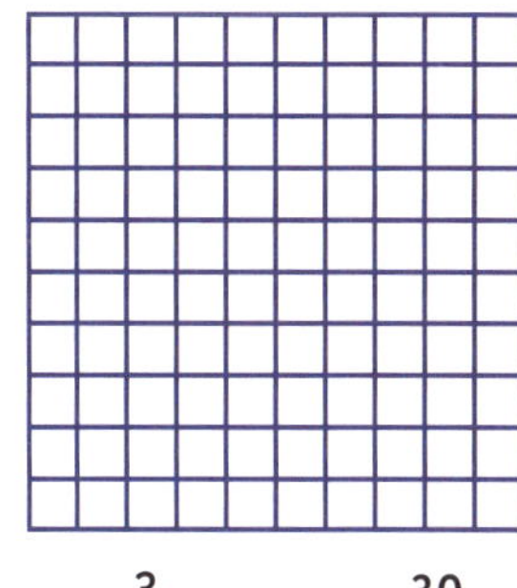

d $\frac{3}{10}$ equals $\frac{30}{100}$

Mastery Checklist I can:
- ☐ connect denominators to one whole
- ☐ colour to show fractions
- ☐ write decimals to hundredths
- ☐ connect fractions and decimals.

Unit 34 Centimetres and millimetres

1 a Is a millimetre smaller than a centimetre? ________

b How many millimetres in one centimetre? ________

estimate and measure cm

2 Measure in centimetres:

a the width of the house. ______

b the height of the window. ______

c the short side of the chimney. ______

d the height of the house wall. ______

e the height of a fence paling. ______

f the width of a tree branch. ______

3 Without measuring, name three things that are about 2 cm.

a ____________ b ____________ c ____________

4 Measure the three things to see how close you are.

a ____________ b ____________ c ____________

5 Draw a line that is: a 4 cm 6 mm long.

b 3 cm 2 mm long.

Unit 34 m, cm, mm

m is metre
cm is centimetre
mm is millimetre
10 mm = 1 cm
100 cm = 1 m

1 How many centimetres in:

a 2 m? _____ b 5 m? _____ c 3 m? _____ d $4\frac{1}{2}$ m? _____ e $1\frac{1}{2}$ m? _____

2 How many millimetres in:

a 3 cm? _____ b 7 cm? _____ c 10 cm? _____ d 1 cm? _____ e 9 cm? _____

3 Change these to metres.

a 100 cm _____ b 700 cm _____ c 900 cm _____ d 350 cm _____ e 550 cm _____

4 Change these to centimetres.

a 50 mm _____ b 10 mm _____ c 40 mm _____ d 20 mm _____ e 70 mm _____

5 Name three things you might measure in millimetres.

a _______________ b _______________ c _______________

6 Draw these straight lines and label them.

A 10 mm B 40 mm C 55 mm D 25 mm E 38 mm F 73 mm

7 Give each alien a name then measure its height.

Name _____
Height _____

Name _____
Height _____

Name _____
Height _____

Name _____
Height _____

Challenge! Measure your height in: centimetres. 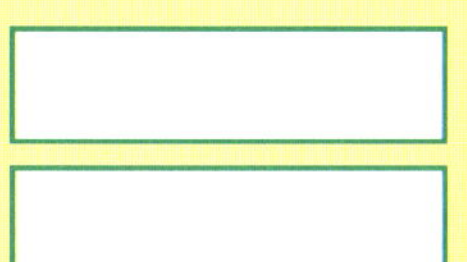

millimetres.

Unit 34 Comparing lengths

Length

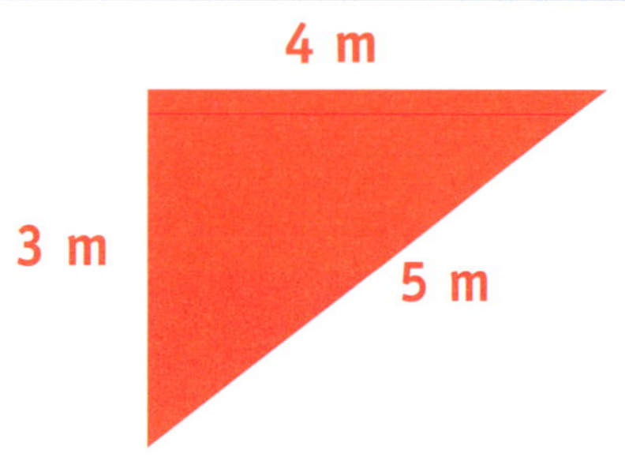

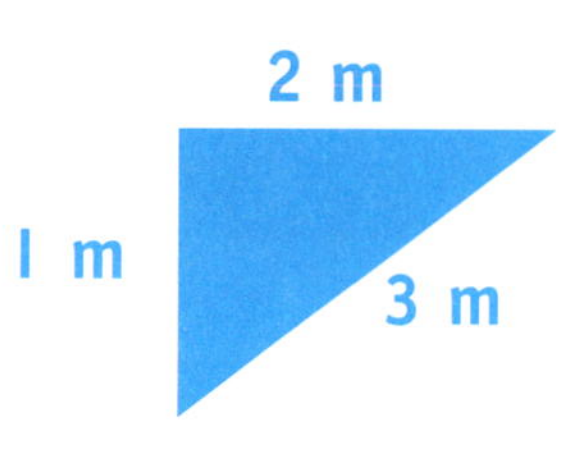

The length around the red triangle is 3 m + 4 m + 5 m = 12 m

The length around the blue triangle is 1 m + 2 m + 3 m = 6 m

The difference in the lengths around the triangles is 12 m − 6 m = 6 m

1 Add the lengths around each rectangle and write the total.

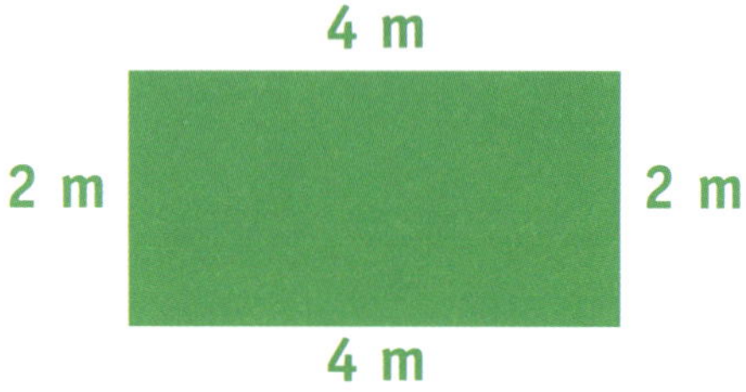

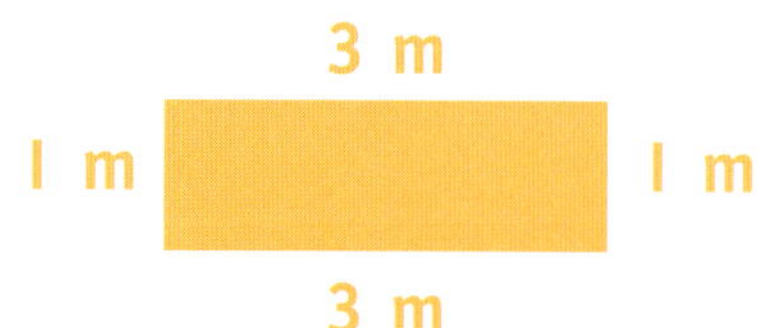

a Length around = ________ m

b Length around = ________ m

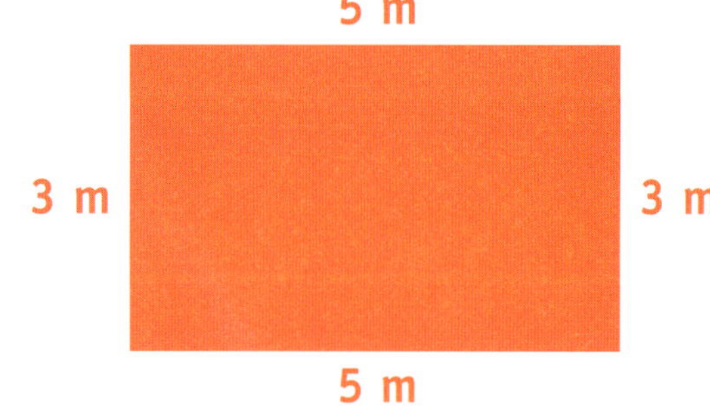

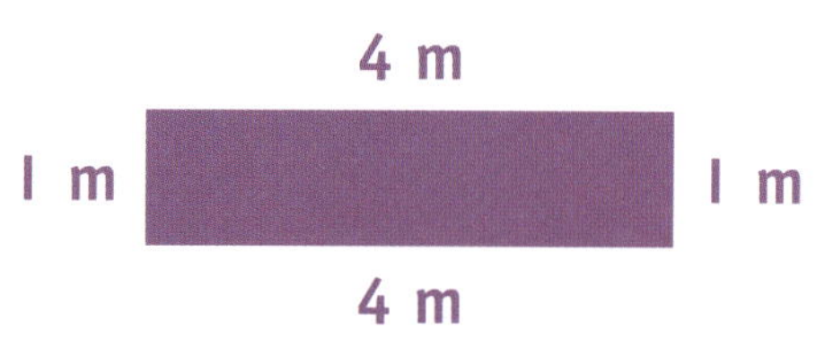

c Length around = ________ m

d Length around = ________ m

2 Fill in the gaps.

a The ________ rectangle has the longest length around the outside.

b The ________ rectangle has the shortest length around the outside.

c The difference in the lengths around the ouside of the green rectangle and the yellow rectangle is ________ m.

d The difference in the lengths around the outside of the orange rectangle and the green rectangle is ________ m.

e The difference in the lengths around the outside of the purple rectangle and the yellow rectangle is ________ m.

Problem solving

Flag heights

Three flagpoles are being put up.

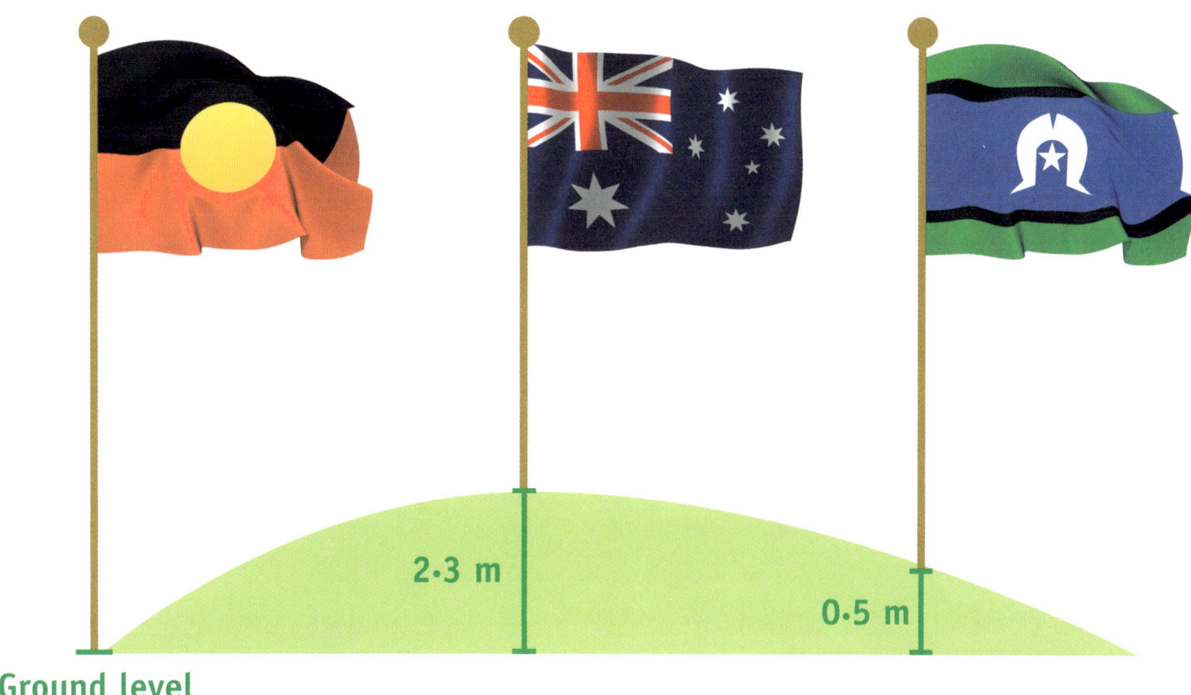

The tops of the flagpoles have to be at equal heights. The Aboriginal flagpole is 3·7 metres tall.

1 What will be the height of the Australian flagpole? ____________

2 What will be the height of the Torres Strait flagpole? ____________

If each flagpole has an extra 1·2 m of pole underground to hold it steady, what is the total height of each flagpole?

3 Aboriginal flagpole ____________

4 Australian flagpole ____________

5 Torres Strait flagpole ____________

I can solve problems by:

☐ understanding length ☐ comparing the lengths of different objects.

Unit 34 Area

Area is the size of the surface. It is measured in squares.

A B C

1 a Estimate the area of these robots in squares.

A = ______ squares B = ______ squares C = ______ squares

b Now count the squares.

A = ______ squares B = ______ squares C = ______ squares

2 Which robot has: a the largest area? _____ b the smallest area? _____

3 Draw a robot with an area of 30 squares.

4 This is half a robot. What will be the area of the whole robot?

5 a Are the squares in questions 1, 2, and 3 the same size? ______

b Will the area of robot A be the same if it is drawn on smaller squares? ______

c Will the area of robot B be the same if it is drawn on bigger squares? ______

6 a Cover your desk with counters. What is its area? ______ counters

b Cover your desk with books. What is its area? ______ books

c Are the answers the same? ______ Why not? ______________________

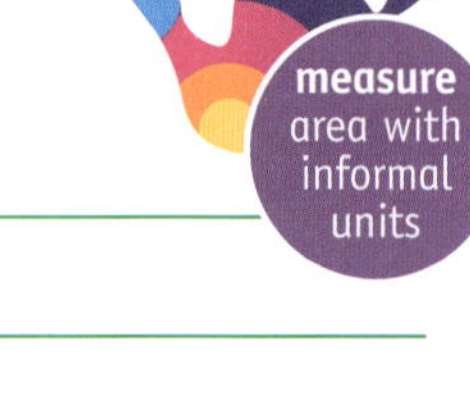

7 What would you use to find the area of the board? ______________________

Unit 34 Square centimetres

To measure area we can use square centimetres.
We write 1 square centimetre as 1 cm^2.

1 This is a square centimetre grid.
What is the area of these shapes? Estimate first.

A B C H D E F G

Area **A** = _____ cm^2 Area **B** = _____ cm^2 Area **C** = _____ cm^2

Area **D** = _____ cm^2 Area **E** = _____ cm^2 Area **F** = _____ cm^2

Area **G** = _____ cm^2 Area **H** = _____ cm^2

a Which shape has the largest area? _____

b Which shape has the smallest area? _____

c Which shapes have the same area? _____ _____

2 On this grid draw and colour 5 different shapes that each have an area of 5 cm^2.

Challenge! Use a 1 cm^2 sheet to work out the area in square centimetres of:

- this book cover. ☐
- your desk. ☐

Mastery Checklist I can:
- ☐ compare millimetres, centimetres and metres
- ☐ measure in cm and mm
- ☐ add lengths around a shape
- ☐ count squares to find the area
- ☐ use square centimetres.

Paper planes

Investigation 4

1 Construct three different paper planes.

2 Draw your paper planes:

Paper plane A
Paper plane B
Paper plane C

3 Conduct three throws with each paper plane. Record in metres how far the plane travelled. Then add to get the total distance for each plane.

	First throw	Second throw	Third throw	Total distance
Paper plane A				
Paper plane B				
Paper plane C				

AC9M3M02 Measurement **MA2-GM-02** Geometric measure A • Length: Measure and compare objects using metres, centimetres and millimetres • Geometric measure B • Length: Use scaled instruments to measure and compare lengths

Paper planes

4 Which plane flew the greatest distance? ________________

5 Which plane flew the smallest distance? ________________

6 Draw a column graph to show the total distance travelled by each plane.

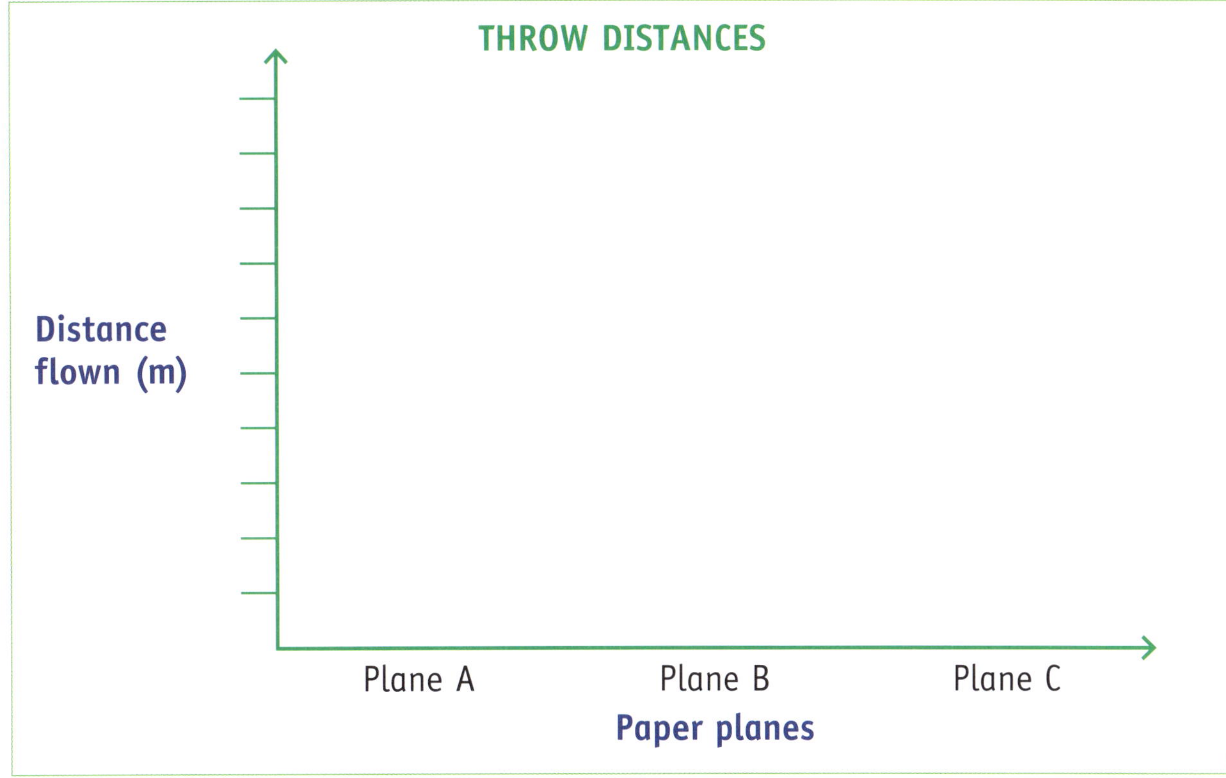

7 How could you improve your paper plane designs? Draw and label your ideas.

To carry out these tasks I need to:

- ☐ construct 3 different paper planes
- ☐ throw the planes and measure and record the distances
- ☐ graph the results
- ☐ think of ways to improve my paper plane designs.

I enjoyed this task!

Revision

1 Which operation shows these shells divided into 6 equal groups?

$18 \div 3$ ◯ $18 - 6$ ◯ $18 - 4$ ◯ $18 \div 6$ ◯

2 Which statement is true?

$\frac{1}{4}$ is less than $\frac{1}{2}$ ◯ $\frac{1}{3}$ is more than $\frac{1}{2}$ ◯ $\frac{1}{4}$ is less than $\frac{1}{10}$ ◯ $\frac{1}{10}$ is more than 1 ◯

3 Mum cut some oranges into quarters.

How many whole oranges did she cut?

16 ◯ 4 ◯ 8 ◯ 6 ◯

4 This fruit was placed in a bag.
Jay closed his eyes to pick one piece.
What is the chance he picked a banana?

certain ◯ impossible ◯ likely ◯ unlikely ◯

5 What shape is second from the left in the top row?

 ◯  ◯  ◯  ◯

Revision

6 Which number is 356 written to the closest ten?

Write your answer.

7 Multiply.

a	5 × 8 = ______	f	10 × 11 = ______	k	4 × 4 = ______
b	3 × 5 = ______	g	4 × 9 = ______	l	5 × 10 = ______
c	5 × 7 = ______	h	3 × 6 = ______	m	4 × 3 = ______
d	10 × 0 = ______	i	3 × 1 = ______	n	5 × 2 = ______
e	3 × 12 = ______	j	10 × 10 = ______	o	4 × 11 = ______

8 What is the height of this alien?

Shade one bubble.

4 cm　4 mm　4 m　40 cm

9 Fifi thought of a number. She then doubled it and added 3. The answer was 19. What number did she first think of?

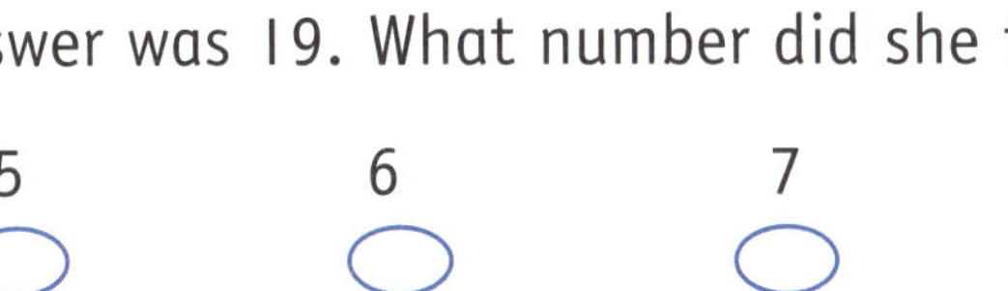

10 Which star shows a number that is not a multiple of 4?

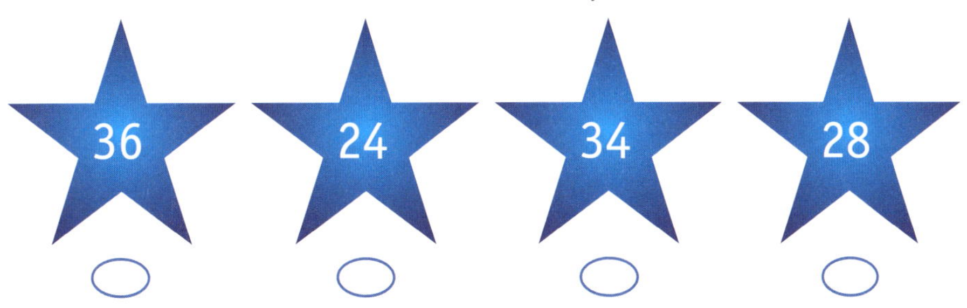

Unit 35 Changing numbers

A + 10
B + 9
C + 8
D + 12
E + 7
F + 11
SUPER-DOOPER NUMBER MUNCHER
OUT

In this amazing machine, numbers are changed into a pattern of four more numbers.

1 What comes out if these numbers are put into A?

a 10 ______ ______ ______ ______ b 35 ______ ______ ______ ______

c 24 ______ ______ ______ ______ d 9 ______ ______ ______ ______

2 What comes out if these numbers are put into F?

a 3 ______ ______ ______ ______ b 25 ______ ______ ______ ______

c 12 ______ ______ ______ ______ d 38 ______ ______ ______ ______

3 What comes out if these numbers are put into D?

a 7 ______ ______ ______ ______ b 9 ______ ______ ______ ______

c 4 ______ ______ ______ ______ d 11 ______ ______ ______ ______

4 What comes out if these numbers are put into B?

a 24 ______ ______ ______ ______ b 19 ______ ______ ______ ______

c 16 ______ ______ ______ ______ d 27 ______ ______ ______ ______

5 What comes out if these numbers are put into E?

a 3 ______ ______ ______ ______ b 15 ______ ______ ______ ______

c 30 ______ ______ ______ ______ d 41 ______ ______ ______ ______

Unit 35 Matching answers

1 True (T) or false (F)?

a $6 + 4 = 4 + 6$ ____ b $8 + 5 = 5 + 8$ ____ c $1 + 7 = 7 + 1$ ____ d $3 + 9 = 9 + 3$ ____

e $5 + 8 = 8 + 5$ ____ f $7 + 6 = 6 + 7$ ____ g $3 + 7 = 7 + 3$ ____ h $4 + 5 = 5 + 4$ ____

i What rule can you make? ______________________________

____

2 True (T) or false (F)?

a $3 \times 9 = 9 \times 3$ ____ b $7 \times 4 = 4 \times 7$ ____ c $8 \times 5 = 5 \times 8$ ____ d $5 \times 9 = 9 \times 5$ ____

e $3 \times 5 = 5 \times 3$ ____ f $6 \times 5 = 5 \times 6$ ____ g $9 \times 4 = 4 \times 9$ ____ h $10 \times 8 = 8 \times 10$ ____

i What rule can you make? ______________________________

____

3 Are the rules the same? ______________________________

4 True (T) or false (F)?

a $6 - 2 = 2 - 6$ ____ b $9 - 5 = 5 - 9$ ____ c $8 - 3 = 3 - 8$ ____ d $7 - 4 = 4 - 7$ ____

e Can you make a rule? ______________________________

5 True (T) or false (F)?

a $18 \div 3 = 3 \div 18$ ____ b $25 \div 5 = 5 \div 25$ ____

c $40 \div 4 = 4 \div 40$ ____ d $9 \div 3 = 3 \div 9$ ____

e Can you make a rule? ______________________________

6 True (T) or false (F)?

a $9 + 7 = 7 + 9$ ____ b $21 \div 3 = 3 \div 21$ ____

c $14 - 6 = 6 - 14$ ____ d $9 \times 3 = 9 + 3$ ____

e $8 + 11 = 11 + 8$ ____ f $6 + 8 = 8 - 6$ ____

g $90 \div 10 = 10 \div 90$ ____ h $26 + 42 = 42 + 26$ ____

i $68 \times 97 = 97 \times 68$ ____ j $42 - 36 = 42 + 36$ ____

7 What happens to all numbers if they are multiplied by 1?

____

Challenge!

a Add these numbers together in four different ways. Are the answers always the same? [ ]

b Use a calculator to multiply the numbers together in four different ways. Are the answers always the same? [ ]

Unit 35 Making patterns

Patterns

Mary used matches to make some shapes. Draw the next shape in the box, then complete the table. Look for patterns.

1 a

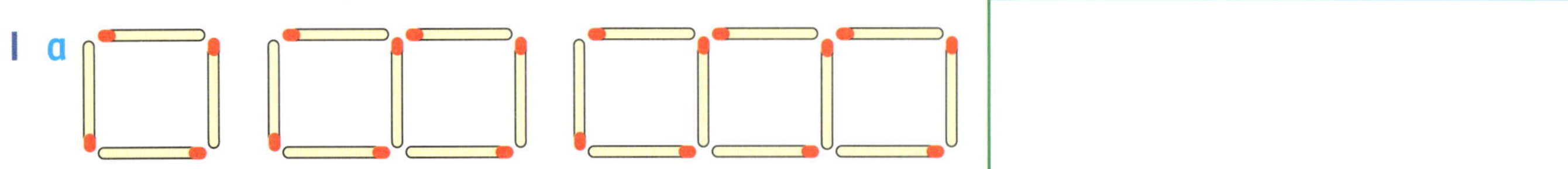

b

Number of shapes	1	2	3	4	5	6	7	8
Number of matches	4	7	10					

2 a

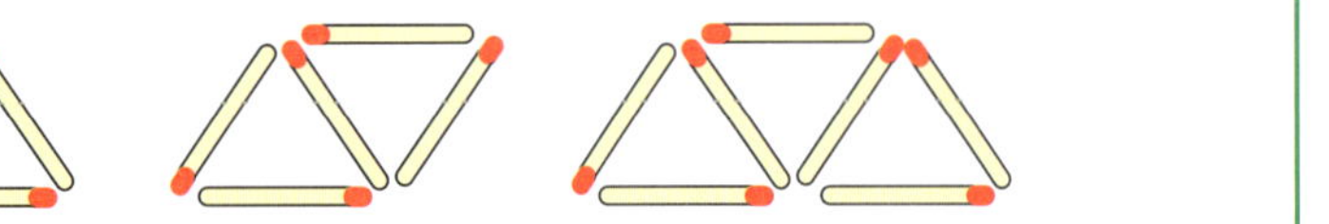

b

Number of shapes	1	2	3	4	5	6	7	8
Number of matches								

3 a

b

Number of shapes	1	2	3	4	5	6	7	8
Number of matches								

4 a

b

Number of shapes	1	2	3	4	5	6	7	8
Number of matches								

Mastery Checklist I can:
- ☐ follow algorithms to make a pattern
- ☐ investigate patterns with +, −, ×, ÷
- ☐ investigate shape patterns with matches.

Unit 36 Angle search

When two straight lines meet, they make an angle.
eg 

1 a What shape is the aquarium? ____________________

b What type of angles are at the corners? ____________________

2 How many angles can you see inside:

a the red fish? ______ b the purple fish? ______

c the green fish? ______ d the yellow fish? ______

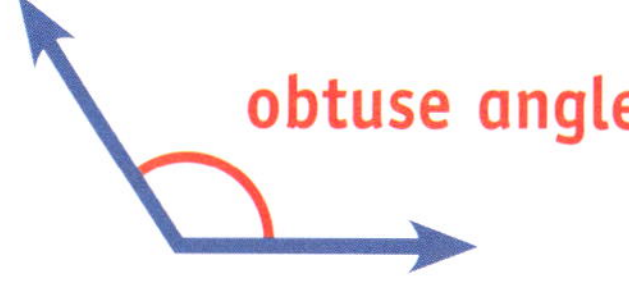

3 How many right angles can you see inside:

a the red fish? ______ b the purple fish? ______

c the green fish? ______ d the yellow fish? ______

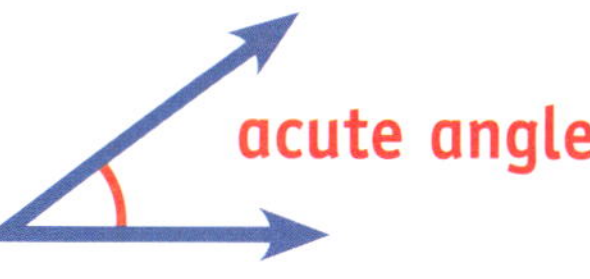

4 How many obtuse angles can you see inside:

a the red fish? ______ b the yellow fish? ______

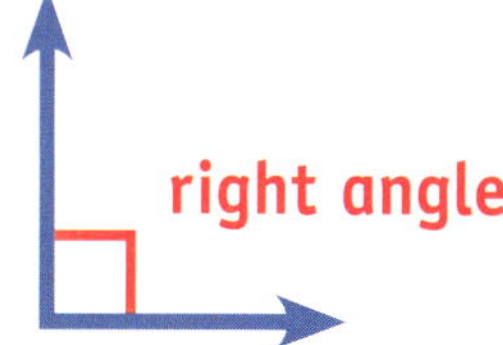

5 How many acute angles can you see inside:

a the green fish? ______ b the purple fish? ______

6 Draw another angle fish.

Unit 36 Angle size

1

A Here are 4 angles.	B Copy the angle.	C Draw a larger angle.	D Draw a smaller angle.
a	b	c	d
e	f	g	h
i	j	k	l
m	n	o	p

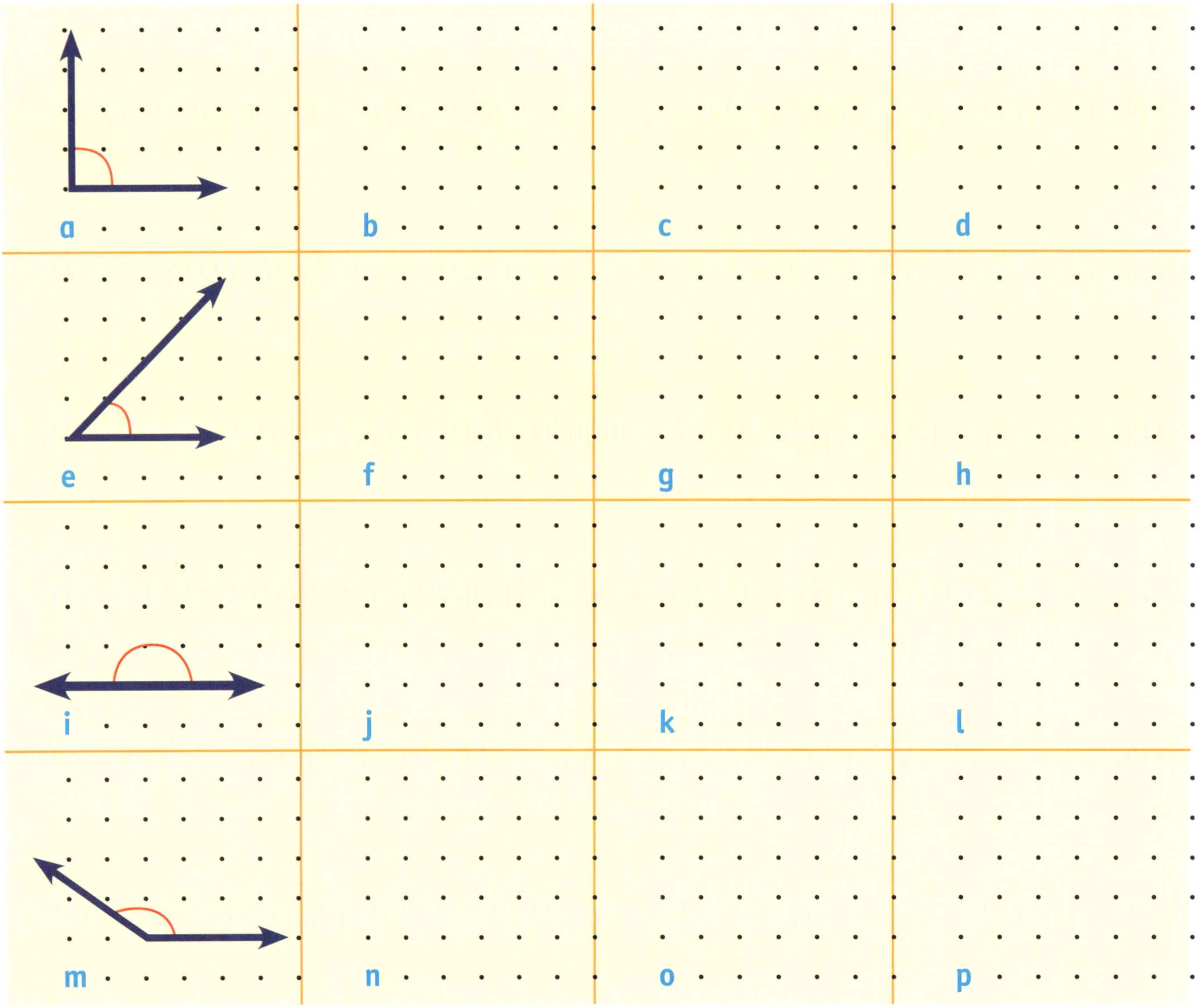

2 Which angle is the largest in:

a column A? _____ b column B? _____ c column C? _____ d column D? _____

3 Which angle is the smallest in:

a column A? _____ b column B? _____ c column C? _____ d column D? _____

4 Look around the classroom and write 3 places where you can see right angles.

_______________ _______________ _______________

Draw a diagram

Draw a house. Colour the right angles blue, colour the acute angles pink, colour the obtuse angles orange.

Unit 36 Comparing angles

The corners of this page are square corners.
A square corner is called a right angle.

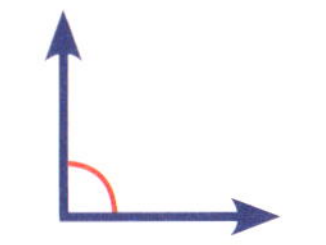

Acute angles are smaller than right angles.

Obtuse angles are larger than right angles.

1 Colour the right angles red; the angles bigger than a right angle green; the angles smaller than a right angle yellow.

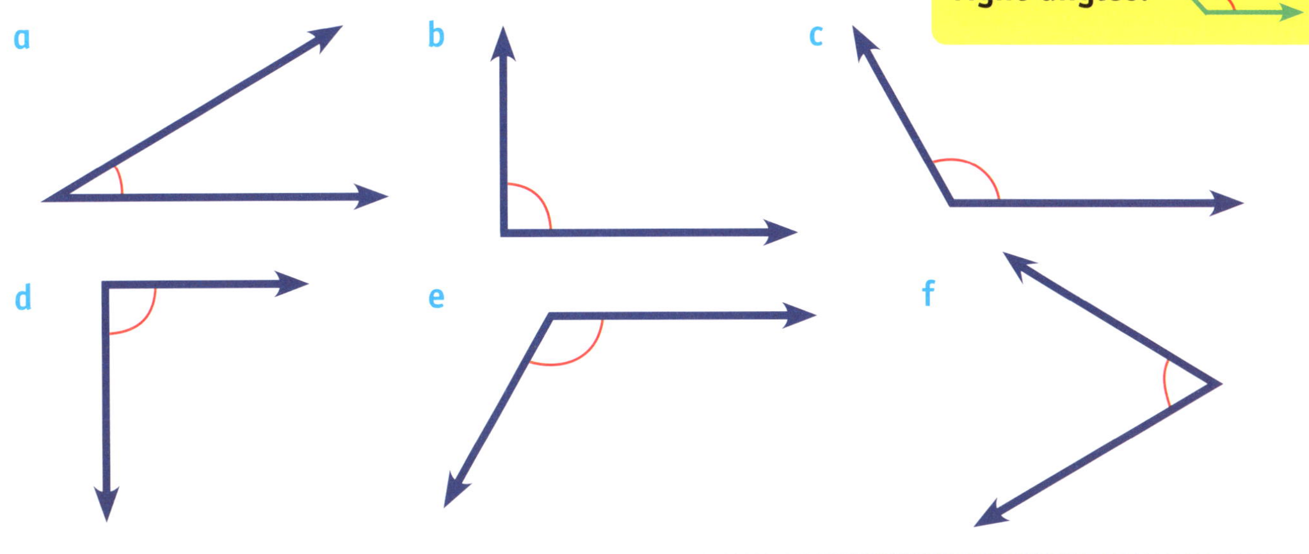

2 a Draw a right angle.

b Draw an acute angle.

c Draw an obtuse angle.

3

Make a movable angle with 2 strips of cardboard and a fastener.

Use your movable angle to find and circle angles the same as A.

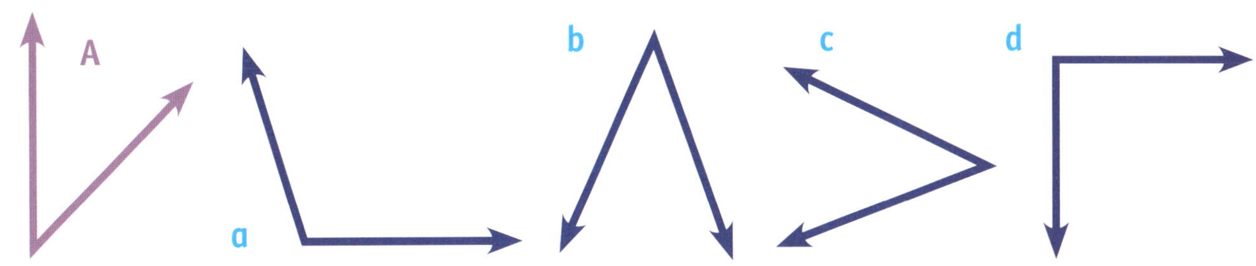

Unit 36 Reading a timetable

This is Tim's school day.

A		B	
7:15	Wake up	12:30	Lunch break
7:20	Shower and clean teeth	1:10	Back to class
7:30	Get dressed	3:10	School finishes
7:45	Have breakfast		Arrive home and have a snack
8:00	Feed dog, cat and rabbit	4:00	Begin homework
8:20	Walk to school	5:00	Finish homework
8:45	Arrive at school	5:05	Play
9:00	Start school	6:15	Dinner
10:55	Morning recess	7:00	Watch TV
11:10	Back to class	8:30	Bed

1 Which column shows pm time? ________

2 When does Tim begin his shower? ________

3 How long does it take for him to get dressed? ________ minutes

4 Does Tim have any pets? ________ How do you know? ____________________

5 a How long does it take for Tim to walk to school? ________ minutes

b It takes him the same time to walk home from school.
Complete the timetable by writing the time Tim arrives home.

6 How long is school lunchtime? ________ minutes

7 How many minutes does Tim spend on his homework? ________ minutes

8 How long in hours and minutes does Tim spend watching TV? _____ hours _____ minutes

9 Tim watches the same amount of TV each night from Monday to Friday.
How much TV is this for the 5 days? ________ hours _____ minutes

Mastery Checklist I can:
- ☐ identify obtuse, acute and right angles
- ☐ draw larger and smaller angles
- ☐ compare angles
- ☐ answer questions about a timetable.

AC9M3M04 Measurement **MA2-NSM-02** Non-spatial measure B • Time: Represent and interpret digital time displays • Time: Use am and pm notation

Unit 37 Design a classroom

Here is an aerial view of a classroom you have been asked to design.

First, think about what you like about your own classroom. What could be improved?

Here are the things you must include:

- seats for 28 children
- 1 teacher's desk
- 1 computer desk
- 2 bookshelves
- 2 storage cupboards

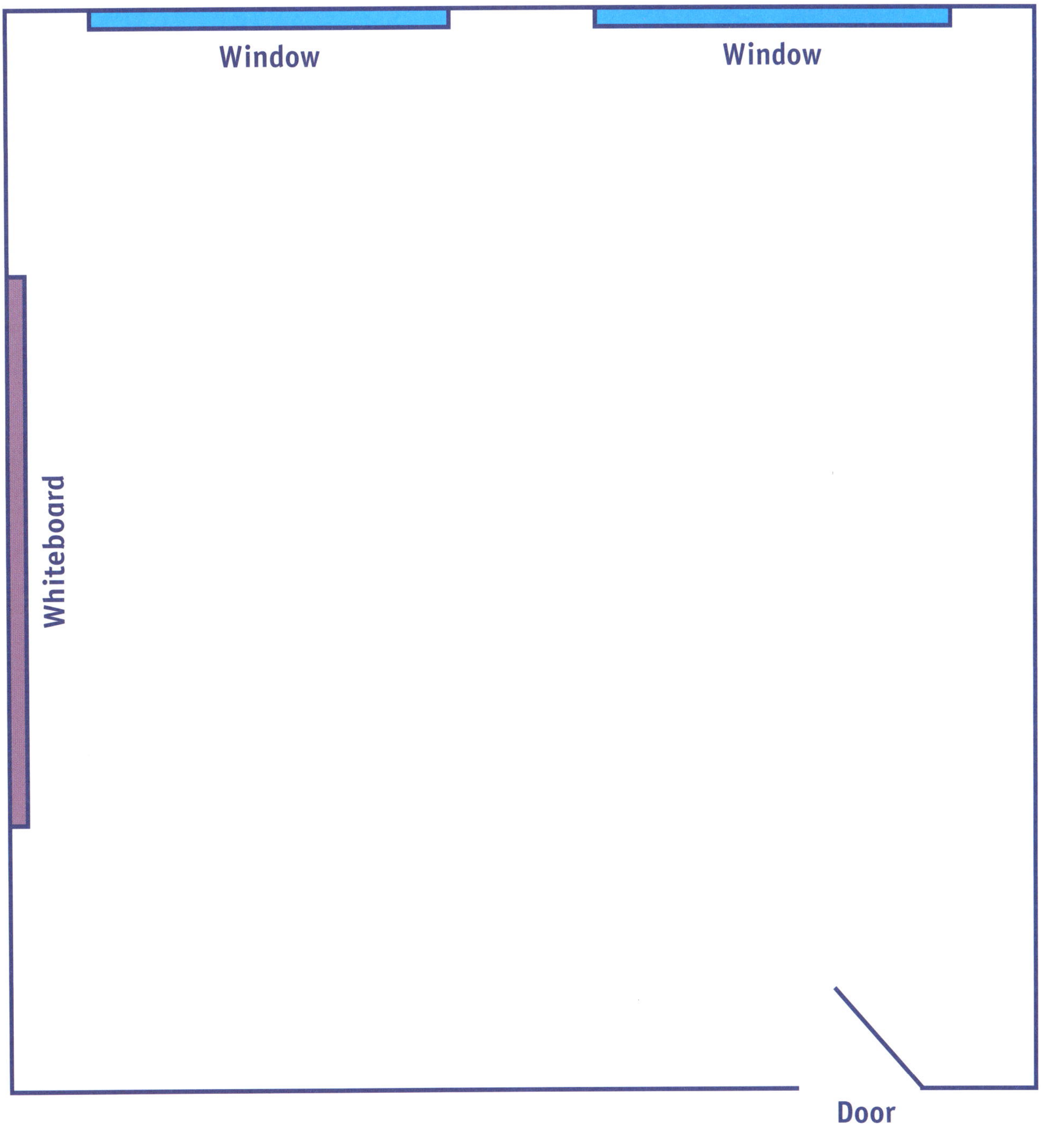

Window

Window

Whiteboard

Door

Unit 37 Position

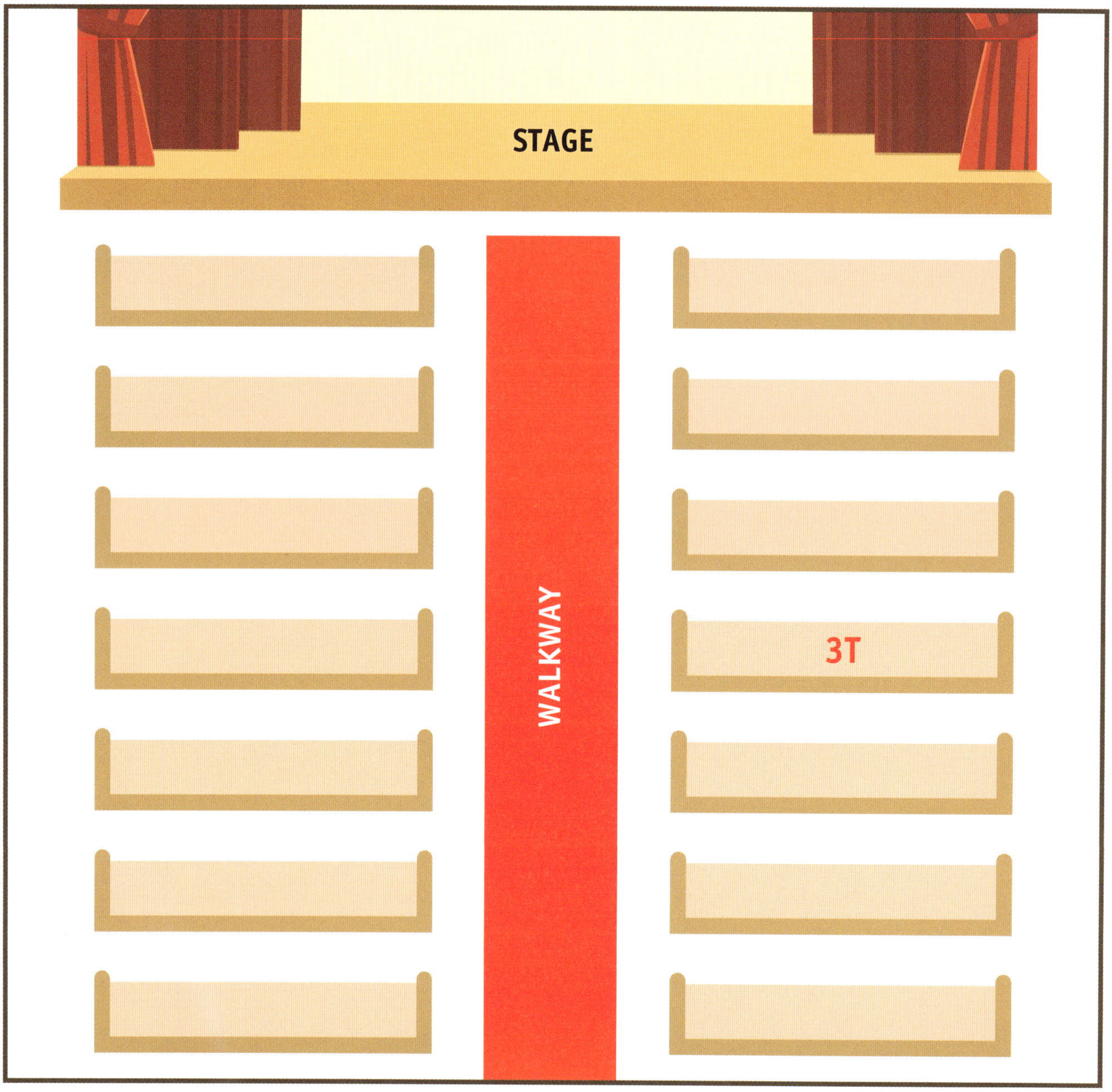

STAGE

WALKWAY

3T

At Boorloo Primary, there is an assembly every Friday. You are in class **3T**.

Use the clues below to label the assembly class chart.

- KG is at the front of the assembly on the left side.
- KJ is three classes in front of 3T.
- 4C is seated behind 3T.
- 5Z is seated behind 4C.
- 6A is seated behind 5Z.
- 1D is seated behind KJ.
- 3F is seated in front of 4B.
- 1N is seated behind KG.
- 2P is seated in front of 3T.
- 5M is seated to the left of 5Z.
- 4B is seated three classes behind 1N.
- 2C is seated to the left of 2P.
- 6G is seated behind 5M.

Unit 37 Following directions

1 Write the moves made on the grid. Start at *.

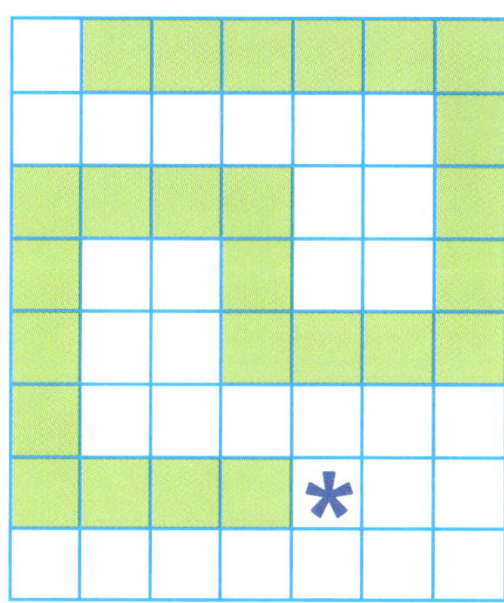

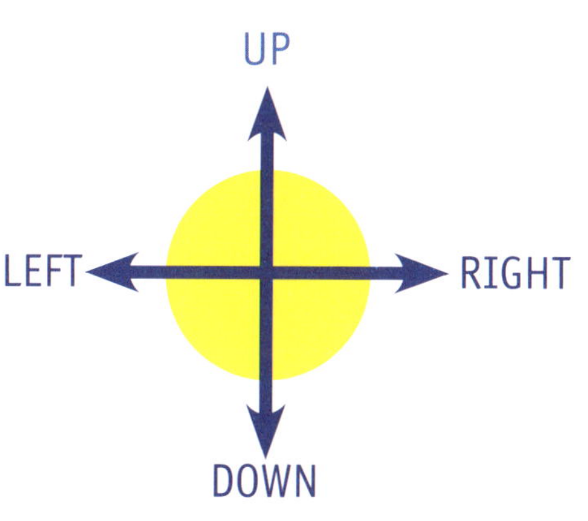

4 left
4

2 Start at * and follow the directions.

The first two moves have been done.

a 1 right b 2 down c 1 right

d 1 down e 2 right f 1 up

g 1 right h 2 up i 1 left

j 1 up k 3 left l 2 up

m 1 right n 1 up o 3 right

p 1 down

q What number have you drawn? ______

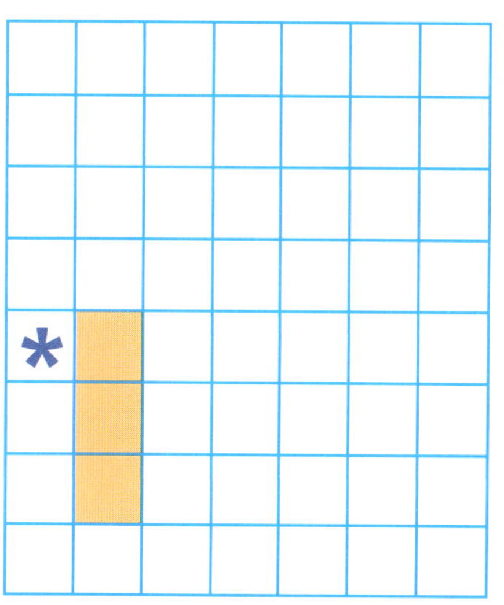

3 Ari has made a path for Caleb to follow. There is a mistake in the directions. Correct the mistake.

Start

Start
Go up 4
Right 5
Up 3
Left 3
Down 1
Left 2
Up 1
Right 5

Problem solving

Zoo directions

1 Place the following animals on the map and write their location.

Monkeys ______ Giraffes ______ Platypus ______ Red panda ______ Kangaroo ______

2 Give instructions on how to find two of the animals, starting at the entrance. Use direction words: North, South, East, West, right, left and ahead.

A ______________________________

____

____

B ______________________________

____

____

I can solve problems by:

☐ understanding position ☐ following directions on a grid.

AC9M3SP02 Space **MAO-WM-01** Working mathematically • communicating thinking and reasoning coherently and clearly • **MA2-GM-01** Geometric measure B • Position: Use directional language and describe routes with grid maps

Unit 37 Possible paths

Larry's house

MARLIN

Larry

Larry likes to look at different things when he walks home.

1 Colour red his shortest way home.

2 Colour blue a very long way home.

3 Find another 4 ways Larry could walk home. Show each way in a different colour.

4 How many different ways do you think he can walk home? ☐

Mastery Checklist I can:
- ☐ make a floorplan of a classroom
- ☐ use descriptions to work out positions
- ☐ follow directions for a path on a grid
- ☐ draw paths on a map.

Unit 38 Possible outcomes

Chance

Main Course

Spaghetti

Fish

Hamburger

Chicken

Dessert

Ice-cream

Cheesecake

Fruit salad

1 This is the menu for Claire's Cosy Cafe.

a How many main courses are there? __________

b How many desserts are there? __________

c Hal ordered spaghetti. How many different desserts could he have with it? __________

d Ivy ordered ice-cream. How many different main courses could she have with it? __________

e List all possible combinations of meals.

Main Course	Dessert	Main Course	Dessert

2 Sam painted different shapes on some tiles and put them in a box.

a How many circles? __________

b How many triangles? __________

c How many squares? __________

Without looking, he took one tile out of the box.

d What shape was the most likely? __________

e What shape was the least likely? __________

Unit 38 Chance

1 a How many faces on a die? ________

b Which three faces are showing on this die? ______ ______ ______

c Which three faces are not seen? ______ ______ ______

d If the die is tossed, what numbers could be on top?

______ ______ ______ ______ ______ ______

e Is there any chance 7 dots could appear? ________

Why? ________________________________

2 Match one of the words in the list with each of these statements.

a I will watch television tonight. ____________

b It will snow today. ____________

c The sun will rise in the morning. ____________

d I will grow taller than my mother. ____________

e I will see a horse on the road. ____________

impossible
unlikely
likely
certain

3 a How many different outcomes are possible with this spinner? ________

b Do all shapes on this spinner have the same chance of being selected? ________

c Draw the shape that is most likely to be selected.

d Draw the shape that is least likely to be selected.

e True or false?

(red cross) is more likely to be selected than (star). ________

(four-point star) has more chance of being selected than all the other shapes together. ________

f What is the chance that the arrow will point to (half yellow, half purple circle)? ____________

Mastery Checklist I can:
- ☐ work out outcomes and combinations
- ☐ compare the likelihood of events happening
- ☐ understand impossible, unlikely, likely and certain.

Revision Term 4

1 Write as many multiplication facts as you can for this group. p 144

____

____

2 What is the product of: p 145

a 3 and 7? _____ b 5 and 10? _____

3 Colour the multiples of 8. p 146

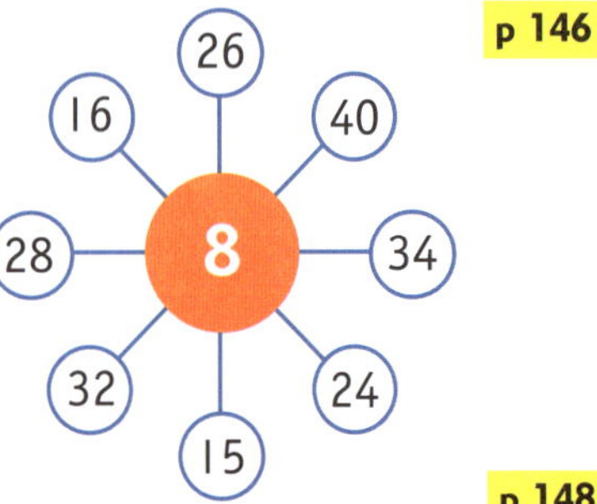

p 148

4 What do seven 5c stamps cost? _______

5 a 40 ÷ 10 = ______ b 18 ÷ 2 = ______

c 21 ÷ 3 = ______ d 55 ÷ 5 = ______

6

Divide the stars into: p 149

a 2 groups. 1 group = ______ stars

b 3 groups. 1 group = ______ stars

c 9 groups. 1 group = ______ stars

d 6 groups. 1 group = ______ stars

7 p 152

Use the numbers to make:

a the largest number. ____________

b the smallest number. ____________

8 Round to the nearest thousand. p 153

a 4695 ________ b 2398 ________

c 9003 ________ d 5802 ________

9 Write the number 100 more. p 153

a 479 ________ b 1280 ________

c 1005 ________ d 3600 ________

10 Write the number 100 less. p 153

a 749 ________ b 1820 ________

c 1500 ________ d 3006 ________

11 7426 is the same as: p 154

a _____ tens _____ ones

b _____ hundreds _____ tens _____ ones

c _____ thousands _____ ones

12 Colour the fraction. p 155

a $\frac{1}{5}$

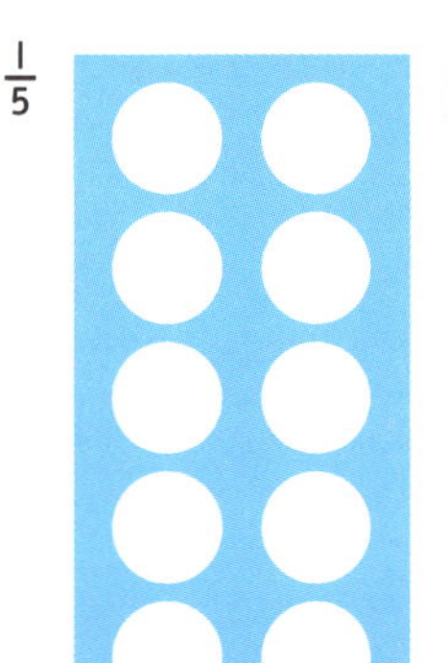

b $\frac{1}{2}$

13 Colour five tenths. p 157

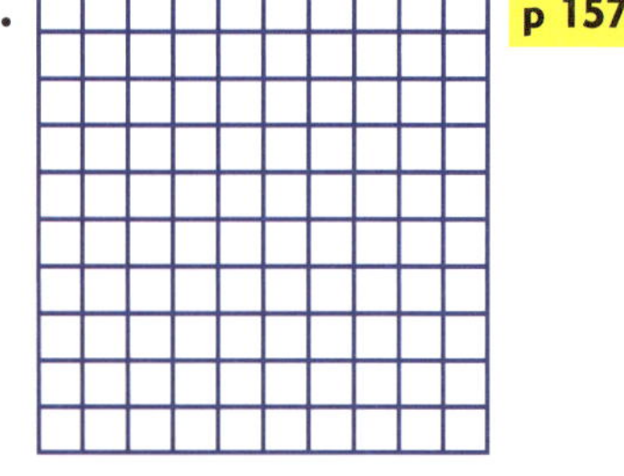

14 Colour $\frac{75}{100}$. p 157

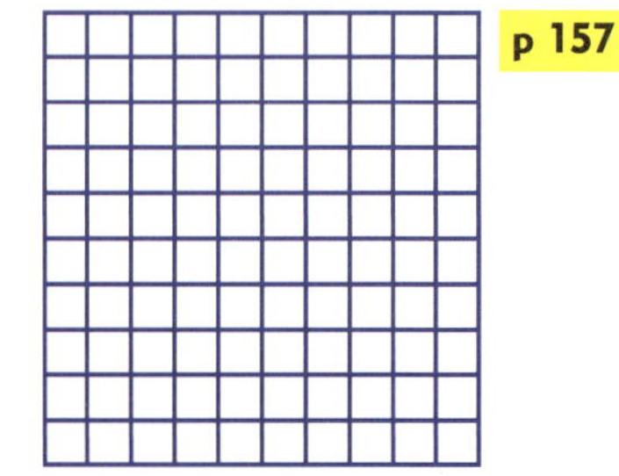

Revision Term 4

15 How many centimetres in: p 159

a 2 m? ______

b $\frac{1}{2}$ m? ______

16 How many millimetres in: p 159

a 5 cm? ______

b 12 cm? ______

17 a Draw a line 38 mm long. p 159

b Measure this line in mm.

18 p 160

2 m

4 m

What is the length around the rectangle? ______

19 Draw a shape that has a length around the outside that is 10 cm. p 160

20 This magic machine changes numbers four times to make a sequence. p 168

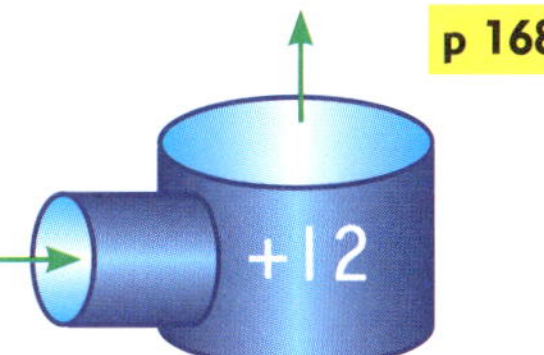

What will these numbers become?

a 7 ______, ______, ______, ______

b 25 ______, ______, ______, ______

These number sequences came out. What number went in?

c 28, 40, 52, 64 ______

d 42, 54, 66, 78 ______

21 True or false? p 169

a $6 \times 8 = 8 \times 6$ ______

b $32 \div 8 = 8 \div 32$ ______

22 p 170

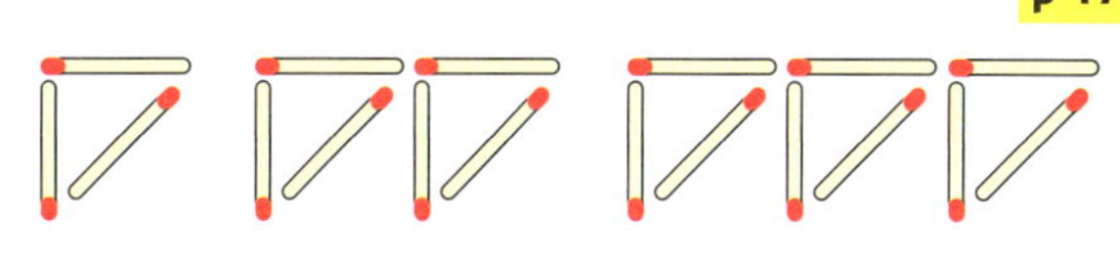

Number of shapes	1	2	3	4	5
Number of matches	3				

23 Draw: p 171

a an acute angle.	b an obtuse angle.

24 Write two places where you can see a right angle. p 172

a ______

b ______

25 p 173

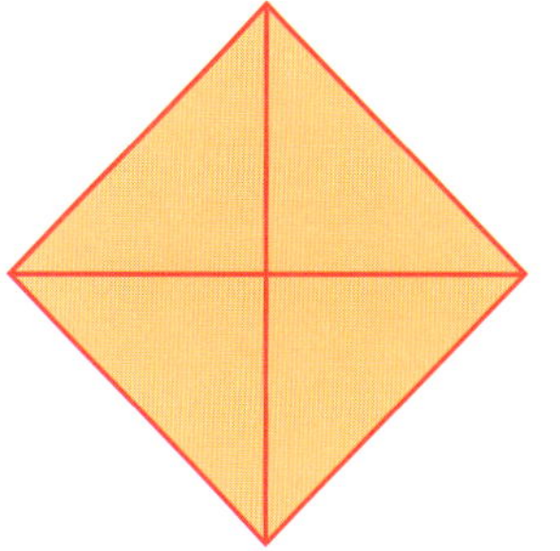

Which statement is true about this diagram? ______

a There are 8 right angles.

b There are 4 right angles and 8 acute angles.

c There are 8 right angles and 8 acute angles.

Revision Term 4

26 p 174

3:30	Finish school
3:45	Afternoon tea
4:00	Play with Jan
5:10	Homework
5:30	Have bath
6:00	Watch TV
6:35	Eat dinner

This is part of Bill's timetable for Monday.

a Is it am or pm? ________

b What did he do at $\frac{1}{4}$ to 4?

____

c How long did he watch TV? ________

d What else did he do between 5:30 and 6:00?

____

e How long was it from finishing school to eating dinner? ________

27 Draw an aerial view of your bedroom. p 175

28 Draw the path by following the directions. Start at * and move: p 177

a 1 up b 3 right
c 2 up d 1 left
e 2 up f 2 left
g 2 up h 2 left
i 2 down

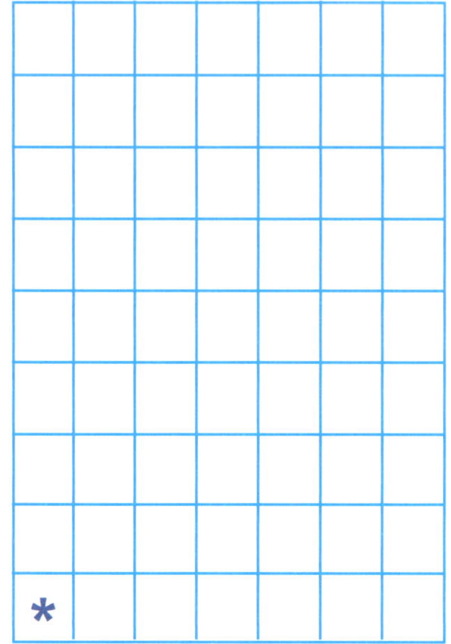

29 Helen has cheese, tomato, ham and lettuce for sandwich making. What are the different two-filling sandwiches she can make? p 180

________ ________
________ ________
________ ________
________ ________
________ ________
________ ________
____

30 Sam wanted ham with one other thing. How many different sandwiches could he have? p 180

____